CW00972970

Estimating the Prevalence of Problem Drug Use in Europe

Papers arising from a Scientific Seminar on
Addiction Prevalence Estimation: Methods and Research Strategies
held in Strasbourg, France, 10-14 June 1996

Jointly organised by the Pompidou Group of the Council of Europe
and the European Monitoring Centre for Drugs and Drug Addiction

PLANNING GROUP

Richard Hartnoll
Peter D.A. Cohen
Antònia Domingo-Salvany
Roland Simon
Martin Frischer
Colin Taylor

EDITORIAL GROUP

Gerry V. Stimson
Matthew Hickman
Alan Quirk
Martin Frischer
Colin Taylor

Council of Europe
Co-operation Group to Combat Drug Abuse
and Illicit Trafficking in Drugs (Pompidou Group)

E.M.C.D.D.A.
European Monitoring Centre
for Drugs and Drug Addiction

A great deal of additional information on the European Union is available on the Internet. It can be accessed through the Europa server (http://europa.eu.int)

Cataloguing data can be found at the end of this publication

Luxembourg: Office for Official Publications of the European Communities, 1997

ISBN 92-9168-006-0

Printed in Italy

Contents

CONTENTS

PART V: NOMINATION METHODS

PART VI: COMBINING AND COMPARING DIFFERENT ESTIMATION METHODS

ACKNOWLEDGEMENTS

*T*his monograph reflects the efforts and scientific reflections of many people. In particular, thanks are due to the participants of the Scientific Seminar on 'Addiction Prevalence Estimation: Methods and Research Strategies', held in Strasbourg from 10 to 14 June 1996, and to all those involved in the planning group, namely: Richard Hartnoll, Peter Cohen, Antònia Domingo-Salvany, Martin Frischer, Roland Simon and Colin Taylor, together with Florence Mabileau-Whomsley and Patrick Buchmann of the Pompidou Group secretariat and Lucas Wiessing and Kathy Robertson of the EMCDDA.

Thanks also go to the authors whose presentations make up this monograph, especially Professor Gerry Stimson and those who assisted him in editing the text into a more scientifically and linguistically consistent manuscript. The editorial group comprised Martin Frischer, Matthew Hickman, Alan Quirk and Colin Taylor and was assisted by Véronique Sérafinowicz, Steve Monk, Christopher Fitch and Robert Lilly. Last but not least, my thanks are extended to Chris Luckett of the Pompidou Group and Richard Hartnoll of the EMCDDA whose support for, and involvement in, the Seminar made this monograph possible.

**Georges Estievenart,
Director,
EMCDDA.**

GENERAL INTRODUCTION

GENERAL INTRODUCTION

by Richard Hartnoll

Why this monograph?

'How many addicts are there?' is a question commonly asked. Unfortunately, the answer tends to be either that 'no one knows' or that 'experts consider that the number could be more than 100,000', with no indication of what counts as an addict or of whether there is any sound scientific basis for the figure. The problem is compounded when the question is phrased in terms of comparative figures for the prevalence of 'addiction' in different countries.

This scientific monograph directly addresses the question of how to obtain prevalence estimates that, scientifically, are more valid and comparable. It does not aim to offer a definitive answer to the question of how to estimate prevalence, but rather to reflect the state-of-the-art in European countries and to provide guidance for future studies.

The monograph is the result, although by no means the final outcome, of a process that began in 1993 when epidemiology experts of the Pompidou Group of the Council of Europe began to discuss how to improve prevalence estimates in Europe. These discussions, and a review of approaches used in different countries, led to a proposal to hold a Scientific Seminar. The proposal finally came to fruition in June 1996 in a joint seminar on *'Addiction Prevalence Estimation: Methods and Research Strategies'* organised in Strasbourg by the Pompidou Group and the EMCDDA. Over 80 scientists from 30 countries attended the meeting and many of the papers they presented at the event form the basis of this book.

Following the Seminar, the papers were sent to other experts for 'peer review' and then passed on to Professor Gerry Stimson who, together with an editorial group, organised and edited the material into its present format, in some cases asking the authors to revise their contributions.

A separate follow-up to the Seminar was the initiation, by the EMCDDA, of two pilot projects to develop and improve prevalence estimation at local and national levels respectively. The first project focuses on comparative three-sample capture-recapture estimation methods in different cities while the second looks at whether the definitions, methods and assumptions used in national prevalence estimates in certain countries can be applied in others so as to provide more comparable results. The reports from these two projects will be submitted to the Centre at the end of 1997 and the work further developed in the coming years.

Prevalence of what, and why?

One of the traditional methods used to measure the prevalence of drug use in a population is a survey based on random sampling of the population concerned. However, there are some types of drug use which often cannot be assessed reliably by this method, notably rarer and/or more stigmatised or problematic patterns of drug use, such as drug injecting or heroin addiction. Thus, alternative strategies are needed to complement the information obtained from population surveys.

The title of the Strasbourg Scientific Seminar used 'addiction' as a short-hand term to indicate that the emphasis was on methods for investigating the prevalence of heavier patterns of drug use (e.g. frequent or high-dose consumption or drug-injecting) that have a higher risk of problematic consequences, such as dependence or HIV infection, and that may require interventions such as treatment or secondary prevention.

This, however, raises a problem. What is to be counted? Or in other words, what is the case definition? In some studies, the definition refers to heroin dependence, in others, to daily or almost daily use of any illegal drug (including cannabis) and/or any drug injection. How can researchers be sure of the criteria actually used (e.g. by treatment staff or police officers) to record cases in the original databases on which they rely? If this is not clear, then what population does the estimate describe? The theme of case definition, and of the uncertainty that this implies for any estimate, runs through many chapters of this monograph. It is one of the central issues that must be addressed and discussed honestly whenever presenting or comparing the results of prevalence studies.

The answer to the question of what is being measured is closely linked to the purpose of the estimate. If the purpose is to assess possible treatment needs, then the definition should relate to potential clients, either now or in the future. If it is to assess the possible demand, and thus the illicit market, for a drug such as heroin, then all heroin users should be included, regardless of whether they are likely to seek treatment. More overtly, political demands for prevalence data may push the definition in other directions. There is no simple answer to this, apart from stressing the vital point that it is essential to specify, as clearly and as consistently as possible, what criteria have been used and what these might imply about the resulting estimate.

A further point regarding the uses of prevalence data is that a prevalence figure is only a starting point for obtaining relevant information about a largely hidden phenomenon. In itself, a number or a rate does little more than establish the approximate dimensions of 'addiction' or 'problem drug use'. Putting a figure to a problem may reduce some of the anxiety and wild estimates that are aroused by an unknown and apparently threatening phenomenon. It may also indicate, in a general fashion, whether there is a problem and whether there are sufficient treatment or other services to cope with it. In some cases, it may also be used to justify a decision to increase spending on such services. However, it is the information that lies behind the bald prevalence figure that is important: not simply how many addicts there are, but what kind of addicts, with what problems and needs, and living in what sections of the community, under what circumstances.

It is thus important that prevalence estimates lead on to other more discriminating studies that provide information that is relevant to action, policy development and service provision. Good prevalence estimates may help to establish a consensus about the dimensions of the phenomenon and reduce the energy wasted on arguments about the problem based on uninformed and unscientific points of view. However, this is only the beginning.

Overview of the state-of-the-art of prevalence estimation in Europe

A variety of methods are available for estimating the prevalence of heavier or more problematic patterns of illegal drug use, for example drug dependence. These include: population-based surveys (although, as mentioned earlier, these are often unreliable for rarer, stigmatised and hidden patterns of drug use); case-finding studies; capture-recapture estimates; multiplier techniques (e.g. based on the number of addict deaths and the mortality rate amongst addicts); nomination techniques, including snowball sampling; synthetic estimates, based on social or demographic variables assumed to correlate with drug prevalence; and a variety of more sophisticated statistical modelling approaches.

Some of these methods have been applied in different European countries, although only in a few countries has a body of expertise and experience in prevalence estimation begun to develop. In most cases, the more scientific and rigorous methodologies have been applied at local (e.g. city) rather than national level. Reliable national estimates are rather rare. At all levels, more attention needs to be paid to the question of case definition.

Table 1 (overleaf) summarises the different methods that have been tested in European countries. In many instances, they are based on data produced by various registers or case-reporting systems (e.g. treatment notifications or police registers) or by active case-finding methods. An increasingly popular method uses such sources to apply statistical estimation techniques, in particular capture-recapture, whilst others use them to make extrapolations, for example by taking account of the time-lag between starting to use drugs and first entering treatment, or by applying multipliers obtained by nomination techniques. Various other multiplier methods are used, especially the addict-death multiplier, although it is all-too-frequently applied without paying sufficient attention to important sources of error. A few countries derive estimates from population surveys, whilst in others, a less scientific approach involves combining estimates obtained from a range of key persons. Several snowball studies have been conducted, but these do not usually generate prevalence estimates *per se*, unless they are combined with nomination techniques (which is unusual). More sophisticated statistical models have not often been applied.

In a few cases, attempts have been made to compare and cross-validate the estimates produced by different methods. These indicate that, when careful attention is paid to the likely directions of bias in each estimate, it is possible to arrive at a reasonable 'best estimate' of the probable range within which prevalence lies. They also show, however, that it is rare to achieve identical estimates, underlining one of the important conclusions of this monograph, that there is no one ideal method that can be considered as a 'gold standard', and that it is always wise to compare different methods in the knowledge that the answer will be an approximate range rather than a precise figure. Thus, apart from improvements in specific methods, it is also important to develop research strategies for obtaining estimates based on more than one method or set of assumptions. At European level, it is also essential to develop common instruments and methodologies so that the results can be better compared.

Table 1: "Addict" Prevalence estimates - methods tried

| | POTENTIAL BASIS FOR ESTIMATES | | | ESTIMATION METHODS TRIED (NATIONAL OR LOCAL) | | | | | |
	Registers[1] (T)	(P)	Case Finding	Capture Recapture	Death Multiplier	Nomination	Survey	Other[2]
Austria	?	✓						
Bulgaria	?					✓?		✓(k)
Croatia	?	?						✓(k)
Czech Rep.	✓					✓?		
Denmark			✓		✓			✓(k)
France				✓				✓(e)
Germany		✓	✓	✓	✓		✓	✓(e)
Hungary			✓			✓?		
Ireland	✓		✓					
Italy	✓			✓	✓			
Luxembourg	✓	✓	✓					✓(e)
Malta	✓							
Netherlands	✓			✓		✓	✓	
Norway		✓						
Poland	✓	✓		✓	✓			
Russia	✓							
Slovenia	?					✓?		✓(k)
Slovakia	?							
Spain	✓		✓	✓	✓	✓	✓	
Sweden			✓	✓				✓(k)
Switzerland	✓			✓?	✓			✓(k)
United Kingdom	✓		✓	✓	✓	✓	✓	✓ (e

[1] Registers: (T) = treatment; (P) = police.
[2] Other: (k) = key persons; (e) = extrapolation.

Finally, prevalence estimates are only as good as the data on which they are based. The science of estimation cannot improve unless the data collection and databases on which they rely also improve. This means that it is as important, if not more so, to invest time and energy in achieving good data quality in the reporting systems, registers, surveys and other studies as it is to develop ever more sophisticated methods for analysing these data.

Structure of the monograph

The outline of the monograph follows the broad structure of the Strasbourg Seminar. It begins with chapters on the relationship between scientific prevalence estimates and policy since, as noted earlier, prevalence estimation takes place within a political context. It then deals with case-finding methods, not because they provide a prevalence estimate in themselves, but because they are a basis for many of the more reliable estimation methods and because discussing them raises key issues of case definition, double-counting and data quality.

The following three sections deal with the methods most commonly used in Europe. The first of these is capture-recapture, which directly uses data collected through techniques such as case-finding. Whilst this is a promising and interesting approach, the elegance and deceptive simplicity of the basic model hides difficult methodological issues of sampling bias, interdependence between samples and interpretation of the results.

The subsequent two sections deal with other single-method approaches to prevalence estimation: multiplier methods and nomination techniques. The former, especially the addict-death multiplier, also appears deceptively simple but is based on assumptions about the quality of mortality data and the relationship between mortality and prevalence that are often unjustified. At national level, however, some sort of multiplier approach may at times be the only way forward, especially in larger countries.

Nomination methods, which may be linked to snowball sampling techniques, are an alternative approach to obtaining multiplier estimates. Under certain circumstances they may also be used in estimates based on analysis methods similar to those found in capture-recapture.

The final section of the monograph is concerned with combining and comparing different estimation methods. This makes it clear that there is no standard combination of methods that can easily be applied in all circumstances. Rather, it is the local or national conditions that provide the context, and the limitations, within which researchers have to work. It is for this reason that information exchange, dialogue and collaboration between researchers is essential to understand better, not only which methods are most appropriate under what conditions, but also to improve mutual understanding between researchers of how far, and in what way, estimates can be compared and how far they cannot. We hope that this monograph contributes to this understanding.

SCIENCE AND POLICY

PART I

INTRODUCTION

by Gerry V. Stimson

*I*n this first section of the monograph, the authors examine the relationship between epidemiological work on the estimation of drug problems, and the development of drugs policy and strategy. A recurrent theme is that there is a complex relationship between science and policy.

Gerry Stimson and Ali Judd examine different models of the interaction between science and policy. They warn against undue optimism that epidemiological data will be used by policy makers and influence policy, and suggest that both epidemiologists and policy makers need to find ways to bring evidence into the policy-making process. They identify several key questions to which policy makers might expect answers. These concern: the extent of drug use; who is using drugs; the nature of the health, social and criminal problems connected with drug use; the scale of costs to the individual and society; whether the problem is getting worse or better; whether (and what) can be done; and the impact of interventions.

Peter Cohen also explores the relationship between prevalence estimation and policy interests. He argues that epidemiological data are not neutral. Epidemiologists may – quite rightly – argue about technical issues. However, the kinds of data that are collected, and the manner in which they are analysed and interpreted, depend on the policy framework. Estimation issues, he suggests, are not merely technical but are also strategic. He illustrates this argument by examining the data requirements – i.e. what to estimate – under three different policy models – repression, harm reduction and cultural integration. He ends the chapter with a discussion on whether there can be general indicators that are useful across different models of drug policy.

Philip Lazarov presents a case study of the utilisation of data on drug use for the development of drug policy and interventions. Drawing on experience in Bulgaria, he highlights the responsibilities that drug policy makers have in educating governments and the public. He makes a strong plea for the usefulness of good data in sensitising society, and in helping to implement and develop policies, programmes and projects. In many contexts, good prevalence data and estimations will often be hard to obtain. Following the experience of the Pompidou Group Multi-City Study, he argues for the strategic use of both qualitative and quantitative data.

CHAPTER 1

ESTIMATING THE SCALE AND NATURE OF DRUG PROBLEMS: THE RELATIONSHIP BETWEEN SCIENCE, POLICY AND DRUGS STRATEGY

by Gerry V. Stimson and Ali Judd

The European Monitoring Centre for Drugs and Drug Addiction and the Pompidou Group of the Council of Europe have a key role to play in initiating scientific debate and development in the drugs field, and in making the science of epidemiology understandable and relevant to the needs of policy makers.

The task of estimating the scale and nature of drug problems, and of encouraging policy makers to use that information, is ambitious and will span many years to come. The task is ambitious for two reasons. Firstly, the science of estimating drug problems is still in a relatively undeveloped state. Considerable international work has already been undertaken in this field and there are many landmark methodological achievements in both the direct and indirect estimation of the scale and nature of drug problems (Brodsky, 1985; Cormack, 1992; Hartnoll *et al*, 1985; Woodward *et al*, 1985). This monograph has many examples from across Europe of the development, application and comparison of different methods of indirect estimation.

However, despite growing concern about drug problems, there is still much to know about the actual extent, nature and consequences of illicit drug use in Europe. Epidemiological expertise and methodological sophistication have to develop consonant with the demands for information and understanding. There is a need for more reliable and valid information about the extent, patterns and distribution of illicit drug use, changes in patterns of drug use over time, and the natural history of consumption and the development of associated health and social problems. It remains unclear to what extent the use and misuse of drugs is associated with increased morbidity and mortality. Existing indicators inadequately reflect the range of health and social problems that are linked to drug misuse. This monograph aims, therefore, to give a European overview of the current 'state-of-the-art' in the field of epidemiological estimation of drug problems.

The second difficulty regards the state of drug policy-making in Europe. There is no lack of interest in drug problems in Europe. A concern that drugs and drug addiction *are* problems is one thing about which governments of Member States in the European Union agree. There is an instinctive feeling that something is wrong, and that something needs to be done about it. However, instinctive reactions are not always a good basis for policy-making: whilst politicians may have passionate debates about 'drugs and drug addiction', it remains unclear how far policy makers are currently using scientific evidence in setting policy agendas and developing strategic responses.

Many researchers believe that they can contribute scientific evidence to policy-making and strategic development. Therefore, the issue to be considered is whether science can influence the policy-making process and influence the development of evidence-based policy-making.

The relationship between science and policy

There is a growing interest in the relationship between science and policy. However, at present, it is little more than an act of faith that science can lead to sensible policy-making. Recent events concerning Bovine Spongiform Encephalitis (BSE) in Europe serve as a good example to show that this relationship is not straightforward.

In an analysis of drug and alcohol research and policy, Virginia Berridge and Betsy Thom have pointed out that the potential 'for social science research to guide and inform policy-making has, at various times, been greeted with enthusiastic optimism and cynical pessimism' (Berridge and Thom, 1996). There are some instances which demonstrate the contribution of social science to policy debate and decision, but there are also many instances where social science research has been ignored.

Social policy analysts have described several models of the relationship between social science research and the policy-making process.

A *rational model* of policy-making is based on the belief that 'policy-making is a rational process which calls on the scientifically derived facts of research to provide the empirical evidence needed in decision-making' (Berridge and Thom, 1996). In this model, scientists are seen as being relatively autonomous and producing objective evidence which can be used and referred to by equally autonomous and objective policy makers. Due to the objective nature of the evidence, ideological differences between scientists and policy makers should not be of concern. However, technical issues, such as a lengthy timescale for research, may hinder the implementation of research results into policy. Although it is possible to sympathise with such a concept of the relationship between science and policy, the model can be criticised for its over-simplification of this association in reality.

An alternative model promotes the concept that science offers enlightenment to the policy-making process, rather than directly influencing it. The *enlightenment model* suggests that the work of scientists, including their theories, ideas and findings, influences the policy process in a rather diffuse way. In this model, as Berridge and Thom point out, policy and science are not separate spheres, but are 'linked through networks of influence and policy communities where information and ideas are constantly reviewed and exchanged' (Berridge and Thom, 1996). Research permeates through many channels of influence, including the mass media, professional journals, and conversations with colleagues, thereby shaping the way that policy makers and the general public think about social issues (Weiss, 1986). Rather than enabling policy makers to refer to the findings of specific studies, in this model, policy makers 'have a sense that social science research has given them a backdrop of ideas and orientations' (Weiss, 1986). Research sensitises policy makers and others to emerging issues. It may indeed change the debate and help define the policy agenda, turning what were once non-problems into policy problems and *vice versa*.

Another, more cynical, model describing the relationship between science and policy subscribes to the view that science legitimises decisions that have already been taken. This *legitimation* or *political model* (Weiss, 1986) suggests that research may often *follow* key policy decisions and be used to justify changes that are already under way and to deflect criticism of decisions that have already been made. Decision makers may not always be receptive to new evidence elicited from scientific research, and 'for reasons of interest, ideology or intellect, they have taken a stand that research is not likely to shake' (Weiss, 1986). Research evidence is then utilised to strengthen this predetermined stance of policy makers. Less cynically, this relationship is understandable given the temporal link between the political imperatives for funding scientific research and the timescale of this research. The political decisions need to be made now; the evidence for the decisions may take much longer to produce.

Other models of the relationship between science and policy are discussed elsewhere (see Weiss, 1986), and there may be some truth in all the various models. However, the reason for highlighting them here is that they serve as a reminder that social scientists work within political contexts. They also reveal that the relationship between science and policy-making is not straightforward, that it brings both benefits and dangers and holds out the prospects of triumphs and disappointments. The optimal relationship between science and policy therefore needs to be developed.

Prevalence estimation and the policy decision-making process

Estimating the scale and nature of drug phenomena *could* have an important role in drug policy-making but, as indicated, this role is in need of development. Social scientists are not in the business of counting things for the sake of counting things. As Peter Reuter has pointed out, 'for conscientious policy makers dealing with drug problems at the national and local levels, prevalence estimation ought to be a fundamental element of sensible decision-making' (Reuter, 1993). In practice, prevalence estimation has not been important in policy-making, either in setting the policy agenda, or in the formulation and implementation of policy and its evaluation. Policy-making decisions are all too often determined without consideration of prevalence data.

Thus far, much of the interest in prevalence estimation has been in providing gross measures to show that a city or a nation has a large drug problem (Reuter, 1993).

These measures are relatively simplistic and have had limited relevance to policy makers. It may be important for them to know what percentage of the population has had some experience of illicit drug use, and what proportion has had recent experience of it. It may be considered important to know what percentage of the population has been exposed to particular risks, such as injecting, and what proportion has problems linked with their drug use – for example, dependency or criminal justice problems. However, it is doubtful that the knowledge that 15 *versus* 30 per cent of young people are regularly using cannabis, or that 0.5 or 1.5 per cent of the population has injected drugs, is going to make that much difference to the policy decision-making process.

As Reuter (1993) points out, what may be more important is the use of prevalence estimates in order to improve decisions about the investment of resources in different kinds of interventions, and in the assessment of the impact of these investment decisions. For example, estimating the size of the population of problem drug takers that may benefit from substance misuse treatment should be crucial in making a decision about what resources to allocate to drug treatment. Similarly, investment in a harm reduction programme, such as syringe exchange, needs to be based on evidence about the size and location of the population at risk. Furthermore, estimating the scale of drug-related crime, or the size of drug markets, can also lead to informed decisions about investment in different kinds of interventions.

Prevalence estimates can hopefully be used to help in making decisions about where public money should be spent. Of course, this requires some consensus about what the problems of drug use are and how they are to be addressed (see Chapter 2 by Peter Cohen). If drug use itself is seen as a harm, measures of the scale of drug use, and estimations about how different interventions might influence the scale of drug use, are needed. If it is specific harms to health that are of concern, such as overdose or risk of infectious disease, then estimates of the specific target populations at risk of these problems are needed. If the concern is about the size of drug markets, or the scale of drug-related crime, again the target population and measures will differ, as will the interventions.

Key questions to which policy-makers might expect epidemiologists to provide answers

It is helpful to anticipate the kind of questions that sophisticated policy makers might ask. They might reasonably expect epidemiologists to provide answers to eight key questions concerning the prevalence of drug use. These questions are phrased here in lay, rather than scientific, terms.

The *first* question that might be asked is 'What is the extent of the phenomenon?' There are a number of ways in which the extent of the phenomenon might be described, for example in terms of: the number of people involved; the number of drug use events, exposures or risks; the amount of drugs consumed; or expenditure on drug use. Note that many epidemiologists tackle the estimation problem in terms of the number of *people* who are affected. The questions asked by policy makers may not require people as the units of analysis.

The *second* question that policy makers might want to ask is 'Who uses drugs?' Do drug use and drug problems affect different sectors of the population? Where are these people located, both geographically and socially? What are the correlates and characteristics of different kinds of drug use?

The *third* question is 'What is the nature of the problem?' Predominant concerns have been about harms to the health of the individual, such as drug dependence, risk of infectious disease for those who inject drugs, acute accidents linked to consumption, such as overdose and drug interactions, and drug-related behavioural incidents, such as risks related to driving motor vehicles. There are also concerns about criminal activities and drug use, including the cost of drug-related crime, threats to public order and public safety through to drug-related intoxication and affronts to public sensibility. There are also concerns about the ability, or otherwise, of the individual to perform social roles in the family, as an income earner and in terms of social relationships.

The *fourth* question pertains to the costs incurred from drug use, including the health care costs of helping and treating people, the costs to victims of crime, criminal justice costs, and the cost of morbidity and mortality on lost productivity.

The *fifth* question that policy makers will want to ask is 'Is the problem getting worse, or is it getting better?' Many estimates are *point prevalence figures*, but policy makers are more interested in trends over time. Situations may be deteriorating because more people are involved or because they have worse outcomes. This may strengthen the arguments for interventions. On the other hand, drug use trends may reverse and this might give policy makers an opportunity to congratulate themselves and divert resources elsewhere.

Drug use patterns and practices change rapidly. The growth of injection of illicit drugs in Europe is a good example. The first diffusion of drug injecting occurred in Europe in the early 1960s. Whilst each country within Europe has its own specific history of drug injecting, it is significant that trends in the diffusion of drug use often transcend national boundaries. Increases in the use and injection of heroin were seen across Western European cities in different stages and waves in the early 1970s and again in the 1980s (Stimson, 1996). The spread of unwanted consequences may also be fast. Here again injecting provides a good example, with the rapid spread of HIV infection associated with injecting in many European cities in the mid-1980s.

The epidemiological task must, therefore, move beyond *point prevalence estimation* and towards an understanding of the dynamics of changes in drug use over time (see Chapter 18 by Ludwig Kraus). This involves *serial estimation of incidence and prevalence*. Prospective developments in social epidemiology are the application of the diffusion of innovation theories (Rhodes *et al*, 1996), the use of social geographic techniques to describe and predict the spread of new substance consumption patterns and practices, and socio-demographic mapping of the links between drug use and social condition (Giggs *et al*, 1989; Pearson and Gilman, 1994; Squires *et al*, 1995).

The *sixth* question is about the causes of new patterns of drug use. This is not a question which many politicians like to ask in public, particularly those in governments that have been in power over the period in which drug problems have developed. It is notable also that social scientists have been unable to give clear answers to such questions. It is necessary to examine causal issues at the level both of the individual and the community. Regarding the latter, a *social epidemiology* would attempt to explain and predict, as well as to describe, the epidemiology of drug use (Rhodes *et al*, 1996). The sub-regional diffusion of injecting may provide important case material. However, because epidemiologists have mostly been concerned with trends within their own cities and countries, there has been no attempt to develop a model for the diffusion of drug use practices across Europe as a whole. Cross-regional studies of past and current epidemic dynamics are required.

The *seventh* question on which policy makers might seek advice is 'Can anything be done about drug use? and, if so, what?' It is here that the relevance of epidemiology to the development of interventions is apparent. Epidemiology should be able to describe the characteristics of the target population in order to indicate the scale and nature of interventions required, but it requires other expertise to advise on the appropriate kinds of interventions.

The *eighth* question on which policy makers may require advice is about the impact of their policies. Epidemiology should contribute to the assessment of the impact of interventions. For example, if treatment is effective for certain drug problems, one indicator of whether an intervention is successful is the ability of services to attract problem drug users into treatment – therefore, it is necessary to develop measures to determine the ratio of those problem drug users in and out of contact with helping services.

Why estimate?

The above questions may seem relatively straightforward, so what are the difficulties? Why is it necessary to be concerned with the methodological issues of estimating drug problems? Difficulties in describing the extent, nature and impact of substance use and misuse present considerable scientific challenges, as described in other chapters of this book. Drug use is usually illicit and hidden and subject to rapidly- changing fashions. Routine surveillance sources remain only partially validated, are of variable coverage, and measure only a part of the phenomenon. Research studies are usually conducted on selected populations of unknown representativeness, and with little opportunity for methodological development or collection of time-trend data. Some household surveys have included questions on illicit drug use, but doubts remain about their ability to elicit reliable and valid data about illicit and socially-disapproved behaviour. Properly conducted population surveys require large samples in order to identify behaviours that may only be quite rare in the population (but see Chapter 7 by Paul Griffiths and colleagues).

Therefore, the reasons for estimating are connected with the nature of the pheno-menon – serious drug problems are sufficiently rare to be difficult to measure through other means, and estimation may be cheaper than more direct methods. This monograph describes a number of methods that are used for indirect estimation including capture-recapture (Part III), the use of multipliers (Part IV), and nomination (Part V). These are under-pinned by case-finding methods (Part II).

Conclusions

Two emerging problems which were identified at the beginning of this paper were the need to develop epidemiological expertise and the need to educate policy mak-ers in the uses of information for making decisions about policies and strategies. This is a critical time for scientific advances. The European Monitoring Centre, the Pompidou Group and the scientific community have a major opportunity to show policy makers that scientists can make an important contribution to policy-making. However, scientists must be cautious – one of their first tasks is to convince policy makers of the worth of the product that they are selling.

Inevitably there will be tensions between the desire for scientific rigour *versus* the adequacy of information for decision-making. Scientists want precision, whilst policy makers want only sufficient information to be confident that they have made the correct assessment and taken the right decisions. There will be a tension between the time required to conduct good scientific work, and policy makers' needs for quick information relevant to immediate action. There will also be ten-sions about the cost of providing information and about whether investment in pro-viding such information leads to an improvement in policy-making.

Finally, epidemiologists need to be modest in what they think they can achieve and the contribution that this will make to policy-making. Prevalence estimates are but one kind of information that will be assessed along with a wide range of other infor-mation. The astute policy maker needs to be able to understand the relevance of prevalence estimates alongside a range of other information which provides a pic-ture of the unfolding state of drug problems within our countries.

References

Berridge, V. and Thom, B. (1996) 'Research and policy: what determines the relationship?' *Policy Studies*, 17 (1), 23-34.

Brodsky, M.D. (1985) 'History of heroin prevalence estimation techniques', in B.A. Rouse, N.J. Kozel, L.G. Richards (Eds) *Self-report methods of estimating drug use: meeting current challenges to validity*, Rockville: NIDA.

Cormack, R.M. (1992) 'Interval estimation for mark-recapture studies of closed populations', *Biometrics*, 48, 567-576.

Giggs, J., Bean, P., Whynes, D. and Wilkinson, C. (1989) 'Class A drug users: prevalence and characteristics in Greater Nottingham', *British Journal of Addiction*, 84, 1473-1480.

Hartnoll, R.L., Lewis, R. and Mitcheson, M. (1985) 'Estimating the prevalence of opioid dependence', *Lancet*, 1, 203-205.

Pearson, G. and Gilman, M. (1994) 'Local and regional variations in drug misuse: the British heroin epidemic of the 1980s', in J. Strang and M. Gossop (Eds) *Heroin addiction and drug policy – the British system*, New York: Oxford University Press.

Reuter, P. (1993) 'Prevalence estimation and policy formulation', *The Journal of Drug Issues*, 23 (2), 167-184.

Rhodes, T.J., Stimson, G.V. and Quirk, A. (1996) 'Sex, drugs, intervention and research: from the individual to the social', *Substance use and misuse*, 31 (3), 375-407.

Squires, N.F., Beeching, N.J., Schlecht, B.J.M. and Ruben, S.M. (1995) 'An estimate of the prevalence of drug misuse in Liverpool and a spatial analysis of known addiction', *Journal of Public Health Medicine*, 17 (1), 103-109.

Stimson, G.V. (1996) 'Preventing HIV-1 infection among drug injectors in Europe: the challenge for social and behavioural scientists', in J. Georgas, M. Manthouli, E. Besevegis and A. Kokkevi (Eds) *Contemporary psychology in Europe: theory, research and application*, Gottingen: Hogrefe and Huber.

Weiss, C.H. (1986) 'The Many Meanings of Research Utilisation', in M. Bulmer (Ed) *Social Science and Social Policy*, London: Allen and Unwin.

Woodward, J.A., Bonett, D.G. and Brecht, M.L. (1985) 'Estimating the size of a heroin-abusing population using multiple-recapture census', in B.A. Rouse, N.J. Kozel, L.G. Richards (Eds) *Self-report methods of estimating drug use: meeting current challenges to validity*, Rockville: NIDA.

CHAPTER 2

THE RELATIONSHIP BETWEEN DRUG USE PREVALENCE ESTIMATION AND POLICY INTERESTS

by Peter D. A. Cohen

My comments will focus on the local level of drug use prevalence estimation. It is at the local level – often the city or local municipality – that most decisions are taken, and where the relevance of good data and understanding for drug policy practice is highest. Furthermore, national estimation of drug use, or related behaviours and events, is difficult without reliable local data. If local data collection is good, and covers the most important areas of a country, national data have a chance of being of relatively sound quality.

In this chapter, I would like to discuss some problems related to the selection of appropriate methods for the estimation of drug use or heavy drug use. I do not propose to cover everything, but will look at the kind of problems that have to be solved before one begins this task or while analysing, interpreting and digesting the data. I will also discuss questions about how clarity regarding a general model of drug policy can improve the relevance and interpretations of local drug use data and estimations.

Data of reasonable quality are often available only in part or not at all, but once the importance of collecting reliable data is recognised on the political level, this problem may be solved. Then, by means of good sampling, sound survey instruments and by means of good police registration techniques, prevalence and patterns of different kinds of drug use can be studied on a regular basis. Moreover, once treatment institutions are in place, reliable treatment registration can also supply interesting data sets. The inherent problems and potential for error in using particular methods are not always fully grasped by those who use them. This means that the match between type and quality of data and technique of analysis is sometimes poor.

I will not discuss here ways of making available reliable sets of local data or the statistical techniques to digest them. Solutions to 'technical' problems will only come if the perceived political importance ascribed to data and good estimation rises to a sufficiently high level. Therefore, most important for the selection of the most appropriate objects and methods of drug use research in general, and prevalence estimation in particular, are problems of drug policy and the way drug policy is made. As long as it is made without a heavy input from systematic and scientific data analysis, the political basis for drug policy is not much more than emotion or orthodoxy (Ehrenberg, 1996; Cohen and Sas, 1996; Boekhout van Solinge, 1996).

Every estimate has to be tailor-made to its proper use or functions. This implies that estimation problems should not only be seen as technical, but also as strategic. What exactly is there to estimate? To what broad or narrow policy aspect is the estimate of relevance related? What precision of the estimate is required? Do we need the estimate to be comparable to estimates made in other areas? What are the political implications of the estimates? In other words, the sophistication of drug policy itself has a strong influence on the quality of the estimation process.

Drug policy models and what to estimate

Let us take the example of general prevalence estimation of frequent and/or heavy heroin use. In what policy model can such an estimate perform a role? Let us assume, for the sake of brevity, that we have three distinct policy models. One is a predominantly punitive and repressive model, the second a harm reduction model and the third what we might define as a cultural integration model.

In the *repressive* model, the dominant aim is to suppress all drug use. Estimators will probably work with a definition of 'drug addiction' that includes all types of heroin use since, in this model, all types of heroin use are considered harmful and abusive. Estimation needs will encompass all forms of heroin use, intravenous or not, regular or not, and problem-related or not. The size of the heroin problem is more or less the size of heroin use prevalence. The function of this estimate repeated over time is to assess the success of suppression. If estimates are reliable and go down, suppression is deemed successful. If estimates go up, suppression is not considered successful enough and has to be increased or changed in scope and implementation.

Prevalence estimates in the punitive model are used to evaluate the short-term success of suppression techniques and not their intrinsic merits in relation to another model of drug policy. It is also possible that, in a particular version of the punitive model, the size of the heroin-using population is not so important, but the number of heroin-overdose deaths is. The number of emergency room visits of heroin consumers may also be deemed important. The latter data probably say more about the conditions surrounding drug use than about the seriousness of the problem (in terms of the number of users) but the public or politicians often do not perceive this. In a repressive model, these types of data represent deterrence, and giving them a high profile is part of the policy. In such a case we will sometimes find that extremely high prevalence estimates may play a role, either in the press or in the speeches of politicians. Such estimates may simply be anecdotal (if not worse) but this fact is easily clouded behind the emotional appeal which is the real function of such estimates.

In a *harm reduction* model, the aim is still to reduce drug use in general, however, the emphasis is not placed on punitive action but on the prevention of potential harmful effects of drug use behaviour and drug distribution. It allows for the fact that drug use exists and will continue. In spite of the goal being to reduce its prevalence, reducing individual and social risks of the existing types of drug use is seen as a major concern.

As far as this model is concerned, the need for data could be very different from demands made in the repressive model of drug policy. Policy makers who work within a harm reduction model are mainly interested in the number of heroin users who are clients and potential clients for harm reduction intervention, be it medical or non-medical. Such clients could belong to quite different sub-groups. One sub-group may consist of drug injecting prostitutes working on the street under marginalised conditions, another might be prostitutes working in a completely different site of the sex market, such as clubs or expensive brothels. Other sub-groups might consist of homeless users, inmates, ethnic groups or students and employees. Providing assistance to each of these sub-groups – where needed – is deemed important. However, the attention given to these different groups will probably have different policy priorities, different budget consequences and different kinds of political usefulness.

Estimates in this model serve for the assessment of the treatment and assistance needs of particular groups based on knowledge about drug use and risk patterns in these groups. The estimates may also be needed to find out if some groups remain without adequate assistance. For instance, one may have data that generate estimates of high injecting drug use in certain ethnic groups, but these groups are rarely seen in institutions which give assistance. In that case, the treatment system will have to be able to relocate or devise new options. Similarly, in the Dutch city of Rotterdam, a general increase in the use of base cocaine by heavy drug users has been reported (Grund, 1993; Visser, 1996; van Swol, 1996). The adequacy of the present methadone-based treatment system – designed for heroin users – has to be investigated in the light of these developments.

Another function of estimations in a harm-reducing policy model is related to evaluating the level of harm reduction that is characteristic of the context of particular kinds drug use. For instance, if drug overdose deaths are reliably estimated (by excluding double counting, by including corrections for false cause of death registration and by maintaining unambiguous definitions) and these estimates rise, something may be wrong with the style of police activity in a city. Crude suppression may result in high variability of drug purity, unavailability of quiet drug use locations and so on. This, in its turn, could result in rising numbers of drug overdose deaths. Since drug policy in a harm reduction model aims at reducing risks, changes in the style and intensity of police suppression may be more important for risk reduction than the development of accessible assistance institutions.

If one investigates the prevalence of injecting drug use in a particular city and finds that it is much higher than elsewhere, one might start to investigate the possible reasons for this. In Amsterdam, among the population of heavy heroin users, only a minority inject and a large majority (about 70 per cent) are smokers of heroin (Korf, 1995; Grapendaal et al, 1995). In Amsterdam, those who inject have a higher mortality than the non-injectors (van Haastrecht et al, 1996). Although this difference might not apply in other settings, it is very interesting from the point of view of local mortality prevention. Would it be possible to decrease heroin-related mortality in cities by having heavy users change their route of ingestion? Could we find out under what conditions (heavy) current heroin users abandon injection as the route of ingestion, or new users start by smoking heroin rather than injecting it? Might cheap heroin base, of stable and relatively high purity, provide such a condition? Is such a condition attainable if law enforcement against individual heroin use and sales is given a low priority, as is the case in Amsterdam? In this example, the availability of the estimate of low prevalence of injecting drug use among heavy heroin users in Amsterdam is the starting point for broader drug policy questions.

In the third policy model, that of *cultural integration*, the main aim is no longer to suppress drug use *per se*. The overall aim is to bring drug use under the normal regulatory mechanisms societies have for controlling accepted behaviour and attributing meanings to behaviour. Drug use in this model is as 'normal' as are its problems. In the Netherlands, this approach is called 'normalisation of drug use' (Engelsman, 1989) and it implies explicitly that possible problems are no longer treated as extreme or principally different from other social problems, such as traffic, broken marriage or stress in the office. In this policy model, the basic aims are exactly opposite to those of the suppression model: in the latter, drug use is maximally ostracised and marginalised. In this model, it is integrated into the normal social process.

In the cultural integration model of drug control, the need for data is different. One may want to know how many heavy drug users are treated in the normal care system (e.g. by general practitioners and hospitals) and how many are still referred to special institutions. Taking care of heavy drug users in special institutions pertains more to repressive and harm reduction models where heavy drug use is so deviant and its problems so special that those concerned need these special institutions. But, as we can see in the field of alcohol use (which is culturally integrated in the Netherlands), much of the treatment takes place in the normal system. In the Netherlands, it is mostly general practitioners who prescribe vitamins, monitor health status and refer to other health care when needed. Only very few of the heavy alcohol users are referred to specialised institutions. In repressive and harm reduction systems, heavy drug users are still seen as so deviant that most do not have a chance to be treated in regular psychiatric institutions, although a certain percentage of them would need such treatment. (In spite of 'normalisation' attempts in Amsterdam, the Municipal Health Service has had to set up a small psychiatric care unit within the Municipal Health Care system for heavy drug users).

Other data that could be needed in a cultural integration model would focus on what social processes hinder cultural integration. A good example is the shift from a repressive policy model around homosexuality in the Netherlands towards a cultural integration model. With the latter, it is relevant to enquire into the prevalence of teachers that are denied employment because of their homosexuality, or what career problems homosexual officers in the military might have, and how to redress them.

This short overview illustrates that 'estimates of the prevalence of heroin addiction' or related estimates can only have meaning and function within the local models of policy. If such functions are not well ascribed, estimation will probably never reach an acceptable level of accuracy, nor will it have very much impact on drug policy. Fuller accounts of types of estimates and their possible uses are given by Reuter (1993) and by Anglin, Caulkins and Hser (1993).

On a higher level of abstraction, one could say that, in all countries, there is some sort of local construction of the drug problem. This construction appears in the kind of problems that are considered relevant, the causal attributions that are made to 'explain' these problems, the policy interventions that are produced to 'do something about it', and the type of expertise (e.g. medical, social or legal) that is considered mostly relevant in the situation. It is usually a change in the latter factor (the dominance of particular expertise) that shows the introduction of a change in the type of paradigm that governs the problem construction.

In the Netherlands, this was very clear in the late 1960s when drug policy commissions, which included not only medical but also many criminological and social scientific experts, were created. This made a broader view of drug use possible, with dramatic consequences for the way the 'drug problem' was viewed and responded to (Cohen, 1997). Latterly, in the USA, a military general has been made the director of drug policy (a 'Drug Czar') after this function had previously been in the hands of a police officer. This might point to a new way in which the problem is perceived and a new direction for policy development.

What precision is needed for estimates?

Functional considerations for precision

Creating estimates for the size of small – albeit well-defined – groups is an intricate procedure. For some groups, it may entail case-finding and nomination techniques or costly survey and/or fieldwork methods to provide data which, combined with other registries, might yield reasonable estimates. The highest possible precision of the estimates is always important from a scientific point of view, precision being defined here as a narrow band of confidence intervals. However, since policy makers will have to provide the funds for estimation-making, the elevated costs for higher levels of precision will, unfortunately, not always be considered legitimate.

The required precision will often be dictated by drug policy aims, budgets, simple technical skills, and by the quality of the raw data which are available, but most of all by the political agendas of those who will fund and use estimations. Estimating the prevalence of rare or hidden behaviours or events is a matter of combining results of different methods for estimating. If estimates vary considerably among methods, something is wrong and precision probably low. Fieldwork and databases must be improved. But if really independent estimates are not too far apart for each method, or if variations are clearly understood as artefacts of data collection, one could be relatively satisfied with the results. For instance, if one knows that a database of drug-related arrests is biased towards certain ethnic groups because of unequal arrest probability between ethnic groups, the error resulting from this will be reflected in estimates using capture-recapture in which arrest databases are used. This can be dealt with to a certain degree simply by allowing a certain correction for such an error. But, if such errors are not well quantifiable, one might have to decide to set up the estimates from different assumptions on arrest probability, to set up capture-recapture using other data or to move to different methods altogether.

Political considerations for precision

An important aspect to be discussed when speaking about the desired level of estimate precision is the political use that is made of estimates. Since political differences about the right kind of drug policy occur quite frequently, an estimate might be of use to a particular type of drug political rhetoric and not to another.

Imagine a situation in which the size of the group of 'addicts' is an important political issue. If someone responsible for drug policy can say that this group has diminished during his/her administration, this can be used as support for the particular policy. In the recent exchange of opinions on drug policy between France and the Netherlands, the Dutch Prime Minister used French estimates of addiction prevalence to show that addiction was less prevalent in the Netherlands than in France. The quality of the Dutch addiction estimates, even if marginally better than the French, is not high enough to play a role in a serious comparison of addiction prevalence between the two countries. This leaves untouched the question of the relevance of such a comparison for an evaluation of drug policy; addiction prevalence is probably determined more by broad economic and cultural conditions, immigration and quality of social security than by drug policy. So, estimates can become weapons in a political struggle. This gives the researchers behind these estimates a particular responsibility. It requires the provision of estimates of the highest possible quality and precision, with a clear minimum standard. It is hard to give a standard 'bottom line' but this topic cannot be ignored.

Sometimes strong pressure is applied by politicians to drug policy functionaries to supply estimates of drug use or addiction – 'Just give me some figure that looks like something'. But if decent estimates cannot be produced, this should be made very clear, for instance by stating how uncertain the estimate is, and why. One could supply different estimates and not just one, by making use of different assumptions and data sets. If, under conditions of high uncertainty, more than one estimate is systematically provided, this prevents the development of quasi-knowledge. The absence of 'clear figures', due to insufficient data, should be used to legitimate the funding of the research and registration improvements needed to be able to make good and firm estimations. Specialists in the area of epidemiology should not be forced, or let themselves be forced, to supply unwarranted estimates; they are not magicians. They should stick to the adage that if the data do not exist, estimates cannot be provided.

Another problem attached to the results of estimations is the realistic threat that these results may pose to particular groups of professionals within the field of drug policy and treatment. One does not need much imagination to see that particular groups of professionals may have an interest in these estimates to be high or on the rise. Such groups could be specialised forces in the police, customs, treatment personnel, etc. By providing their own estimates, they can influence the political debate in whatever way they wish. If a scientifically sound, independent and regular estimate of the most important drug use phenomena is in place, such interest-related estimates pose less of a danger to serious discussion about drug policy.

Standardised estimates for purposes of comparison

Up to this point, this chapter has focused on the thesis that well-described local policy needs should be the basis for all local prevalence estimation work. I will conclude with some remarks about estimates that can be used as general indicators.

It is possible to create particular prevalence estimates which are relevant across different models of drug policy. If it were possible for the same phenomenon to be estimated reliably in different places (which does not necessarily mean in the same methodological way), thinking about the impact of drug policy in relation to the drug use phenomenon can be improved. In spite of the fact that an estimate of all heroin use is seen as not very important in a drug policy model that focuses on harm reduction for heavy users, an overall estimate of all heroin use in the general population is very useful as a general descriptive indicator, which can be seen as a baseline. This means, for instance, that if one were to find relatively high prevalence of heroin use among homeless adults, one would want to know if heroin use prevalence among the household population is relatively high as well. The meaning of estimates or measurements relating to sub-groups in a city can only be established if one knows the extent of the same phenomenon in the city population as a whole, if one knows the relative extent of the same phenomenon in more cities and if one knows the sub-group data in these different cities. In order to make such measurements and comparisons thereof, one needs to standardise the definitions of a phenomenon and the methods of looking for it. Some of the epidemiological work of the Experts in Epidemiology of the Council of Europe's Pompidou Group is an example of this drive for comparability between cities.

To be able to evaluate the total level of heroin, or other drug, use in a population, one would need estimates valid for the general household population (from 12 years and above) and for the most important population sub-groups that cannot be measured via household surveys (e.g. prison inmates, the homeless in some cities, etc.). The type of drug use experience to be measured could be recency and frequency: lifetime experience with a drug, and experience in the last year, the last 30 days and the last 24 hours. Within each of the time spans one could measure the frequency of drug use. In this way, it becomes possible to define many different patterns of drug use including long-term frequent drug use. The advantage of this simple way of measuring recency and frequency is that an overview is created of all drug use. One will often see that long-term frequent drug use is rare. This is true in different drug control systems and slowly we start to see that drug policy may have less impact on drug use level than politicians assume. Total heroin use would be near the sum of household and sub-group use, and this summation should be done in different cities according to standardised methods. This could yield massive information on the effects (or the lack of effect) of drug policy, the effects of economic or cultural factors on levels of use, and the prevalence of particular patterns of use or the prevalence of particular problems (such as overdose, first treatment, crime).

Conclusions

Estimation of drug use and the interpretation of such data are, as in all other drug use data collection, very much a function of the drug political situation in a city or country. Technical matters, such as statistical techniques, are only a small part of the problems with which epidemiologists and other researchers of drug use have to struggle. This chapter has attempted to give some insight into these problems and to show that these other problems have a much larger impact on data collection and interpretation than normally acknowledged.

Acknowledgements

Marieke Langemijer of *Centrum voor Drugsonderzoek* provided useful comments on an earlier version of this essay.

References

Anglin, D. Caulkins, J. and Yih-Ing Hser (1993) 'Prevalence estimation: policy needs, current capacity, and future potential', in Rachin, R. L. (Ed) Prevalence Estimation. Techniques for Drug-Using Populations, *Journal of Drug Issues*, Spring 1993 (special issue).

Boekhout van Solinge, T. (1996) 'Heroine, cocaine en crack in Frankrijk. Handel, gebruik en beleid', Centrum voor Drugsonderzoek, Universiteit van Amsterdam.

Cohen, P. and Sas, A. (1996) 'Cannabisbeleid in Duitsland, Frankrijk en de Verenigde Staten', Centrum voor Drugsonderzoek, Universiteit van Amsterdam.

Cohen, P. (1997) 'The case of the two Dutch drug policy commissions. An exercise in Harm Reduction 1968-1972.' Forthcoming in: P. Erickson *et al* (Eds) *New Public Health Policies and Programs for the Reduction of Drug-Related Harm*, Toronto, University of Toronto Press.

Ehrenberg, A. (1996) 'Contre les théologies antidrogue', *Libération*, 15 February.

Engelsman, E. (1989) 'Het Nederlandse drugbeleid in W. Europees perspectief', 137-144, in: M.S. Groenhuijsen en A.M. van Kalmthout (Eds) Nederlands, *Drugsbeleid in Westeuropees Perspectief*, Arnhem, Gouda Quint.

Grapendaal, M. Leuw, E. and Nelen, H. (1995) 'A world of opportunities. Lifestyle and economic behavior of heroin addicts in Amsterdam', New York, State University of New York Press. SUNY series in *New Social Studies on Alcohol and Drugs*, H.H. Levine and C. Reinarman (Eds).

Grund, J-P. C. (1993) 'Drug use as a social ritual: functionality, symbolism and determinants of self-regulation', Rotterdam, Instituut voor Verslavingsonderzoek.

van Haastrecht, H.J.A. *et al* (1996) 'Predictors of mortality in the Amsterdam cohort of Human Immunodeficiency Virus (HIV)-positive and HIV-negative drug users', *American Journal of Epidemiology*, 143, 4, 380-391.

Korf, D.J. (1995) 'Dutch treat. Formal control and illicit drug use in the Netherlands.' Thesis Publishers, Amsterdam.

Reuter, P. (1993) 'Prevalence estimation and policy formulation', in Rachin, R. L. (Ed) Prevalence Estimation. Techniques for Drug-Using Populations, *Journal of Drug Issues*, Spring 1993 (special issue).

Visser, H. (1996) 'Perron Nul. Opgang en ondergang', Zoetermeer, Meinema Uitgeverij.

van Swol, C. *NRC* Handelsblad, 1 juni 1996.

CHAPTER 3

POLICY MAKERS
AND THE USE OF PREVALENCE DATA

by Philip Lazarov

Experience in the development of drug policy and practical interventions in Bulgaria indicates that the policy maker in the field of drugs and drug-related problems has rather unusual roles and functions. In this context, we use the term 'drug policy maker' to refer to those who use their expertise to sensitise society towards the nature and extent of drug use and drug problems and to help facilitate changes in attitudes to drugs.

The 'drug policy maker' has a crucial advocacy role in persuading and motivating policy planners and politicians in government about the need to adopt and implement policy, programmes and projects. 'Drug policy makers' are professionals who have specialised education and training in the drugs field and who often create and run programmes and projects at a national, community or local level. Sometimes they act as temporary policy planners. Their work involves relationships with people working in many different parts of the 'drug system', including politicians and policy planners working at the strategic level, and those engaged in concrete practical works in the areas of prevention, treatment, harm reduction, rehabilitation and law enforcement.

Due to being involved with a wide variety of people, the policy maker needs to develop a large number of activities according to the different target levels of the drug system. The policy maker also has another very significant obligation which is to be a vehicle for the transmission of information and ideas and to provide links between people working in the respective services. Additionally, he or she should also be a professional and experienced person with social and institutional support.

Taking into account this definition, it is possible to conclude that the policy maker is one of the most important elements in the very complicated structure which we refer to as the 'drug system'.

The role of the policy maker will vary according to the different audiences and relationships within the drug system. For example, in Bulgaria, at the level of society and policy planners, there is a need to: increase information about drug use, drug problems and the overall drug situation; sensitise members of the wider society and people working in various institutions dealing with drug problems; encourage a more humanising view towards drug users and people with drug problems; and help find the best balance between drug demand reduction and drug supply reduction in national and local policy.

At the level of practical implementation of policy, there is a need to: increase the knowledge of professional workers; provide them with ideas for the development of different approaches and programmes; and help them in their efforts to recognise the local drug situation, including patterns of use and associated problems.

In general, there is a primary need to describe the current drug situation at both a national and local level. This requires addressing the following questions:

- Are there any drug problems in the community?
- If there are, what kind of problems are they and are they of a major social significance nationally or locally?
- If they are significant, and depending on the kind of problems, what measures should be taken in order to establish and develop appropriate and effective policies and interventions?

The role of the policy maker is, therefore, to describe the concrete drug situation using data from scientific studies using mainly, but not exclusively, the methods and techniques of both epidemiology (which includes direct and indirect estimation) and in-depth research. On the basis of this information, it is possible to see the overall framework of drug issues, and the policy maker can provide expert evaluation and help people working in different sectors to develop proposals for appropriate interventions.

Epidemiology

The methods of population surveys can be used to assess the prevalence of experience with psychoactive substances and of problematic drug use. The prevalence of problematic or addictive use is very difficult to estimate by population surveys because it affects a relatively small group, and population surveys are rarely economical for assessing the size of relatively rare groups. Other chapters in this monograph focus on this crucial issue of estimating the size and nature of problem drug use. However, estimation of the prevalence of drug experience in the general population, or in major sectors of the general population, is still important for the needs and aims of policy makers, particularly for the development of preventive programmes.

Such surveys, like those which target specific populations such as school children, can provide useful information on the socio-demographic characteristics of drug users and risk factors such as lifestyle, tobacco smoking, use of alcohol, availability of drugs, peer pressure and so on. One example is the surveys which have been conducted in schools in Bulgaria by the National Centre for Addictions in Sofia. The first was carried out on students aged between 14 and 18 in four cities in 1993 (n = 998). The second was a representative sample of 1,111 students from ten schools in Sofia, again aged 14 to 18. Both aimed to examine the use of drugs, alcohol and tobacco among students, and to assess the level of information and attitudes of students, teachers and parents. Figure 1, for example, shows data which indicate that most often the onset of use of alcohol and tobacco was in the 13-16 age range. There is a correlation between the first use of alcohol, tobacco and drugs. The implication for policy planners is that the early onset of smoking and drinking appears to be a marker for the development of drug use.

More than 50 per cent of students in the ten schools surveyed in Sofia in 1995 knew people – most often their peers – who were using drugs, and a third had close friends who were using drugs. More than 25 per cent had been to a party where drugs were being used, and the same proportion had been offered drugs. From the point of view of preventive activities, this provided important confirmation of the well-known role of teenage peer influence for the establishment of drug use.

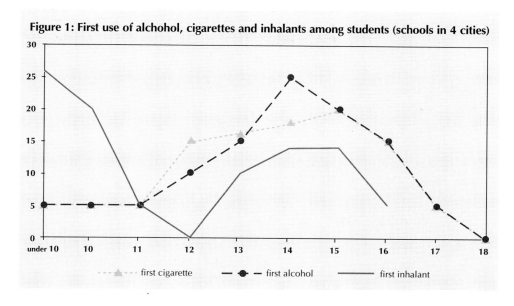

Figure 1: First use of alchohol, cigarettes and inhalants among students (schools in 4 cities)

In the ten-school survey, the most common drug used was cannabis, which was reported by 15 per cent. Of those who reported using drugs in this survey, marijuana was the most popular, reported by 79 per cent of the drug using students, followed by hashish (33 per cent). Sixteen per cent reported using drugs such as stimulants and hallucinogens, which is a new trend in the drug situation. Heroin and cocaine were reported by 4 per cent of the drug users.

Such surveys can also provide summary information on students' perceptions of reasons for using drugs. When we examined reasons for using drugs, students viewed their own drug use in a different way to that of their peers. For themselves, 'curiosity' was overwhelmingly mentioned as the most common reason – by two-thirds of them – and only 6 per cent mentioned 'escape'. When they were asked about reasons why others used drugs, 'escape' was the most important. These attributions can help in the design of educational materials.

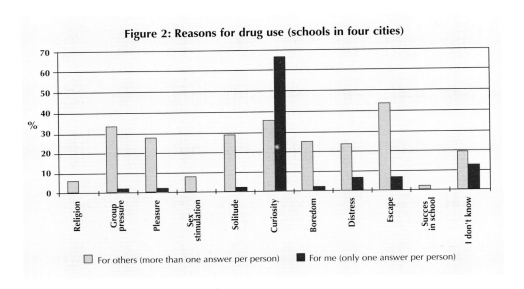

Figure 2: Reasons for drug use (schools in four cities)

In Bulgaria, this type of information has been useful to describe the prevalence of drug experience and for helping to encourage responsible institutions to develop appropriately targeted preventive programmes.

Pompidou Group methods

In order to describe other aspects of the drug situation, especially regarding problematic and addictive use, we have drawn on data from multi-sectoral studies. A good example for us has been the model promoted by the Multi-City Network Project developed by the Council of Europe's Pompidou Group. This model uses a number of different indicators including treatment demand and first treatment demand; drug-related morbidity; non-fatal drug emergencies; drug-related deaths; HIV-1 and AIDS prevalence; and data from the customs, police and the courts.

The Multi-City Network approach gives an overall picture of the drug situation in each respective city. Being a longitudinal study, this project provides an extremely important source of information on the dynamic of the drug situation, which can be used to encourage the development of long-term programmes for the health and criminal justice systems. Data from these studies provided policy makers with important evidence to argue for new interventions, and helped them both to develop and enlarge a number of harm reduction programmes (including methadone maintenance, syringe and needle exchange, and outreach) and to address issues of risk of infection with HIV and hepatitis among hidden populations. The information was also used to improve educational programmes for students and professionals.

In-depth research

Both the planning and implementation of drug policy needs much more detailed information about detailed aspects of problematic and addictive use of drugs than can be provided by epidemiological surveys and indirect estimation. Such in-depth information is important for designing and developing therapeutic approaches, harm reduction programmes and rehabilitation. In order to propose suitable programmes, there is a need for very concrete information. Such knowledge can only be obtained from in-depth studies using, for example, social network recruitment of different populations of drug users.

In 1995, we conducted a snowball sampling study among heroin addicts in Sofia, using the methodology recommended by the Pompidou Group. Forty-nine people were recruited from eleven network chains. They were all recruited from street locations by specially trained interviewers. This approach gave important information about the kinds of drugs being used, the age of onset of first and regular heroin use and the quantity of drugs used. This study found that more than two-thirds of the heroin addicts had started using heroin by injecting it. The most common age for commencing heroin use was between 16 and 18 (52 per cent). The earliest age was 14 and the oldest was 37. Sixteen to 18 years was also the most common age range for first regular use (52 per cent). The mean age for first use and first regular use were 20.1 and 20.3 years respectively, with the mean skewed by some people who started at an older age – 20 per cent were 25 or older. The similar age for first use and first regular use indicates how quickly regular use was adopted. About two-thirds continued to use by injection. Most (60 per cent) were using between 0.50g and 1.00g a day (the mean was 0.87g), with the highest dose around 2.50g a day.

Conclusions

Data from such studies help policy makers develop programmes and activities in a very sensitive area. Drug use – and drug problems – are increasing in Bulgaria, in a situation where there is both attractive information about drugs for some sectors, and a more general restrictive social attitude to their use. Surveys can help supplement the work and experience of professionals such as doctors, psychologists, social workers and their respective organisations. Policy makers can draw on such data to help change attitudes and develop effective demand and supply reduction activities.

Scientific studies in epidemiology – whether using direct estimates as described here or indirect estimates as described elsewhere in this monograph – need to be combined with in-depth studies of drug use and drug-related problems. This can help policy makers provide an expert assessment of the drug situation. This assessment should cover the main aspects of the drug process in each respective country, city or community, including: the dynamic spread of drug use and drug problems; trends in average age of onset of drugs; the appearance of new drugs and new patterns of use; developments of drug markets and drug-related crime; consequences of drug use such as the prevalence of HIV-1 and AIDS, hepatitis and other harms; and the establishment of specific drug sub-cultures.

Such information is one of the cornerstones of effective policy making. On the basis of such knowledge and expert evaluation, suggestions can be made on the development of suitable measures, approaches and programmes directed at the different levels of the drug system, including: the national level (e.g. legislation, national networks, etc.); the level of structures such as the community, schools and the family; and the level of the individual.

CASE-FINDING METHODS

PART II

INTRODUCTION

by Matthew Hickman

Case-finding has a long and honourable history, starting with the first descriptions of death and disease in the population – such as John Snow's maps of cholera in London. It is also the basis of many of our on-going surveillance systems. Alone, however, it is not an exact science. The increased use of statistics and the development of sampling techniques have relegated it to a secondary role for providing reliable estimates of the prevalence of ill-health or associated risk factors in the population.

Not all health problems, however, have a ready-made sampling frame or lend themselves to investigation by large population surveys. Problem drug taking (including injecting behaviour and/or heroin use) – as a comparatively rare, illicit and opprobrious activity – is a classic example of one of these problems.

The authors in this section respond to two problems. The first is the failure or inability of large-scale population surveys to provide prevalence estimates. Here, Roland Simon states the need for case-finding studies; Börje Olsson deals with this at a national level; Conchi Moreno Iribas and Mikel Urtiaga Dominguez at a regional level; and Paul Griffiths, Michael Farrell and Samantha Howes at a small area level. The second problem is that it is not only unlikely, but impossible, for any case-finding exercise to enumerate completely the population of problem drug takers (unlike, for example, diagnosed cases of lung cancer). Case-finding, therefore, plays a crucial role in providing the raw material for indirect methods to estimate the total population (including unreported cases and drug-takers unrecognised or unknown to any data source).

Good case-finding, as outlined by Simon, is systematic. It involves appropriate and feasible case-definition, the proper assessment of available data sources and potential reporters, and validation of the quality of data obtained. Poor case-finding is likely to lead to poor estimates of prevalence or, as Olsson says: 'garbage in, garbage out'.

Olsson highlights problems and solutions to collecting data on drug-takers with reference to the remarkable national case-finding exercises carried out in Sweden in 1979 and 1992. These were prodigious in their scale, ambition and planning – but perhaps also unique and not translatable as a national study to other countries in Europe.

Iribas and Dominguez illustrate the strategies outlined by Simon – clear case-definition and assessment of the availability and quality of data sources – for a region (Navarra) in Spain. They show how data can be obtained on 'visible' drug-takers from a number and variety of sources, mostly routine, by utilising their own data collection or reporting systems. They reinforce the impressions gained from Olsson's chapter that, undertaken properly, case-finding is exhausting and time-consuming.

The outcome of prevalence estimation is often a single number or range. Of equal importance, as shown by the work in Navarra, can be the opportunity case-finding provides for describing the population of visible drug takers: their age, sex, area of residence, occupation and pattern of drug taking. The value of this information is also associated with the quality and thoroughness of the case-finding.

Griffiths, Farrell and Howes demonstrate how a sample survey to estimate the level of drug-taking may be carried out – but at a small area level – at a housing estate in a deprived area of London. Such an area is too small to generate a sufficient number of cases from legal or medical sources to use indirect estimation methods reliably, but it is small enough to carry-out a comprehensive household survey and has high enough levels of reported drug-taking to measure prevalence and provide some further descriptive information.

However, as they admit, there was great difficulty in defining the sampling-frame, and, at very best, the project achieved only a 50% response rate, which would need to be improved for general use elsewhere. Also to be considered further is the importance to policy-makers of determining small area variations in drug-taking, over and above what existing data sources on numbers of arrests or drug-takers in treatment can tell us about geographical variation.

The difficulties with case-finding, and subsequent prevalence estimates, is that usually they are time-consuming, discrete, one-off exercises. Yet most of the data on drug-takers are obtained from existing data sources – crucially treatment and law enforcement agencies. One solution is to work on improving and co-ordinating these main sources of data: to develop an information strategy, and to create an on-going or periodic surveillance system. This should do away with the great deal of work and energy that is currently expended on collecting data from different data sources; will provide regular reports on the number and characteristics of visible drug-takers; and will allow periodic estimates of prevalence with one or several of the methods described in later chapters.

ESTIMATING PREVALENCE
USING THE CASE-FINDING METHOD:
AN OVERVIEW

by Roland Simon

Case-finding is a standard epidemiological method for obtaining an adequate number of cases for observation and research, especially when investigating rare health events in a population (Pflanz, 1973). An extensive literature search of published studies found few studies of illegal drugs citing this method (exceptions include Bishop, 1976; Skarabis and Patzak, 1981; Frischer *et al*, 1992). However, case-finding is important, as seen by the fact that nearly every study discussed in the Scientific Seminar (such as those involving nomination techniques or capture-recapture) started with case-finding procedures. Pure case-finding studies are rare, but the findings are used in different ways to establish valid prevalence estimations.

As there is no single way or information source which can find all, or at least most of, drug users, a combination of different strategies is needed. Multi-source enumeration is one method widely used to overcome the lack of completeness and representativeness of single sources and can provide estimates of the prevalence of drug users.

Case-finding is applicable to studying drug use for several reasons. Firstly, drug use is rare. Secondly, as an illegal activity, it is largely hidden. Therefore, general population sample survey techniques will be too costly, inefficient, and may be ineffective for identifying drug users. Thirdly, a ready-made sampling frame or register does not exist; which, in part, is the reason for carrying out a case-finding study.

Central methodological aspects and common information sources

Although several methodological aspects may be important and different strategies may be employed to meet different requirements, the common and most important aspects are described below:

Coverage and representativeness

It is unlikely that coverage will be complete (100 per cent enumeration). Ideally, the subjects identified through case-finding are representative of the total population of drug users under study, in order to enable the generalisation of characteristics and other findings. The number of all existing drug users in a given population, which can be found using one specific source, depends very much on the specific characteristics of this source, but it is likely that the number identified will be smaller than the total number.

Sensitivity and specificity

It is important that strategies are used which enable all drug users under examination to be identified (sensitivity) and that no cases are included which do not meet the definition of the target group (specificity).

Feasibility, reliability and comparability

The case-finding study must be acceptable to reporters and drug users. Information sources and screening strategies may need to be assessed in order to test whether they can provide the data required by the study. For example, it can be difficult to involve more deeply in research studies subjects who are contacted by the police. Also, obtaining reliable and comparable data (with other studies or countries) especially when using narrow definitions of the target group (e.g. based on ICD 10 or DSM IV) may require specially designed procedures and trained and supervised interviewers.

Double-counting

When different sources are combined, there is a considerable risk of over-estimating the total number of cases unless personal identifiers are available in a reliable and standardised way in all of the sources to enable identification and removal of duplicates.

Cost

Total cost is directly related to the number and amount of staff and time spent per case. This can be reduced if routine data sources are used, even when additional efforts by staff working in these sources are necessary.

Target groups

The term *drug user* is often used as if it refers to a clear and homogeneous group of people, whereas this is far from being the case. For example, therapeutic research projects focus on subjects who have already developed considerable drug problems; primary prevention studies focus on persons who are at risk of starting drug use or of developing problematic drug use; and secondary prevention studies may include ex-users. The typology of target groups becomes even more complex when different types of drugs are considered.

Thus, as depicted in Figure 1, the target group could embrace subjects who are *current users* defined in terms of frequency and recency of use; *problematic drug users* defined in terms of the risk of medical, psychological and/or social problems arising directly or indirectly from drug use; or *drug addicts* defined in terms of specific survey instruments assessing tolerance, withdrawal syndrome and the inability to cease drug use. These may vary in size and in the degree of overlap. In 1990, in Germany, the range was between 0.5 per cent for drug addiction, 0.9 per cent for current drug users and 2.0 per cent for ever use of 'hard' drugs.

Figure 1: Target groups

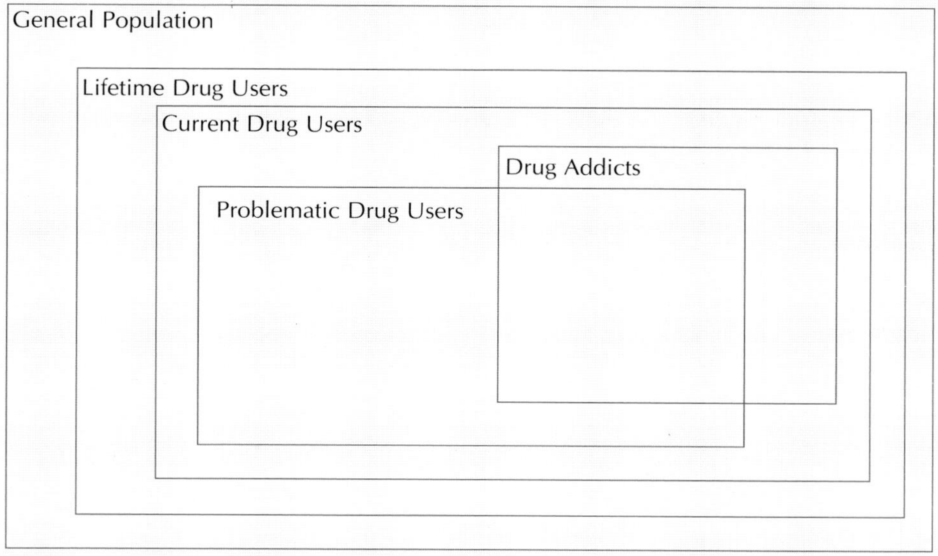

It is essential that the target group should be clearly defined in advance of the case-finding exercise. This will enable a strategy to be drawn up describing how this target group will be found and what biases may affect the representativeness of the sample.

Visibility of drug use and problems of access

Although a proportion of the drug-using population will always remain hidden, there are times when drug users are more 'visible'. These instances include: the process of buying and selling drugs; places where drug users meet; contact with law enforcement as a result of the need to buy or sell drugs or generate income illegally to obtain drugs; or when drug users seek attention for social, psychological or somatic consequences of drug use.

In each of these areas and situations, drug users may be contacted and asked to participate in research projects. Alternatively, an existing information source may be obtained.

Direct access

Direct access (Figure 2) is usually carried out by interviewers who have special training or have some background in the field that enables the targeting of specific drug users, especially for less problematic drug users who may not be in contact with any drug-related agency.

For example, Holmberg (1985) selected cases of drug abusers from a fifteen-year-old school population based on a school questionnaire, premature drop-out or participation in special classes. Such studies, however, are usually small and highly localised.

Figure 2: Access to different target groups - direct access

	Current Drug Users	Problematic Drug Users	Drug Addicts	Comment
Coverage	+	-	-	Less marginalised groups are less visible
Sensitivity	0	0	0	Unknown
Specificity	+	+	+	
Feasibility	+	+	+	Difficult access No additional information available
Costs	-	-	-	Many staff needed for contacting
Comparability	-	-	-	Unclear

For all figures: + = high; 0 = medium; - = low

Routine information sources

Data on drug users already collected by the agencies for their own purposes are cost-effective to obtain. Often people working with these routine sources already have a basic knowledge of drug users and drug use. It may be possible to contact drug users through these sources for further information if necessary. Drug users may be in contact for long periods allowing serial data to be collected over several years.

However, collecting extra data may be burdensome. Data can be incomplete and unreliable. Unless the target population is specific to the information source, it usually offers a very partial picture of drug users in the population.

Some sources do not cater solely for drug users, for example general hospitals, and the need for selection procedures can impose considerable practical, organisational and financial problems on the researcher.

Law enforcement agencies

In most European countries, law enforcement agencies record the biggest number of drug users (Figure 3). Coverage may be high for more marginalised groups of drug users but not so effective for less marginalised groups, such as cocaine users who are not part of the heroin scene. To interview cases personally is often difficult and may not be possible, limiting the use of this information source for more demanding studies. For drugs other than heroin and cocaine, the practice of law enforcement varies between different countries, reducing comparability.

Figure 3: Access to different target groups - law enforcement agencies

	Current Drug Users	Problematic Drug Users	Drug Addicts	Comment
Coverage of total population	0	+	++	Less marginalised groups are less visible
Sensitivity	+	++	++	Only relevant cases, by definition
Specificity	+	-	-	No information on patterns of use
Feasibility	-	-	-	Difficult access No additional information on patterns of use
Costs	+	+	+	Limited additional costs
Comparability	0	+	-	Acceptable for heroin and cocaine in most countries No uniform definition of addiction

Social services

Many drug users are in contact with social services agencies owing to their on-going drug use and financial needs (Figure 4). In regions and city districts, where drug use is more frequent, this can be a useful source to find relevant cases. Even if information on drug use is not directly available, it may be possible to collect further information or employ screening procedures to identify the target population.

Harm reduction projects

Harm reduction projects operate in many countries and are clearly targeted to drug users (Figure 5). They include methadone maintenance and syringe exchange programmes. In some countries these institutions are believed to be in contact with more than 70 per cent of all addicts. Screening procedures may be required in more general services.

Figure 4: Access to different target groups - social services

	Current Drug Users	Problematic Drug Users	Drug Addicts	Comment
Coverage	0	++	++	Some are not visible
Sensitivity	-	+	+	Screening necessary Denial
Specificity	-	+	+	Screening procedure necessary
Feasibility	++	++	++	Good
Costs	-	-	-	High costs for the interviewer
Comparability	-	-	-	Difficult because of differences in national structure of social services

Figure 5: Access to different target groups - harm reduction projects

	Current Drug Users	Problematic Drug Users	Drug Addicts	Comment
Coverage	-	0	++	Primarily high risk groups and heavy patterns of use
Sensitivity	+	+	+	Only contacted population
Specificity	++	++	++	No false positives
Feasibility	0	++	++	Good access via staff
Costs	+	+	+	Small additional costs
Comparability	0	+	-	Acceptable for heroin and cocaine in most countries

General health care

Contact with general medical facilities and emergency rooms is, on average, higher among drug users than the general population (Figure 6). However, drug users may not be identified routinely and screening procedures are important in order to capture the target population.

Figure 6: Access to different target groups - general health care

	Current Drug Users	Problematic Drug Users	Drug Addicts	Comment
Coverage	++	+	+	More marginalised groups may be less reached by the general health care system
Sensitivity	-	-	-	Only some cases detected
Specificity	++	++	++	No false positives Based on clinical and client information
Feasibility	0	0	0	Good for inpatient treatment Bad for GP and emergency rooms
Costs	+	+	+	Small additional costs
Comparability	0	+	-	Acceptable for heroin and cocaine in most countries

Specialist addiction treatment centres

In most European Union countries, a developed treatment system exists for addicted people (Figure 7). According to national estimates, between 10 and 80 per cent of the total number of addicts are in contact with these centres.

For example, in the Netherlands, more than 75 per cent are thought to be in contact with treatment centres, while in Germany the proportion is estimated to be 10 to 25 per cent within a given year. Therefore, it is possible to gain a representative picture of addicts as well as gain easy access to the subjects.

Also, when only basic information is needed, it is, in many cases, already available.

Figure 7: Access to different target groups - specialist treatment centres

	Current Drug Users	Problematic Drug Users	Drug Addicts	Comment
Coverage	0	+	++	Only part of population seeks treatment Differences between total population and treated population
Sensitivity	++	++	++	100% valid cases by definition
Specificity	++	++	++	No false positives
Feasibility	+	+	+	Easy access via therapeutic staff
Costs	++	++	++	Small additional costs
Comparability	-	0	0	Different national system of health care

Multi-source enumeration

Each information source used in case-finding studies gives only a partial picture of the population of drug users and will severely underestimate the total number of drug users. As a first step, therefore, different sources are combined to produce a more complete and valid estimate.

The intention is to create a common frame where the relationship between different data sets is clearly defined. Often the case definition in different sources is not exactly the same, though there may be considerable overlap.

Diagnosis based on DSM or ICD may be available from the treatment sector but might have to be inferred from patterns of drug use found in drug offenders. Information on problematic drug use, however, could be obtained more easily from both sources.

In Germany, a working group based their first estimates of the prevalence of hard drug use on information on offenders, drug-related deaths and treatment demands (*Institut für Therapieforschung*, 1993), which provided a much clearer description and understanding of the different groups defined and used.

The simplest model of multi-case enumeration is based on a common register, where personal information from several sources is collected. The bigger the number of sources, the more complete the picture of drug use. Often only one incident – the first contact of the drug user with law enforcement or social services – is registered.

In time, some of these people will stop using drugs.

Information on current status may be available from central treatment-based registers if all treatment units are participating. For police data, an update can be a new offence registered or – after a period without any more offences – an automatic deletion from the register. As the use of a central register raises important questions on data security and privacy, it is used only in some countries.

Another option used for AIDS surveillance would be the use of personal identifiers for all subjects contacted by different information sources, with some basic information on the persons identified (sex, age, drugs) kept centrally. As only minimum data are collected, it is not possible in practice to identify the person while also allowing duplicate reports to be identified. Where data protection laws are very strict, even this procedure might not be possible.

Dekker and Cohen (1993) have shown that the methods, as well as the selection of sources used for prevalence estimation, differ considerably in Europe. In some countries the numbers of subjects treated or contacted by different institutions were simply added, in other cases estimations were based on different information or assumptions.

Specific methods are dealt with elsewhere in this monograph. The basic problem remains, however, that a model which integrates the different sources and links them to the case definition has to be constructed.

The quality of the estimate depends very much on the success of the case-finding as well as the validity of the model used.

References

Bishop, R.(1976) 'A city looks at its problems of drug abuse by injection', *British Journal of Psychiatry*, 129, 465-471.

Dekker, S. and Cohen, P.D.A. (1993) *Estimating the number of 'problematic drug users'. Review of methodologies used within some European countries*, Council of Europe, Pompidou Group. P-PG/Epid (93) 12 rev.

Frischer, M., Green, S.T., Goldberg, D.J., Haw, S. , Bloor, M., McKeganey, N., Covell, R., Taylor, A., Gruer, L.D., Kennedy D. *et al* (1992) 'Estimates of HIV infection among injecting drug users in Glasgow', *AIDS*, 6(11) 1371-5.

Holmberg, M.B. (1985) 'Longitudinal studies of drug abuse in a fifteen-year-old population. 1. Drug career,' *Acta Psychiatrica Scandinavica*, 71, 67-79.

IFT, Institut für Therapieforschung, Institut für Rechtsmedizin, Universität Hamburg, Bundeskriminalamt, Wiesbaden (1993) *Report on methods to estimate the extent of the drug problem in Germany*, München: IFT reports no. 71.

Pflanz, M. (1973) *Allgemeine Epidemiologie. Aufgaben – Technik – Methoden*, Stuttgart: G. Thieme.

Skarabis, H. and Patzak, M. (1981) *Die Berliner Heroinszene. Eine epidemiologische Untersuchung*, (The Berlin heroin scene. An epidemiological study), Weinheim und Basel: Beltz.

CHAPTER 5

A CASE-FINDING STUDY
TO ESTIMATE THE PREVALENCE OF HEROIN USERS
IN NAVARRA, SPAIN

by Conchi Moreno Iribas and Mikel Urtiaga Dominguez

Epidemiological studies in Spain, aimed at determining the number of heroin users, are relatively recent and based on several indicators: the number of people starting treatment, deaths from overdose, and drug-related emergency admissions. These three indicators comprise the State Information System on Drug Addiction *(Grupo de Trabajo del SEIT*, 1990) which is used in order to assess geographical differences in the 17 regions within Spain (total population 40 million), as well as to monitor changes in drug use, routes of administration and the introduction of new drugs.

Further work has been carried out in some of the regions to obtain more precise estimates of the number of users. This chapter provides a practical example of the case-finding method. It describes a case-finding study carried out in Navarra, an area in the north of Spain with a population of half a million inhabitants, where all health and social services are directed and managed at the regional level. It demonstrates the kinds of data available from different sources, counts the number of cases in different agencies and the overlaps between agencies, and provides a final count of the number of known heroin users.

Methods

Since 1984, responsibility for strategic planning and provision of treatment for heroin use lay with the mental health services of the region (Varo, 1991; Varo and Aguinaga, 1984). Initially, the development of therapeutic services, although receiving public support, was in the private sector. In 1986, as part of the Mental Health and Alcoholism and Drug Addiction Plan, provision of treatment for heroin use was included in the mental health centres and integration with social services fostered. This led to a broadening and diversification of the resources for the treatment of drug users.

The support of the Public Health Management was vital for carrying out the study, facilitating access to the hospitals, epidemiological service, social services and institutions dependent on the Justice Ministry (forensic doctors, prison medical service).

Case definition

Information was sought retrospectively on all heroin users in contact with, or known to, the above services during 1990, who were residents of Navarra. It was recognised that some of the data sources would have no information about the frequency of use (occasional, regular, etc.) and a few (clinical and social services) would be expected to deal with more problematic heroin users.

Data sources

Table 1 shows the sources that provided information, outlined in more detail below, including all the public centres for the treatment of drug dependence in Navarra. A number of services which have contact with, or potentially have information on, drug use were not included: these were GPs and private doctors; over half of the social services; the press; private hospitals; courts and police stations; and non-psychiatric hospital emergency departments.

Mental health centres for assistance to drug users

All services for treatment in public centres were included: eight mental health centres; two units for hospital detoxification; two day hospitals; and one day centre. All relevant cases were extracted directly from computerised registers.

Therapeutic rehabilitation centres

Under the region-level National Drug Plan, data were requested on all residents of Navarra who had requested public financial assistance for entry to a therapeutic centre, irrespective of whether funding was obtained.

General hospitals and psychiatric emergency units

Computerised summaries of patients' clinical records for two of the three large hospitals were extracted with the following ICD-9 admission codes: 304 – dependence on drugs; 305 – drug abuse without addiction; 292 – psychosis due to drugs; 070 – hepatitis; 571.4 – chronic hepatitis; 573.3 – toxic hepatitis; 279 – immunity disorders.

All episodes occurring in 1990 were checked manually from registers held at the two psychiatric emergency units.

Criminal Justice

The prison register (admissions and releases) for 1990 was consulted and subsequently checked with the prison doctors' individual clinical files to identify cases with antecedents of opiate use.

Table 1: Information sources contacted during the study

Sources	N	Coverage	Observations
Mental health centres for assistance to drug users:		100% of treatment in public centres	Excludes treatment by private centres or doctors
- mental health centres	8		
- hospital detoxification units	2		
- day hospitals	2		
Therapeutic rehabilitation centres	11	In private sector, funded with public support; 5 in Navarra; 6 in other regions	
General hospitals	3	Hospital admissions in 3 of 4 main centres	Drug-related admissions identified from clinical codes ICD. 9
Psychiatric emergency units	2	All emergencies due to heroin	Excludes non-psychiatric emergencies
Criminal Justice:		Total population for Pamplona Prison	Excludes arrests, and offences not resulting in prison sentences
- provincial prison	1		
- social assistance to detainees	2		
Forensic doctors	1	All heroin overdose deaths	Deaths in 1990 with cause of death due to heroin overdose
Social services units	6	42% coverage of the population	Pamplona and environs
Hepatitis B case register, Public Health Institute	1	All cases with injecting risk factor	
HIV surveillance system			Cases of HIV where route of transmission classified as injecting drug use

Social assistance service of the Justice Ministry

Cases using this service, which aims to find employment and to provide economic support in situations of provisional freedom, were obtained through the General Director of Prison Institutions.

Forensic doctors

Data were obtained on all the deaths in Navarra in 1990 which required forensic reports where the cause of death was attributed to overdose of opiates.

Social services

Service users identified as heroin users were collected through the managing director of the Navarra Institute of Social Welfare.

Hepatitis B records

Incident cases of hepatitis B attributed to injecting drug use were obtained.

HIV surveillance system

At the same time as this study, the epidemiological service was conducting a case-finding study of cases of HIV infection from the Infectious Diseases Unit and Hospital Laboratory, which carried out confirmatory testing of HIV infection and provided treatment. Information was obtained on HIV positive persons fulfilling the case definition, that is heroin users identified during 1990.

Study variables

Data gathering was retrospective and mostly made use of information routinely collected by the centres themselves, though extra work was required in some cases (e.g. in prison and hospital emergency services). The data items provided by the different sources are shown in Table 2.

Table 2: Data items available from different sources

	Surname and first name	Initials of surname	Initials of first name	Sex	Date of birth	Municipality of residence
Mental health centres	*no*	*yes*	*yes*	*yes*	*yes*	*yes*
Hospital detoxification units	*no*	*yes*	*yes*	*yes*	*yes*	*no*
Day hospitals	*no*	*no*	*no*	*yes*	*yes*	*yes*
Therapeutic centres	*no*	*yes*	*yes*	*yes*	*yes*	*yes*
General hospitals	*yes*	*yes*	*yes*	*yes*	*yes*	*yes*
Psychiatric emergency units	*yes*	*yes*	*yes*	*yes*	*yes*	*yes*
Prison	*yes*	*yes*	*yes*	*yes*	*yes*	*yes*
Social assistance	*no*	*yes*	*yes*	*yes*	*yes*	*yes*
Forensic doctors	*yes*	*yes*	*yes*	*yes*	*yes*	*yes*
Social service units	*no*	*yes*	*yes*	*yes*	*yes*	*yes*
Hepatitis B register	*yes*	*yes*	*yes*	*yes*	*no*	*yes*
HIV surveillance	*no*	*yes*	*yes*	*yes*	*yes*	*yes*

One problem encountered during the study was the large number of cases for which it was not possible to confirm residence in the region. Where possible, non-residents were excluded by matching case reports with the 1986 Municipal Census of Inhabitants; alternatively additional information was requested from the sources.

Duplicates

Duplicate records from the same source and multiple records of the same person between sources were identified manually and removed to compile a record of heroin users who had contacted the institutions participating in the study.

Confidentiality

Personally identifiable data (see Table 2) were dealt with only by the principal researcher and were not made available to any person or institution outside the study project.

Results and discussion

Case-finding

Two thousand three hundred and fifteen records of heroin users were obtained, 2,088 of which met the case definition. Two hundred and eighty-eight records were excluded as being non-resident in Navarra. Removing duplicate records left a total of 1,231 individual cases. Table 3 shows the number of users collected from each source and the number known exclusively to that source. Seven hundred and eighteen persons (58.3 per cent) appeared in a single source; 245 (19.9 per cent) in two sources; and 268 (21.8 per cent) in three or more sources. Nine hundred out of the 1,231 individuals were reported from one of the specific services for the treatment or rehabilitation of drug dependence (mental health centres, psychiatric emergency units and therapeutic centres). The remainder were reported from non-specific health services, social assistance centres and prison.

Of the cases recorded in two sources, 50 per cent of those found in therapeutic centres and 67 per cent of those who attended psychiatric emergency units also appear in one or another of the mental health centres. In contrast, only 28 per cent of those found in the hepatitis B register were found in the mental health centres. In short, it was feasible to carry out a case-finding survey in geographically distinct regions. If possible, it would be desirable to widen the information sources to include police detention centres, GPs, and hospital and outpatient emergency services. However, the data collected can provide the basis for prevalence estimation using capture-recapture methods.

Prevalence and profile of drug users

The prevalence of 'known' heroin users from the selected institutions is a minimum estimate of visible drug use, given that several sources were not included which other studies have shown to be important (Hartnoll *et al*, 1985; Peveler *et al*, 1988; Parker *et al*, 1987).

Table 3: Number of heroin users reported by source, and number reported from a single source

	Number of users	Reported exclusively
Mental health centres	697	344
Hospital detoxification units	103	14
Therapeutic centres	334	111
Day hospitals	160	39
Psychiatric emergency units	341	65
Criminal justice (prison and assistance to detainees)	254	67
Forensic doctors	12	5
Social service units	46	17
Hepatitis B register	40	22
HIV surveillance	101	34
Total cases	2,088*	718**

* Before removal of duplicates; ** cases reported from a single source

Table 4: Prevalence of known heroin users by age and sex

Age	Men (n)	Men (rate 1000)	Women (n)	Women (rate 1000)	Total (n)	Total (rate 1000)
Less than 15	3	0.05	1	0.01	4	0.03
15 to 19	23	1.1	23	1.1	46	1.12
20 to 24	253	11.6	108	5.2	361	8.47
25 to 29	421	22.2	124	6.9	545	14.72
30 to 34	168	8.9	36	2.0	204	5.51
35 to 39	43	2.4	8	0.4	51	1.40
Greater than 40	15	0.15	5	0.04	20	0.09
Total	926	3.63	305	1.18	1,231	2.40

The 1,231 heroin users identified represent a population rate of 2.4 per 1,000 or 1 in 417 residents in Navarra (Table 4). Among men the rate was 3.63 per thousand and for women 1.18 per thousand. The highest prevalence rate was among people aged 25 to 29 at 14.72 per thousand (or 1 in 68), followed by those aged 20 to 24 at 8.47 per thousand (1 in 118). The difference in prevalence between the sexes was lowest for the younger age groups, which may indicate that, in recent years, proportionally more women are becoming heroin users.

Large differences were observed between urban (3.5 per 1000) and rural areas (0.96 per 1000), which we believe cannot be attributed to methodological issues alone, for example the study was carried out with greater intensity in urban areas. Equally, there were differences within Pamplona: Old Town, Chantrea and Berriozar had rates of over 7 per thousand, while Iturrama had a rate of 2.0 per thousand, which may reflect differences in income, facilities, education resources and so on. In summary, the majority of heroin users were men (3 to 1), aged between 20 and 29 (72.9 per cent), and resident in urban areas (3.4 to 1). The number of heroin users identified, though an underestimate of the total population and even of visible drug use, still represents a considerable number.

For the Navarra region, the results of the case-finding study emphasise the importance of assessing need in relation to available resources, not only in fields such as treatment of drug use and social services, but also to other strategies aimed at improving quality of life and reducing morbidity and mortality. We believe it important to diversify the existing treatments on offer to include programmes such as methadone maintenance and to begin initiatives aimed at preventing and treating the important drug-related health problems, such as HIV, AIDS and hepatitis.

Acknowledgements

José Amador, Comisión de Asistencia Social del Ministerio de Justicia en Navarra; Iosune Aramburu, Servicio de Asistencia Social al Detenido del Instituto Navarro de Bienestar Social; M[a] José Arozarena, Servicios Sociales de base del Ayuntamiento de Barañain; Aurelio Barricarte, Instituto de Salud Pública de Navarra; Ana Baruque, Servicios Sociales de base del Ayuntamiento de Olza Jesús Domínguez: Dirección de salud mental del Servicio Navarro de Salud; Miguel García, Médico de la Prisión Provincial de Pamplona; Angeles Granados, Directora General de Instituciones Penitenciarias; Carlos Gurruchaga, responsable de los Servicios Sociales de base de los Ayuntamientos de Berriozar y de Ansoaín; Juan Romero, Psicólogo de la Prisión Provincial de Pamplona; Belén Sancho, Servicios Sociales de base del Ayuntamiento de la Cendea de Elorz y Galar; Rafael Teijeira, Médico Forense de la Audiencia Provincial de Pamplona; José Varo, Dirección de salud mental del Servicio Navarro de Salud.

References

Grupo de Trabajo del SEIT (1990) 'Admisiones a tratamiento por consumo de opiáceos y cocaína en España', *Gac Sanit*, 16, 4-11.

Hartnoll R., Micheson M., Lewis R. and Bryer S. (1985) 'Drug addiction. Estimating the prevalence of opioid dependence', *Lancet*, 1, 203-5.

Parker H., Newcombe R. and Backx K. (1987) 'The heroin users: prevalence and characteristics in Wirral, Merseyside', *British Journal of Addiction*, 82, 147-57.

Peveler R.C., Green R. and Mandelbrote B.M. (1988) 'Prevalence of heroin misuse in Oxford City', *British Journal of Addiction*, 83, 513-8.

Varo J.R. and Aguinaga M. (1984) 'El uso de drogas', en: *Encuesta a la juventud en Navarra*, Fundación Bartolomé de Carranza, Pamplona.

Varo J.R. (1991) 'Drogodependencia en Navarra', en: *Plan de Salud de Navarra*, Nafarroako Osasun Plana.

CHAPTER 6

PROBLEMS OF DEFINITION
AND OTHER ASPECTS OF CASE-FINDING:
THE SWEDISH NATIONWIDE STUDIES

by Börje Olsson

Case-finding studies are one of the most frequently used methods for providing the empirical data for estimating the prevalence of drug use. The validity of these estimates depends largely on the quality of the source data. This paper concentrates on five key factors which influence the results of case-finding and draws upon the experience of two nationwide case-finding studies carried out in Sweden (Socialdepartementet, 1980; Olsson *et al*, 1993).

- case definition;
- sampling procedures;
- informing and training reporters;
- attitudes and perceptions towards drug users, and towards prevailing drug policy misclassification.

Case definition

A prerequisite for proper case-finding is that we know what a 'case' is. However, numerous definitions of drug users are available, covering biomedical, behavioural, psychological and social aspects. For example, an earlier meeting of the Council of Europe asked participating countries to estimate the number of 'hard-core addicts'. Two neighbouring countries of similar size reported there were one thousand and over fifty thousand respectively. The difference did not lie in the prevalence of drug use but in the definitions used: the first country considered a 'hard-core addict' to be someone in long-term treatment while the other estimated the number of people in need of treatment.

The lack of a common, clear-cut, widely accepted definition means that the investigators must set the criteria themselves: the definitions depend on the interests of the investigators. Of course, such a pragmatic approach does not preclude the importance of basic knowledge in medical, pharmacological, psychological and social aspects of drugs or the necessity of clearly stating the purpose of the study.

In practice, the choice is limited to drug users who are known or can be identified and by the extent of information on the nature of the drug use possessed by the reporters. Too lax a definition and reporters may construe a different case than others; too tight a definition and reporters may not have the information to know whether a drug user fulfils the case definition and therefore may not report them.

One solution to this problem used by the Swedish studies is to use a minimal definition. These studies requested reports on every drug user known to have used drugs during the last twelve months. Additional information, if available, was also requested including: type of drugs used, dominant drug, main route of administration, injecting behaviour, how long the person had used drugs, concomitant misuse of other substances such as alcohol, hypnotics, sedatives and solvents, use of drugs during the last four weeks, intensity of use during the last four weeks, and finally, sex, age, area of residence, work, education and contacts with the authorities due to criminality or drug use.

Since case-finding methods rarely cover sporadic or less severe forms of drug use, it is not meaningful to assess the extent of these forms of use. In the Swedish case, separate analyses were made for 'heavy drug abuse' defined as daily or almost daily use of drugs, and any use (regardless of frequency) by injection.

Sampling procedures

In Sweden, the choice was between a study covering the entire country or a sample of geographical units (cities, local communities, parts of a city, etc.). In 1979, a national study was considered more appropriate because knowledge both of the spread of drug use in the population and of the number and characteristics of drug users in contact with services was limited. Furthermore, an important aim of the Swedish study was to provide a comprehensive description of the extent of 'heavy drug abuse' in different parts of the country. In 1992, the investigators chose to select a sample of local communities and police districts because of the information provided earlier by the 1979 study. An additional advantage (and maybe the most important factor) was that drawing a sample made the study cheaper to carry out.

The aim of the study was to estimate prevalence for the entire country, based on an enumeration from the communities and police districts included in the sample. One problem raised through sampling geographical areas was the mobility of drug users over one year, with many reported users moving in and out of the sampled areas or being reported in one area but residing outside that area. The problem was solved by adding a question about area of residence but created new problems for the capture-recapture calculations. Individuals reported from units belonging to the sample but who lived elsewhere were excluded, among other reasons, because they were less likely to be reported by other data sources in the sampled area and, therefore, would erroneously inflate estimates of the 'true' number of 'heavy drug abusers'. In 1992, the final population estimate of the number of 'heavy drug abusers' for the whole of Sweden was 17,000 (confidence interval 14,000 to 20,000). However, if all drug users were included in the calculations irrespective of whether they were resident in the sampled areas, the prevalence estimate would be 30 per cent higher, exceeding the upper confidence interval of the officially accepted estimate.

The two Swedish studies used two different criteria for reporting drug users. In 1979, reporters were asked to record prospectively all drug users with whom they had contact over a six-month period, while in 1992 they were asked to report retrospectively all drug users with whom they had had contact over the last year. The first method provides more up-to-date information but is more demanding on the reporters and the investigators who must keep contact with the reporters to prevent 'reporting fatigue'. The second is faster but relies on patient files and other sources to compile the data. The method employed by the second study was believed to have produced a higher coverage rate, since the capture-recapture adjustment of the cases collected was only 14 per cent higher in 1992 compared to 45 per cent in 1979.

Informing and training reporters

Since case-finding depends upon the goodwill of reporters, the issue of information and education becomes crucial. In the Swedish studies, information about the aim of the study and education on how to participate were very important. If this phase of the investigation fails, the resulting prevalence estimates will be highly questionable.

Explaining that the information obtained will be used for policy and planning may not, on its own, be a sufficient inducement for the reporters, unless the data can be collected and analysed in a way that is relevant to them. Since priority is given mostly to routine daily activities, participation in a case-finding study should be integrated, wherever possible, with routine tasks. Besides providing basic information on different drugs, types of use, doses and multiple substance use, it also may be considered worthwhile to set up a phone line during the study which reporters can use to seek further information or clarification.

Our experience from the Swedish studies also highlights the importance of making the instructions to the reporters (however seemingly trivial) as clear as possible. In both studies, reports were requested on all persons *known (not suspected)* to have used drugs during the last twelve months. In 1992, additional instructions were given to include people who, in their professional opinion, were drug users, in order to recognise cases where definitive proof was not available. It is not my intention to argue for or against either of these ways of phrasing the instructions, but I am convinced that differences like this have a considerable impact on the overall result. Unfortunately, it was not possible to assess the result of the extra instruction.

Attitudes and perceptions towards drug users and towards prevailing drug policy

The two Swedish case-finding studies illustrate some of the problems facing epidemiologists. Important changes occurred in public policy and in perceptions of drug use between 1979 and 1992. In 1979, use of drugs had not yet been criminalised, and protecting the rights and confidentiality of the individual were the prevailing concerns of health and social workers. In 1992, the overall goal of policy was to achieve a drug-free society and drug use was criminalised, reflecting harsher attitudes towards drug use and drug users.

The difference in attitudes between the two studies may explain the higher non-response rate in the 1979 study compared to the 1992 study and that a greater number of persons erroneously classified as 'heavy drug abusers' could be expected in the 1992 study. Prevailing attitudes and perceptions should be borne in mind when planning case-finding studies and interpreting the results.

Misclassification

Misclassification occurs in several ways. Firstly, the illegality of drug use militates against full self-report, in particular, drug users may provide insufficient or false data to distinguish 'heavy' drug use. Secondly, data may not be systematically or reliably recorded in routine data sources. Thirdly, cultural attitudes towards drug use may influence a reporter's perception of a case. Some assessment of the level of misclassification is very important, if not through separate control studies, then at least through comparing data supplied by several sources on the same individual.

In the 1979 Swedish study, a comparison of different reporters' classification of the same individual led to the conclusion that heavy abusers were four times as likely to be classified correctly than incorrectly. It is likely that the number of users is between three and six times higher. Therefore, if we assume that the 'true' number of heavy drug abusers and users is 10,000 and 40,000 respectively, the effect of misclassification would lead to a situation where approximately 17,500 heavy drug abusers were reported. Though a hypothetical example, it shows that misclassification is important and could lead to considerable over-estimation.

Conclusions

Case-finding is a practical exercise. Theoretical considerations are important, especially when employing statistical methods to estimate prevalence, but these should not take precedence over the very practical aspects of carrying out a case-finding study outlined above. In other words 'garbage in, garbage out!'

References

Socialdepartementet (1980) *Tungt narkotikamissbruk - en totalundersökning 1979*, Rapport från utredningen om narkotikamissbrukets omfattning (UNO), Stockholm, Ds S 1980:5.

Olsson, O., Byqvist, S. and Gomér, G. (1993) *Det tunga narkotikamissbrukets omfattning i Sverige 1992*, Stockholm, Centralförbundet för alkohol- och narkotikaupplysning (CAN).

CHAPTER 7

LOCAL PREVALENCE ESTIMATION:
CAN AN INNER-CITY PREVALENCE SURVEY
PRODUCE USEFUL INFORMATION?

by Paul Griffiths, Michael Farrell and Samantha Howes

Patterns of drug use are characterised by acute local variation. In estimating the prevalence of drug use amongst the general population such variations are often obscured. Survey methods may produce reliable information on the extent of use of drugs like cannabis where 'lifetime use' levels may be high and social stigmatisation low. However, the combination of low prevalence rates and highly stigmatised behaviour make such methods less suitable for providing convincing data on drugs such as heroin and cocaine, or on the injection of these or other drugs.

For such behaviours, subjects may be hard to locate and unwilling to be inter-viewed. Clustering also creates problems in these conditions; although overall prevalence rates may be low, high prevalence rates may be found within small dis-tinct geographical locations. These locations are often, but not exclusively, inner-city areas characterised by high levels of deprivation. Such sites are notoriously difficult to gain access to by conventional survey techniques.

In this paper, the rationale for conducting local prevalence estimation surveys will be considered. Data from a pilot household survey of an inner London housing estate of high drug prevalence will be explored. Of particular concern are the prac-tical and methodological problems that researchers face when conducting a local prevalence survey in an inner-city setting. The local prevalence survey may be viewed as a special example of the case-finding study.

What is the purpose of local prevalence estimation?

Much of the debate on the construction of satisfactory prevalence data is pitched at the macro level, towards exploring overall prevalence of drug consumption for the general population. However, such data, even if accurate, are not always helpful to those planning or delivering drug services locally. It is not that national and local estimation procedures are not complementary, but rather that the rationale for each exercise is often different and may result in a separate set of methodological issues.

In this paper, our main concern is to consider variations in patterns of drug use prevalence which occur within small inner-city areas. However, it is important to remember that variation in the scale and pattern of drug use may be found in any exercise. Two indicators of United Kingdom cocaine consumption illustrate this point. Police seizures are skewed toward two large urban areas. Sixty-four per cent of cocaine seizures by police in England in 1994 were in London. A similar picture emerges from treatment indicators. Of the 1,373 new registrations of drug users reported to the Home Office's Addicts Index in 1993, 594 (43 per cent) were from London. In total, only four other districts reported more than 100 new cocaine users. These data suggest that cocaine use in the UK appears to show marked geographical variation which, in turn, questions the utility of national estimation rather than examining drug use prevalence within a more restricted geographical context.

Important variations may still be missed if analyses are confined to a city. The methods presented here form part of a pilot study carried out by the National Addiction Centre in London (Howes *et al*, 1995), which explores the feasibility of complementing a capture-recapture methodology with a local prevalence survey.

The starting point for this exercise was to consider existing prevalence indicators. When the addresses of local drug treatment attenders were mapped, acute variation was evident with two local wards (small areas designated for voting purposes) having much higher numbers of drug treatment attenders. Such clustering also tends to occur in areas which pose the most serious practical problems for conventional population survey methodologies, with the likely result that large-scale prevalence surveys are unreliable and underestimate the number of certain types of drug users.

Can survey methods produce useful prevalence data?

In recent years, conventional survey techniques have been regarded with some scepticism by drug researchers seeking to conduct prevalence estimation studies. However, increasingly it appears that, for some drug types, these objections may be overstated. As prevalence rates increase, estimation techniques are less likely to be affected by sampling biases. Also, stigmatisation of those who use the drug may decrease, which, in turn, may reduce reporting biases.

For example, in the United Kingdom, the Health Education Authority recently commissioned a survey of drug use amongst a national sample of over 5,000 people aged 11 to 35 (HEA, 1996). A stratified random location sample combining quota and random sampling procedures was used. A range of innovative interview techniques were used to increase response rates and improve the quality of the data collected, including computer-assisted interviewing, allowing respondents to key in the answer to sensitive questions.

The sampling procedures relied on a neighbourhood sampling schema grouped according to their social characteristics, though some problems were experienced in accessing subjects in more socially deprived areas, which were less well represented in the final sample. The data suggest an ever use of cannabis of 37 per cent, of amphetamines 15 per cent and of ecstasy 7 per cent. Far lower rates of use were found for heroin, cocaine and crack cocaine use.

Other surveys, conducted at the same time, such as the British Crime Survey, broadly support these findings. Although researchers may have some confidence in the estimates for cannabis use and probably some of the other drug types, it is less clear how reliable the data are for heroin, crack cocaine or the injecting of drugs. In some circumstances, this may not matter (such as the HEA's interest in the design of drugs education material), and it may be sufficient to know that use of these drugs is relatively less prevalent than that of other drugs. However, if the accurate estimation of the prevalence of heroin use or other similar substances is important, other research strategies are likely to be of greater utility.

Can survey techniques be used within a local context?

The London pilot study sought to complement a local survey with capture-recapture methodology (the latter will not be considered here). One of the fundamental questions the research team wished to answer was whether a local survey was practicable within a deprived inner-city area. A local housing estate was selected on the criterion that it was in an area of high deprivation, likely to be considered unsuitable for conventional survey methods, and was within one of the wards with a disproportionately high number of treatment attenders. Police and other criminal justice system data also suggested high levels of local drug problems within the sample area.

In addition to both practical and methodological problems, those wishing to undertake local prevalence estimation studies are often handicapped by a lack of resources. A number of market research companies were approached to cost the surveying of the designated area. The average cost for a sample of 300 households was £15,000, which was estimated to yield 150 interviews. The company would only allow interviewers to work in daylight hours and in pairs. No direct drug use questions would be included in the face-to-face interview for 'safety reasons' but those respondents who answered a drug screening question positively would be contacted by telephone later.

Although the proposed methodology would have overcome some of the practical problems inherent in the research task, it was felt that this method would compromise data quality. Apart from the high cost per interview (£100), interviewing only in daylight hours would be likely to increase non-response bias. Contacting drug users by telephone, if they had one, was also considered unsatisfactory.

A survey design had to be developed that was inexpensive, minimised reporting and non-response bias and was likely to deliver data of a sufficient quality to justify the exercise. In addition to the general problems surrounding the elicitation of behavioural self-reports, there were also concerns about interviewing drug users in their own homes. The selection of a suitable fieldwork force was considered of critical importance, since employing interviewers who might be seen by respondents as 'threatening' may increase response bias.

Non-response errors are a widely documented problem in household surveys, including concerns about whether the sampling frame adequately represents the target population and whether a young and mobile sample group is likely to be at home during the interviewing period. But the most important practical issue was ensuring the safety of the fieldwork team.

A questionnaire was designed which included general lifestyle questions, alcohol and cigarette use, the use of illicit drugs and drug injecting. Attempts to develop a sampling frame from the local council, which was responsible for the estate's upkeep, proved fruitless, as they did not know who was residing there, how many people lived in each household or even whether the properties were occupied. It was decided, therefore, to conduct a census style survey with blanket coverage of the defined area.

For both methodological and practical reasons, the survey used a central interviewing point, a community centre at the base of one of the tower blocks, at which respondents would be encouraged to attend. This procedure was cost efficient and allowed the safety of the fieldwork force to be guaranteed. In addition, the area acted as 'neutral space' where respondents could enter of their own free will.

A fieldwork force of predominantly young interviewers was recruited from a range of ethnic backgrounds and asked to dress casually. Security was provided by a local agency who usually provided doormen for nightclubs and music venues. The security team were also casually dressed and blended in with the interviewers. Every attempt was made to make the interview area as relaxed and non-threatening as possible, as well as to establish a safe working environment for the interview staff.

Letters were sent to 400 households approximately one week before interviewing, inviting one individual aged between 16 and 45 to attend an interview. Interviewing would occur over a one-week period. Late night and weekend sessions were also scheduled. Secondary invitations to other household members were issued to respondents once they had attended for interview and their household's composition had been established in order to increase the number of young people included in the study. Respondents would be paid £10 for attending an interview and, to be eligible for interview, respondents would be required to bring their invitations with them. Originally, invitations were to be posted to households but, since the postal service had been suspended to the estate area, they were delivered by hand.

It proved difficult to estimate accurately the survey response rate. It was known that 80 flats in the estate were reserved for elderly people, making the maximum possible response rate from 320 dwellings. However, it was not known how many of these were occupied or if they included household members who were eligible for interview. In total, interviews were conducted with 180 people from 161 households. The overall household response rate, therefore, was probably 50 per cent.

This was considered disappointing, though the information collected was useful both in terms of informing other methodological procedures and in describing patterns of drug use in the area. Detailed survey results are presented elsewhere (Howes *et al*, 1995). In terms of lifetime drug prevalence the figures were: cannabis 44 per cent; hallucinogens 17 per cent; ecstasy 10 per cent; amphetamines 32 per cent; cocaine 16 per cent; heroin 7 per cent and other opiates 8 per cent.

Four per cent of subjects had used heroin and 7 per cent had used cocaine in the week before interview, confirming that prevalence figures for such drugs were far higher than those found in national studies.

The inclusive cost per interview was £40.

Conclusions

The pilot study shows that it is possible to conduct a low-cost household survey in a deprived and difficult-to-access inner-city community. Significant numbers of problem drug users were interviewed and the findings were useful in describing some hitherto unknown parameters of the existing drug-using population. The survey demonstrated that there is a need to develop sampling methodology techniques to take account of the limited information available in such settings. The use of a room in the community centre appeared successful: it provided a safe environment for interviewers, a less intrusive atmosphere for interviewing and respondents could attend in their own time.

Innovative methodological procedures may allow local surveys to become a useful tool for those wishing to understand patterns of problematic drug use within small areas. They may also have some value as booster samples to improve estimation of prevalence when combined with surveys conducted on a larger scale.

The results of the London pilot study suggest that some of the practical and methodological problems associated with this kind of study may be reduced by the development of appropriate methodological procedures. However, sampling issues remain a paramount concern for those conducting both national and local surveys.

The challenge for researchers working in this area is to discover what gains can be made. This survey formed part of a larger body of work exploring how different estimation techniques can complement one another in calculating prevalence rates. In our view, advances in improving the local estimation of drug prevalence will be likely to involve the synthesis of different estimation procedures. As yet, the elements in such a synthesis remain unclear, though it remains an area where innovative, sensitive and rigorous research design is likely to bear fruit.

Acknowledgements

We would like to thank Colin Taylor and Glynn Lewis for their involvement in the study.

References

Howes, S., Farrell, M,. Griffiths, P. and Lewis, G. (1995) *Estimating local prevalence of drug use, a feasibility study of the complementary roles of capture-recapture and household survey techniques*, National Addiction Centre, London.

HEA (1996) *Drug realities – National Drugs Campaign Survey – Summary of Key Findings*, HEA/BMRB: London.

CAPTURE-RECAPTURE METHODS

INTRODUCTION

by Martin Frischer

*I*n recent years the capture-recapture method (CRM) has become one of the major methods used in epidemiology to estimate hidden populations. Indeed Laporte (1994) regards CRM as being of such importance that it could 'bring about a paradigm shift in how counting is carried out in all the disciplines that assess human populations'.

The chapter by Antònia Domingo-Salvany introduces the main features of the method. Beginning with simple applications involving two lists of drug users, she illustrates the statistical reasoning behind CRM and the assumptions which must be met in order to produce reliable estimates. Extending CRM to more complex scenarios involves greater statistical sophistication, for example, the fitting of log-linear models and the calculation of confidence intervals. The chapter also provides methodological guidelines covering a wide range of practical issues.

Clive Richardson considers lessons that may be learned from the studies of animal populations. Whereas CRM applications in drug epidemiology focus on population estimates, animal studies are often concerned with inward and outward migration and survival rates. At the present time, available data in drug epidemiology preclude the application of these more sophisticated models. However, as data in this field improve, there will be opportunities to employ methods developed in the context of animal studies.

Pierre-Yves Bello and Geneviève Chêne provide a further example of CRM as applied in Toulouse, France. The authors describe difficulties in obtaining data and the practical issues which are often encountered prior to data analysis. The authors also use CRM in an innovative fashion to develop models which take account of interactions between age, gender and data source.

Finally, Martin Frischer describes a CRM study in Glasgow, Scotland, and illustrates how to proceed from simple two-sample models to complex models involving three or more samples. A range of issues is considered, including case definition, case matching, model selection and confidence intervals. The issue of external validation of CRM estimates is also addressed.

Reference

Laporte R. (1994) 'Assessing the human condition: capture-recapture techniques', *British Medical Journal*, 308, 5-6.

CHAPTER 8

ESTIMATING THE PREVALENCE OF DRUG USE USING THE CAPTURE-RECAPTURE METHOD: AN OVERVIEW

by Antònia Domingo-Salvany

One of the major methods used in drug addiction epidemiology to estimate prevalence of drug use is the capture-recapture method (CRM), sometimes known as mark-recapture (Brecht and Wickens, 1993). CRM refers to a technique developed over a century ago to estimate the size of wild animal populations and involves 'capturing' a random sample who are then 'marked' and returned to their habitat. Subsequently, a second random sample are 'recaptured' and the number of marked animals from the first sample are observed. The ratio of marked animals to the recaptured sample size is assumed to be the same as the ratio of the first captured sample to the total population. Thus, if a 'capture' sample of 200 animals is marked and released and a 'recapture' sample of 100 contains ten animals which are marked, the estimate for the total population would be 2,000 (i.e. 10:100 = 200:2,000).

In human sciences, CRM was first used to ascertain completeness of census data by assessing the degree of under-registration of births and deaths in the general registrar (Sekar and Deming, 1949). It has also been used in studies to estimate the degree of under-ascertainment of prevalence studies aimed at intensive case-finding (Hook and Regal, 1992 and McCarty *et al,* 1993).

In view of the real or perceived problems of asking people directly about drug use, CRM affords a means of estimating prevalence indirectly from data on known drug users.

Methods and research strategies

CRM prevalence estimates are based on the analysis of incomplete multiway tables. The term 'incomplete' simply refers to the fact that there is always a missing cell corresponding to individuals not recorded on any of the sample lists and the term 'multiway' simply refers to the fact that there are two or more samples (see Figure 1).

Figure 1: Example of the simplest form of multiway table for CRM analysis

		Sample 1		
		Present	Absent	
Sample 2	Present	a	b	a+b
	Absent	c	d	
		a+c		

The estimate for the missing cell (d) is:	$d = b^* \, c/a$
and for the total population:	$N = a + b + c + (b^* \, c/a)$
The estimate variance of this is:	$\text{Var } N = (a + b)^* \, (a + c)^* \, b^* \, c/a^3$

In this way, we can estimate N with a confidence interval (CI) where $CI = N \pm 1.96 * SE$. If the number of observed individuals is small, formulae should be transformed into:

$$d = b^* \, c/(a + 1) \text{ and } N = [(a + b + 1)(a + c + 1)/(a + 1)] - 1$$

The assumptions of the method are important, particularly for this simplest model (Neugebauer and Wittes, 1994):

- the samples/lists must be representative of the population under study, which has to be 'closed', i.e. random samples of a closed population (closed refers to the assumption that individuals do not enter or leave the population during the study period);
- each list must be homogeneous, i.e. the probability of selection into a sample/list must be constant for all individuals;
- the lists must be mutually independent, i.e. the individual probability of selection into a list must not be influenced by the presence or absence of the person in another list.

These assumptions are interrelated, but each one has some specific features which need to be taken into account in order to apply the method correctly and produce plausible prevalence estimates. Representativeness of the population is crucial. Individuals not seen (those that we wish to estimate) have to have similar characteristics to those who are seen. This assumption is important, as CRM involves extrapolation from available lists which are probably not random samples of the population under study. To assume that the population is 'closed' is only reasonable for short time periods (e.g. up to about one year). During longer periods there will be some individuals who join the group of interest (i.e. initiate regular drug use) and others who leave it (i.e. achieve abstinence or die). If prevalence is to be estimated over a long period of time, other methods considering open populations need to be applied.

Independence between lists needs further clarification. Concepts used in ecological studies may help to understand it (see Chapter 9 by Clive Richardson). 'Trap attraction' can arise when something appealing to individuals happens once they have been caught, so they are more likely to be caught in another sample (positive dependence). 'Trap avoidance' may occur when individuals did not like what happened during the first capture experience and can avoid subsequent captures (negative dependence). In health services, positive dependence may occur when patients like the treatment given at some services (i.e. opioid substitutes in emergency room wards) or because patients included in one list are more frequently submitted to a procedure that is the basis for another list (i.e. treatment patients on one list may be more likely to be easily tested for HIV and appear on a second list – persons tested for HIV). Negative dependence would arise when the fact of being on one list (i.e. in prison) reduces the chances of being included in another one (i.e. attending outpatient clinics). *A priori* information about samples can give an idea of possible dependencies and their direction.

The influence of dependence in the estimates can be understood if we apply these concepts in the formula for 'N': when there is positive dependence the probability of appearing in both samples is higher, thus 'a' (the denominator – see Figure 1) will be higher and the estimate for the unseen population, smaller. Conversely, when negative dependence occurs, the size of the estimate will be too big because 'a' is smaller than it should be.

Heterogeneity has some relation with dependence as individuals likely to fall repeatedly into the 'trap' do not have the same probability as others not caught previously. Heterogeneity, however, is not directly related to the construction of lists. Individuals may have different probabilities of being included in lists for several reasons: severity of disease, geographical area of residence, socio-economic status, etc. The effect that heterogeneity produces in the estimate is likely to be an underestimation since the overlap of sub-groups of people will be higher and some sub-groups are likely to be missed. When three or more samples are available, the independence of samples can be verified by different means:

* calculating the estimate for the different combinations of two-by-two samples;
* pooling together the two dependent samples and comparing the estimate;
* applying a log-linear regression to the data.

Through log-linear regression, heterogeneity can also be analysed and, if necessary, controlled for by dividing the whole group into sub-groups which are known to be more homogeneous in relation to capture probabilities.

Log-linear approach

The log-linear regression model allows interaction terms representing dependencies between samples. Thus, the assumption of independence can be tested and, if dependence is found to exist, interaction terms will modify the estimates of the unknown number of drug users (Cormack, 1989; Wickens, 1993). However, it is not possible to test a saturated model with all possible interactions, as there is one missing cell in the model. Nevertheless, the aim is not to produce a very complicated model but rather the simplest one that has a good fit with the data. The appropriateness of the model is assessed through the residual deviance and can also be assessed through the residuals in each cell. A more formal strategy to select the model, through its likelihood function, can be used following Akaike's Information Criterion (AIC) or the Bayes' Information Criteria (BIC) (IWGDMF, 1995).

It is important to take into account that more complex models may introduce instability and will always diminish precision as variance increases with more terms in the model. If the estimate is sensitive to small modifications of terms in the model (instability), caution is required when interpreting the results. If available statistical packages provide the parameter estimates for the log-linear regression (e.g. GLIM), it will be possible to calculate the missing cell size directly from the regression coefficient. If the statistical package does not give the betas for each parameter and if three samples are being used, it is possible to apply formulae given by Bishop *et al* (1975). There are different formulae according to the number of interactions present between the three samples. It is even possible to calculate an estimate taking into account that all three samples are interdependent. Formulae can also be applied after dependence of samples has been assessed through comparison between different combinations of two-by-two samples.

Confidence intervals

One of the attractive features of CRM is the provision of statistical confidence intervals (CI) for the estimate. The CI will be correct if the model is appropriate. Traditionally, the interval has been calculated through the asymptotic standard error of the estimate in the selected model (i.e. for 95 per cent CI: N ± 1.96 * SE). However, this interval has been criticised for its lack of precision, especially when sample sizes are small. In fact, CIs calculated in this way can give values for the population estimate which are lower than the number of individuals actually seen. A method proposed by Regal and Hook (1984), and also by Cormack (1992), takes into account the goodness-of-fit of the log-linear model chosen to calculate the estimate. In order to apply it, an iteration process is needed. This process tries to find the minimum and maximum missing cell values which produce a statistically significant difference of the model (i.e. inputting differing values of the missing cell until the model deviance changes by a specified criterion, usually p = .05).

With log-linear regression, heterogeneity can also be assessed (Darroch *et al*, 1993). Some prior knowledge about the studied population is needed to be able to apply correct statistical analysis. The structure of the captured population can be analysed and some conclusion drawn about its representativeness of the population under study. To control for different catchability between sub-groups (heterogeneity), stratification built into the regression is used (i.e. break the total population into male and female). However, this may lead to a problem since several strata will produce greater variability of the final estimate achieved by summation and it will be more difficult to obtain a CI for the global estimator.

Recently, Hook and Regal (1995) have proposed a method to ascertain the internal validity of the model(s) used for the estimate. Four or more samples are needed. The test may help to ascertain whether the models used were able to incorporate the different dependencies of the data. In general, it should always be remembered that models are simplifications of a more complex phenomenon and it is not enough simply to achieve a good fit of the model. It is necessary that the unseen part of the population has the same sampling characteristics and has homogeneous catchability with those seen and that no hidden sub-groups exist (Hser, 1993).

Longitudinal data

CRM can also be applied to single samples over a longer time period, still assuming a closed population. This involves subdividing the complete sample in time intervals, considering each one as a separate sample, and then applying capture-recapture to these different samples (Woodward *et al*, 1984). The same assumptions of capture-recapture are needed. The most important problems with capture-recapture applied to a unique sample divided in time periods are as follows:

- the source of information which provides the data may have a retention of the patients not being allowed to appear several times;
- unequal catchability of the population leads to dependence between samples;
- some people have zero probability of appearing at the specific agency, thus the estimate is only for those people likely to appear.

General considerations

In order to evaluate the adequacy of CRM as an estimation method, it is necessary to have a clear understanding of the strengths and weaknesses of all the data used, as well as of the process of data collection. The important points to consider are:

- definition of the disease under study - in the drug field, this refers to characteristics such as type of drug, recency or frequency of use and route of administration;
- adequacy of registers, in terms of completeness and quality of data, especially in relation to identification variables;
- matching difficulties can introduce bias in the overlap and thus in the estimate;
- time elapsed between initiation and appearance in registries (diagnostic delay) can produce underestimation of recent initiates;
- it is desirable to include samples from both the medical care and criminal justice system. The application of CRM should include as many types of list (e.g. medical and legal) as possible;
- results obtained through capture-recapture should be compared with other methods, as a combination of methods may help to ascertain boundaries for the estimate (even if there is inconsistency, this may help to understand the data and the phenomena being studied).

Guidelines on methodological standards

Given the current state of knowledge about the technique, the following guidelines are suggested:

Assumptions of the method

Samples/lists are representative of the population under study:

- persons included in the lists must have similar properties to those not seen;
- the population should not contain hidden sub-groups;
- there should be consistent definition of people across samples in relation to time, geographical area, drug use and age range.

Estimation involves a closed population:

- this requires a cross-sectional design of limited duration or a single longitudinal sample.

Identifiers are required for individuals in all samples:

- information about sensitivity and specificity of identifiers is required;
- the completeness of identifiers must not be related to the number of times subjects are captured in lists.

Homogeneity of the lists:

- severity of the drug problem may affect the likelihood of being captured;
- other variables that might affect homogeneity are geographical differences, route of drug administration and socio-economic status.

Lists are mutually independent:

- this requires at least three samples;
- *a priori* knowledge about interrelation of sources has to be used to help interpret the statistical interactions.

These issues should be addressed when describing a CRM study, i.e. whether the key assumptions are fulfilled, and if they are not, whether they are controlled during the analysis. If the key assumptions are not met, the direction of bias introduced into the estimate should be explained.

Practical issues

When planning to estimate drug abuse prevalence through CRM, it is necessary to ensure that several sources with reliable (and appropriate) data are available. This means that:

- high risk groups of the target population must be covered by the sources used;
- valid indicators of drug use are used in these sources (to allow definition of target population);
- unique individual identifiers can be obtained;
- consistency can be achieved among samples in relation to time, geographical area, population age range and drug use categories (also consistency over time is needed if trends are to be estimated).

Small numbers of people in samples may preclude the implementation of the method. To be confident of the results, it is necessary that there be some overlap between samples. If one has collected a good set of data but one which is insufficient to give a sensible estimate, at least the information gathered could provide a first prevalence estimate through case-finding (lower range). If samples are big enough to apply capture-recapture, the assumptions of the method need to be dealt with in the analyses or at least in the final consideration of the results. The more relevant assumptions at this point are homogeneity of samples and independence between them.

Figure 2: Some recommendations for capture-recapture studies

Do	Do not
• Cover different aspects of drug use (health-related, legal system, etc.) • Take three or more samples from different sources • Use an equivalent target population definition in all samples (in relation to drug use, age range, geographical area and time period) • Consider representativeness and homogeneity of the samples in relation to the studied population • Consider the adequacy of the identifier for individual matching • Test for sample independence (at least three samples are needed) • Control for dependence when it exists (fit log-linear models with interaction terms) • Ascertain stability of the model • Calculate confidence intervals with goodness-of-fit method • Calculate rates: the reference population should be taken consistently according to age range, geographical area and calendar year • Compare the resulting estimate with other prevalence information	• Consider different settings as different samples • Consider a broad time period, as it is then problematic to meet the assumption of a closed population • Consider a wide geographical area as it is more difficult to have homogeneous population groups in it • Take independence for granted • Include too many parameters in the model • Calculate CI with the estimate standard error, if sample sizes are small

In order to explore these issues adequately, sophisticated statistical analysis may be required. The analysis may involve creating different log-linear models, for which the help of a statistician may be needed. It is important to study the stability of the model. Calculation of confidence intervals taking into account the goodness-of-fit of the model can also be fairly complex. Confidence intervals should be calculated with this method instead of through the standard error when some sample sizes are small. In order to provide adequate prevalence rates, the reference population to be used in the denominator should include the same age range and geographical area of the estimated number of drug users. This reference population should also correspond to the year for which estimation was calculated. These guidelines seem reasonable in the light of the present state of knowledge. Some 'dos and don'ts' are shown in Figure 2 above. Capture-recapture is a method still in evolution, particularly with regard to statistical analysis involved in overcoming the problems posed by assumptions.

References

Bishop Y.M.M., Fienberg S.E. and Holland P.W. (1975) *Discrete multivariate analysis: Theory and Practice*, Cambridge, MA., MIT Press.

Brecht M.L. and Wickens T.D. (1993) 'Application of multiple-capture methods for estimating drug use prevalence', *Journal of Drug Issues, 23*, 229-50.

Cormack R.M. (1989) 'Log-linear models for capture-recapture', *Biometrics, 45*, 395-413.

Cormack R.M. (1992) 'Interval estimation for mark-recapture studies of closed populations', *Biometrics, 48*, 567-76.

Darroch J.N., Fienberg S.E., Glonek G.F.G. and Junker B.W. (1993) 'A three-sample multiple capture-recapture approach to census population estimation with heterogeneous catchability', *Journal of the American Statistical Association, 88*, 1137-48.

Hook E.B. and Regal R.R. (1992) 'The value of capture-recapture methods even for apparent exhaustive surveys', *American Journal of Epidemiology, 135*, 1060-7.

Hook E.B. and Regal R.R. (1995) 'Internal validity analysis: a method for adjusting capture-recapture estimates of prevalence', *American Journal of Epidemiology, 142*, S48-S52.

Hser Y. (1993) 'Data sources: problems and issues', *Journal of Drug Issues, 23*, 217-228.

International Working Group for Disease Monitoring and Forecasting (IWGDMF) (1995) 'Capture-recapture and multiple-record systems estimation I: History and theoretical development', *American Journal of Epidemiology, 142*, 1047-1058.

McCarty D.J., Tull E.S., Moy C.S., Kwoh C.K. and LaPorte R.E. (1993) 'Ascertainment corrected rates: applications of capture-recapture methods', *International Journal of Epidemiology, 22*, 559-65.

Neugebauer R. and Wittes J. (1994) 'Annotation: voluntary and involuntary capture-recapture samples – Problems in the estimation of hidden and elusive populations', *American Journal of Public Health, 84*,1068-9.

Regal R.R. and Hook E.B. (1984) 'Goodness-of-fit based confidence intervals for estimates of the size of a closed population', *Stat Medicine, 3*, 287-91.

Sekar C.C. and Deming W.E. (1949) 'On a method of estimating birth and death rates and the extent of registration', *Journal American Statistical Association, 44*, 101-15.

Wickens T.D. (1993) 'Quantitative methods for estimating the size of a drug-using population', *Journal of Drug Issues, 23*, 185-216.

Woodward J.A., Retka R. and Ng L. (1984) 'Construct validity of heroin abuse estimators', *International Journal of the Addictions, 19* (1), 93-117.

CHAPTER 9

CAPTURE-RECAPTURE METHODOLOGY: LESSONS FROM STUDIES OF ANIMAL POPULATIONS

by Clive Richardson

Statistical analysis is employed in so many fields of science and social science that it is not surprising that the same methods appear in various places. Sometimes this means that the same methods are rediscovered and parallel literatures develop almost independently. In other cases, techniques have been so well developed in one area that the needs of another can be met by recognising what can be borrowed and adapted from the existing material. This is more or less the situation with capture-recapture methodology (CRM). It has been applied in several fields, including drug use epidemiology, but has been worked on so extensively in relation to the study of animal populations that it is natural to look there for methodological tools and discussions of problems such as the effect of departures from the assumptions of each model. This paper highlights some of the key differences between applications of these methods in drug use epidemiology and in animal studies, and adds some comments on other areas of application.

Animal population studies

The review papers by Seber (1986, 1992) and Pollock (1991) are important in themselves and also give all the necessary references to the earlier literature. Much has been published on fisheries and wildlife in books and in journals, which may not easily be found by readers of this article. Methodological papers continue to appear in almost every issue of the journal *Biometrics*, while the *Journal of Wildlife Management* is the most important of the other sources.

Epidemiology

There are very recent, comprehensive reviews by Hook and Regal (1995) and the International Working Group for Disease Monitoring and Forecasting (IWGDMF, 1995a, 1995b). The major outlets for both methodological papers and applications are the *American Journal of Epidemiology* and the *International Journal of Epidemiology*. Papers on application to the estimation of numbers of drug users include the contents of a special issue of the *Journal of Drug Issues*, particularly Wickens (1993) and Brecht and Wickens (1993).

Census adjustment

For about fifty years, capture-recapture techniques have been applied to assess the completeness of a census of a human population, particularly in the USA. Dual record, rather than multiple record, systems have been the norm. In other words, the analysis is based on the appearance of individuals in one or both of two lists, one being the census itself and the other a sample survey conducted for the purpose of this check. Thus, it becomes possible to estimate the number of individuals who have been missed by the census. A bibliography on this area of application is given by Fienberg (1992), while Darroch *et al* (1993) discuss a three-sample approach.

Studies of animal populations

Study design

As a first step to understanding the difference between epidemiological and ecological applications, consider the usual form of the study of an animal population (see Figure 1). Each sample involves the capture of animals belonging to a population under study. The first time an animal is captured, it is given a recognisable mark and released. The nature of the mark depends on the animal. Birds are often given rings around the leg, fish a tag attached to one of the fins, insects perhaps dabs of paint. Except in studies involving very large numbers of animals (mainly in fisheries research), the ring or tag usually carries a numerical or other code so that the individual animal can be identified (I assume from here on that this is the case).

Figure 1: Process of a typical capture-recapture study of an animal population

Sample	Time sequence	Action
Capture	1	Mark and release animals
Recapture	2	Recapture and re-release Mark and release animals never captured before
Recapture	3	Recapture and re-release Mark and release animals never captured before
Recapture, etc.	4 etc.	etc.

The samples are usually taken in the same place at different times (theoretically they should be instantaneous; in practice, the sampling occupies a short time compared to the intervals between samples). In most studies, the recaptured animals are released and may be recaptured again in subsequent samples. Many variations on this basic theme are possible. In the first place, some animals may not be released after recapture (for example, if they were injured, or if they were taken for further study) and the basic equations allow for this. In fact, the design of the study may be that there are never any re-releases – this would usually be termed a *tag-recovery* study, since its essence would be the recovery of tags (marks) by recapturing the tagged animals. Another variation is that no physical recapture need take place except on the one occasion when the animal is marked. This tends to arise with animals large enough to carry marks visible to an observer from a distance and is often termed a *mark-resighting* study.

Study size

Applications can be found on all scales. The numbers of animals involved could be tens of thousands, but this is hardly likely to arise other than in fisheries research. Elsewhere, rather small population sizes are likely to be encountered. In a typical ornithological study, the total population size at any time is usually well below a thousand and the number of marked birds recorded in each sample below one hundred (Richardson, Patterson and Dunnet, 1979). However, these smaller studies, as well as many others, tend to be of long duration. The study by Richardson *et al* employed data from eight years' observation while Cormack (1989) used a 25-year period in studying another species of bird.

Models

The basic model for the analysis of data from such a series of samples is known as the Jolly-Seber model. It applies to an open population (i.e. allowing for inward and outward migration), since the longitudinal nature of the study implies that the assumption of a closed population is unlikely to be justifiable. Besides estimating the population size at each sampling time, the analysis gives estimates of birth and death rates between successive samples. 'Birth' includes immigration of an animal into the population (this means that its range of activity has shifted to cover the geographical area covered by the sampling scheme) while 'death' includes permanent emigration from the population. The model does not permit temporary emigration from the population. This is because temporary absence at the time when a sample is drawn means that this animal has zero probability of being captured in the sample, in contrast to the non-zero capture probability of the animals which have remained in the area. In other words, temporary emigration would introduce severe heterogeneity. The other assumptions of the basic model are familiar and obvious assumptions of homogeneity of survival probabilities and capture probabilities. A number of models have been proposed that relax certain assumptions or impose constraints on parameters. The work of Cormack, in particular, shows how many – although not all – of these models can be fitted to the data by applying the standard statistical procedure of log-linear modelling (Cormack, 1989). Another full example of log linear modelling may be found in IWGDMF (1995a).

Differences between epidemiological and ecological applications

Are the similarities between the areas of application only superficial or are the problems essentially the same? The following seem to be the key points of difference:

Definition

Epidemiological and ecological studies face more or less the same problem of defining the geographical extent of the population, but they differ in their ability to define members of the population within this area. Almost any epidemiological study has to start by defining a case: for example, who, for the purpose of the present task, will be defined as a drug user? The definition may be partly imposed by the nature of the lists available to us, which will usually be biased in some way (probably, in most applications, towards problematic users and users of certain classes of drugs). We may be able to try different definitions and find that our methods work out better for one than the other. Or we may define strata, such as frequency of use or main substance of abuse, and carry out a stratified analysis. This is a problem that does not arise in studying an animal species, where there is seldom any difficulty at all in saying whether or not an animal belongs to that species, since objective criteria have been laid down elsewhere.

Matching

The issue of matching, a major problem in epidemiology, also arises in the applications to the census. It refers to our ability to identify correctly the presence of the same individual in more than one list. Identifying information (names, birth dates, addresses) may be incomplete and inaccurate. The problem is exacerbated in drug use epidemiology where the identification information on certain kinds of lists is deliberately restricted. The nearest equivalent problem in ecological applications is tag loss, the loss of the mark (such as the numbered ring on a bird's leg) that allows the animal's individual identification. In this case, matching is an 'all or nothing' situation, being either correct or impossible. In epidemiology, we may make mistakes in matching and may need to try out different criteria.

Cross-sectional versus longitudinal study

Almost all epidemiological studies are cross-sectional; they employ samples that refer to more or less the same time point (e.g. a one year period). In animal studies, as already mentioned, the population is studied longitudinally by taking a sequence of samples over a period of time. One consequence of this is that the log-linear modelling of an ecological study is usually simplified by the fact that many interaction terms are implausible. In epidemiological applications, on the other hand, nothing can be excluded.

Observational study versus planned experiment

In epidemiology, the lists employed in a multiple-capture analysis have usually been assembled for some other purpose. On the other hand, a study of an animal population can usually be planned. In particular, the timing, location and duration of sampling are, to a large extent, under the investigator's control. One consequence of this is that some literature has developed on optimal sampling for particular purposes. As most epidemiological applications are not able to control these factors, they are not able to take advantage of knowledge gained from animal studies. However, this may be an area for future development as epidemiological studies become more sophisticated.

What is being estimated?

In Seber's well-known book entitled '*The Estimation of Animal Abundance and Related Parameters*' (1982), and Pollock's review (1991) referring to 'demographic parameters for fish and wildlife populations', far more than population size estimation is discussed. As pointed out above, an open population is usually being studied, so that birth and death rates are important. In fact, it is often the case that estimates of population size are not even sought.

My own paper cited above is just one of many examples to be found in which the multiple-capture analysis is used solely to estimate survival rates. In contrast, most epidemiological studies have no other purpose than to estimate the population size. Thus, many of the methods, applications and discussions found in the ecological literature are not currently relevant, although there may be scope in future research.

Heterogeneity

It is well known that log-linear models make assumptions of homogeneity. For example, every animal should have the same probability of capture in a given sample, which is equivalent to every drug user in our population having the same probability of appearing on a given list. The effects of departures from such assumptions have been investigated and discussed in both literatures. The difference between the two areas is that, while heterogeneity may or may not arise in an animal study, it is almost certain that there will be severe heterogeneity in a study of drug users even if this is not necessarily the case in all areas of epidemiology.

Heterogeneity may be reduced in various ways, including the choice of a more restricted definition of a user, but above all it should be handled by stratification. Heterogeneity cannot be greater in a sub-population than it is in the whole population and can usually be drastically reduced by wise selection of strata (see Chapter 8 by Antònia Domingo-Salvany for further discussion of this issue).

Dependence between samples

It is also well known that log-linear models make many assumptions of independence. In the extreme, but common, case of the two-sample study, we can only estimate the population size if we assume that the appearance of a member of the population on one list is independent of appearance on the other. The serious consequences of failure of this assumption are well known. Lack of independence is a problem that arises in animal population studies too. There it has been discussed particularly as the problem of *trap addiction* or *trap avoidance* (other terms for the same phenomenon can be found). The former means that an animal that has once been caught has an increased probability of capture in the next, and perhaps in all, subsequent samples.

The equivalent in the study of a drug-using population is that a person who appears on one list is more likely to be on another than a person who is not on the first list. This is highly likely to happen, for many reasons. Trap avoidance refers to the possibility that an animal once captured has a reduced probability of subsequent capture, probably because it has learnt not to repeat the experience. The equivalent would be that a drug user who appears on one list has a smaller chance of being on the other than a drug user who did not appear on the first. This should not be a problem in practice because if, for example, users tend to go to one service or another for treatment but not both, this would often be known beforehand to the investigators, due to their familiarity with the area and the population. The lists could be combined into one for analysis, assuming that there are also other lists available.

Although correspondences on this point can be identified between ecological and epidemiological applications, it should be observed that the features usually arise for quite different reasons. As indicated, it is essentially a behavioural problem among animals. If the drug user, on the other hand, is not going to a second service *because* he or she has been to the first, or is going to the second because of going to the first, this is again most likely to be a known feature of the structure of the services and so this source of heterogeneity could be avoided by selecting and merging the initial lists. For drug users, in fact, the dependence between lists is usually a reflection of heterogeneity. For example, the heavier users may be more likely than lighter users to be on both a police and a treatment list, or on two treatment lists. Stratification could, therefore, be a better way of handling this dependence than attempting to adapt the models that allow for the phenomenon in the form in which it arises in studies of animal populations.

Supplementary information

In every kind of multiple capture study, there is usually further information available on the members of the population, beyond the simple record of their individual capture histories. This may permit a stratified analysis. For example, male and female animals, or adults and juveniles, may be analysed separately. One purpose of this stratification is to obtain greater homogeneity and thus fulfil the assumptions of the statistical analysis more closely.

The difference between ecological and epidemiological applications is that, in the former, there will not usually be much supplementary information available – probably sex, perhaps age, and also location, if the sampling is not all at the same site. In epidemiological applications, on the other hand, there will usually be many pieces of supplementary information. For drug users, depending on the purpose for which the lists have been drawn up, we will probably know not only sex, age and place of residence, but might also have information on treatment history, drug use history, substances of abuse and other behavioural items. How can all these be exploited in the analysis? (Some may already have been used in the matching.) There is a difficulty to be considered in deciding how to use this supplementary information. Our data are generally not totally reliable, so an item which appears on two or more lists may not agree. This seems to be a problem with no real equivalent in the study of animal populations.

Conclusions

Epidemiological applications of CRM differ from their use in animal population studies in many and important ways. Perhaps the key items are that, in the former type of analysis, we are interested in methods applicable to a small number of cross-sectional (rather than longitudinal) samples. There is likely to be a high degree of heterogeneity, but there is the potential advantage of exploiting extra information on the individuals in our population. By and large, papers on CRM in animal population studies are not written with this situation in mind and it is doubtful if much is going to be added to that literature in the future that will be of use in epidemiology. Is the application to census adjustment more relevant? In many ways, yes. Many of the similarities are stronger and the differences fewer. However, there is an emphasis here on the two-sample case, and there is also the difference that sampling is planned.

CRM techniques are important in estimating numbers of drug users because this is the way in which it is possible to make use of partial lists. It seems that, from now on, the special circumstances of this and other epidemiological applications will lead to a more specialised literature. Let us never forget, however, the need for cross-fertilisation and the possibility that what we need can be found elsewhere. Here is one example. The notorious need for independence between lists in a two-sample study can be dropped, at the expense of making other assumptions, by stratifying the data and then imposing some constraints on the parameters of the different sub-tables. For example, tables can be drawn up for each of the two sexes and valid estimates of population sizes obtained for men and women separately, without assuming independence but assuming that the degree of dependence is the same for both sexes. The idea was developed by Wolter for census adjustment (and employed by Choi, Steel and Skinner, 1988) but published in the biometrical literature (Wolter, 1990) and provides a method which could have utility in drug epidemiology.

References

Brecht M.L. and Wickens T.D. (1993) 'Application of multiple-capture methods for estimating drug use prevalence', *Journal of Drug Issues*, 23, 229-250.

Cormack R.M. (1989) 'Log-linear models for capture-recapture', *Biometrics*, 45, 395-413.

Choi C.Y., Steel D.G. and Skinner T.J. (1988) 'Adjusting the 1986 Australian census count for under-enumeration', *Survey Methodology*, 14, 173-189.

Darroch J.N., Fienberg S.E., Glonek G.F.V. and Junker B.W. (1993) 'A three-sample multiple-recapture approach to census population estimation with heterogeneous catchability', *Journal of the American Statistical Association*, 88, 1137-1148.

Fienberg S.E. (1992) 'Bibliography on capture-recapture modelling with application to census undercount adjustment', *Survey Methodology*, 18, 143-154.

Hook E.B. and Regal R.R. (1995) 'Capture-recapture methods in epidemiology: methods and limitations', *Epidemiologic Reviews*, 17, 243-264.

IWGDMF (1995a) 'Capture-recapture and multiple-record systems estimation. I: History and theoretical development', *American Journal of Epidemiology*, 142, 1047-1058.

IWGDMF (1995b) 'Capture-recapture and multiple-record systems estimation. II: Applications in human diseases', *American Journal of Epidemiology*, 142, 1059-1068.

Pollock K.H. (1991) 'Modelling capture, recapture, and removal statistics for estimation of demographic parameters for fish and wildlife populations: past, present and future', *Journal of the American Statistical Association*, 86, 225-238.

Richardson S.C., Patterson I.J. and Dunnet G.M. (1979) 'Fluctuations in colony size in the rook, *Corvus frugilegus*', *Journal of Animal Ecology*, 48, 103-110.

Seber G.A.F. (1982) *The Estimation of Animal Abundance and Related Parameters*, 2nd edition, London, Griffin.

Seber G.A.F. (1986) 'A review of estimating animal abundance', *Biometrics*, 42, 267-292.

Seber G.A.F. (1992) 'A review of estimating animal abundance II', *International Statistical Review*, 60, 129-166.

Wickens T.D. (1993). 'Quantitative methods for estimating the size of a drug-using population', *Journal of Drug Issues*, 23, 185-216.

Wolter K.M. (1990) 'Capture-recapture estimation in the presence of a known sex ratio', *Biometrics*, 46, 157-162.

CHAPTER 10

A CAPTURE-RECAPTURE STUDY TO ESTIMATE THE SIZE OF THE ADDICT POPULATION IN TOULOUSE, FRANCE

by Pierre-Yves Bello and Geneviève Chêne

Estimates of the number of 'hard' drug users in France are not very precise, varying between 150,000 and 300,000 (Lert, 1993). Using health data and a demographic model, Costes (1995) estimated that there were at least 160,000 current heroin users in France and discussed the use of epidemiological information in formulating policy.

As in other countries, there is also a need to estimate the size of the drug-using population at regional or local level. In particular, such estimates enable some assessment of the proportion of drug users using social and health care facilities. The use of a denominator, together with additional specific investigations, can also provide estimates of the prevalence and possibly the incidence of morbidity (HIV, hepatitis, overdose) and mortality. This information can also be useful for epidemiological surveillance of drug addiction and for health and social planning at local and regional level (Frischer *et al*, 1993).

The unusual and clandestine nature of addictive practices is, however, an obstacle to obtaining data, and it is therefore very difficult to carry out studies covering the general population. Methods such as population surveys which work well for alcohol, tobacco and cannabis are not effective for hard drug consumption (heroin, cocaine, LSD, crack). Large samples are needed to identify an uncommon behaviour pattern, and the response is largely dependent on the interviewer/interviewee relationship. The prevalence of drug addiction is highest among marginal populations (in prison or with no fixed address), and it will be difficult to reach such groups with a standard sampling procedure. Several 'indirect' methods of estimating the size of addict populations have been proposed, including the Markov model, synthetic estimation and the capture-recapture method (CRM) (Wickens, 1993).

CRM is increasingly being used to solve estimation problems in 'marginal' populations (Fisher *et al*, 1994). Recently, CRM has been used to estimate populations of drug addicts (Domingo-Salvany *et al*, 1995; Frischer *et al*, 1993; Mastro *et al*, 1994), prostitutes (McKeganey *et al*, 1992) or persons with no fixed address (Fisher *et al*, 1994). The number of cases can be estimated by this method on the basis of two or more case sources, which may be hospital outpatients or inpatient agencies or any other point of contact (specialised care centre, syringe exchange point, police station, etc) as explained elsewhere in this monograph.

In this chapter, we describe a practical case study of the application of CRM to estimating the size of the drug-using population in the Toulouse conurbation.

Subjects and methods

Case definitions and data sources

Toulouse is the capital of the Midi-Pyrénées region (population 2,430,663) and the Haute-Garonne *département* (population 925,000). The Toulouse conurbation is a young and dynamic area containing 37 per cent of the region's jobs, unlike the rest of the region where the population is mainly rural and ageing. The conurbation is an urban zone with a population of over 650,000 (360,000 in the actual city and 290,000 in the suburbs) (INSEE, 1991).

In this study, the term drug user was definied as 'any person residing in the Toulouse conurbation for at least three months who habitually used, and was dependent upon, substances taken orally, nasally, or by injection, at the time of first contact with the source'. The three-month residence stipulation enabled us to exclude persons treated in the conurbation but originating from another place of residence as well as persons with no fixed address who were not 'settled' in the conurbation. The terms 'habitual user of' and 'dependent upon' were intended to exclude one-off users of drugs (for example, attempted suicide by means of psychotropic substances). Drug use must have commenced at least three months prior to the date of contact with the facility; non-injection users must have taken the drug at least once a week over the previous month.

The drugs taken into consideration were heroin, morphine and its derivatives (particularly codeine, buprenorphine, methadone), cocaine, crack, amphetamines, psychotropic drugs other than for therapeutic purposes, hallucinogens (LSD, ecstasy [MDMA] and other dysleptics) and solvents.

The information collected in respect of each person included in the study was as follows: first initial of the surname; forename; date of birth; sex; home address postcode; whether without any fixed address; whether residing in the Toulouse conurbation for more than three months; date when care commenced in 1994; date when care ended; main substance used; secondary substance; main method used (injection, oral, nasal); number of doses during the previous month; and whether by injection. The study covered the year 1994. Data were collected retrospectively, from March to July 1995.

A list of agencies able to treat drug addicts in the Toulouse conurbation was drawn up, which included specialised treatment agencies for drug addicts, hospital agencies (infectious diseases, gastro-enterology, general intensive care and psychiatry), the drug addiction unit of the prison, the urban police narcotics squad and the

Toulouse syringe exchange bus. The head of each agency and, in some cases, his or her assistant, was contacted in order to explain the project, its purpose, method and aims. This enabled the agreement in principle of all heads to be secured and the possible data collection arrangements for each agency to be discussed. In some agencies, case selection was difficult, reducing the quality of data collection. Finally, twelve agencies were actually asked to collect data: the drug addiction unit; four specialised care services for drug addicts; two psychiatric agencies; two intensive care services and three medical agencies. At least one person was trained in data collection at each site.

Data collection

A data collection form was standardised and tested by agency heads and correspondents, and a handbook was produced setting out the objects of the study and the procedure for filling in the form, together with some examples of completed forms. In each participating agency, one person was responsible for collecting data and compiling a form for each addict with whom the agency dealt during 1994. The case selection arrangements were adapted to each agency. When all the forms had been completed, they were sent to the doctor co-ordinating the study. All forms were read and validated before computer acquisition, which was effected with Epi-Info (WHO-CDC) software.

Cases common to several sources were identified by means of a computer file containing all the forms from all the agencies. This file was classified first by alphabetical surname initial and forename, then by alphabetical forename and surname initial, and lastly by order of birth date and surname. Identification variables were the surname initial, the forename, the birth date and the sex. In this way, it was possible to identify both exact overlaps (identity of surname initial, forename, birth date and sex) and inexact overlaps. It was considered, therefore, that two forms could be regarded as identical if there was a single-digit difference between the birth dates, if the forenames were phonetically similar, or if the surname initial was different in the case of a woman (all other variables being identical).

Submission of the collection form and the accompanying handbook provided an opportunity to determine the data actually available for each agency. It proved to be difficult to identify retrospectively cases in agencies not specialising in the care of problematic drug users, since individuals attend such agencies for organic pathology such as HIV or hepatitis C. Clinical files concentrate on this pathology and data regarding drug use are often fragmentary. It was therefore decided that data collection in three clinical medical agencies was too time consuming in relation to the number of potential forms. One specialised care agency was unable to compile the data by the required date because its active caseload was too great and it had difficulty in releasing staff for the task. The Toulouse police narcotics squad did not have enough information for proper completion of the forms retrospectively, and the Toulouse syringe exchange bus was also unable to take part owing to a lack of data concerning its work in 1994. This left nine participating agencies.

All the forms for consumers of substances defined as drugs in the study were recorded, a total of 947 forms covering 721 persons. Forms which did not meet the inclusion criteria, or where the main substance used was not specified, were rejected, as were those where the variables were insufficient to identify overlaps. A series of choices was made. After cleaning the file and selecting the most relevant data for persons attending more than one agency, those not resident in the Toulouse conurbation, i.e. 90 individuals, were excluded. Owing to the difficulties connected with the concept of drug dependence, the 47 persons who used only psychotropic substances were also excluded, leaving only oral drug users (662 forms covering 577 persons), of whom 487 persons (575 forms) were injecting drug users.

The nine agencies were grouped as follows for the purposes of the CRM analysis: (a) University Hospital Centre (UHC), comprising an infectious diseases unit, a psychiatric emergency unit, a psychiatric unit, and two general intensive care agencies; (b) Joseph Ducuing Specialised Care (JDSC), comprising the two specialised care services for drug addicts (AAT and Clémence Isaure) and the medical agency at the Joseph Ducuing Hospital; and (c) the drug addiction unit at the prison (DAU).

Analysis

Estimation of the number of injecting drug users resident in the Toulouse conurbation

Overlaps amongst the three sources were identified and a contingency table drawn up (Table 1). There are eight possible combinations for the whole population, one of which is unknown.

Table 1: Distribution of injection drug users by sex, age and presence at the sources in the Toulouse conurbation in 1994

	J yes				J no			
	C yes		C no		C yes		C no	
	A yes	A no	A yes	A no	A yes	A no	A yes	A no
Men	1	38	7	116	12	109	84	-
Women	0	21	2	47	0	49	7	-
15-29 years	1	37	5	76	8	79	61	-
30-44 years	0	22	4	81	4	79	30	-
Total	1	59	9	163*	12	158	91	-

Six people could not be included in the study stratified by age for lack of information.
J = Joseph Ducuing Specialised Care
C = University Hospital Centre
A = The drug addiction unit at the prison.

Log-linear analyses (see Chapter 8 by Antònia Domingo-Salvany and Chapter 11 by Martin Frischer) were used to estimate the number of unknown injecting drug injectors. The most effective model for this population comprises interactions between the drug addiction unit at the prison (DAU) and the Joseph Ducuing Specialised Care (JDSC); and the drug addiction unit at the prison and the University Hospital Centre (UHC). It enables the number of missing cases to be estimated at 437. The total population is estimated at 930. This model presupposes the absence of interactions between UHC and JDSC. If UHC and JDSC are used for making an estimate by the capture-recapture method for two sources, the result is a population estimate of 923 (CI 95 per cent 752-1,094), very close to that given by the log-linear model.

Table 2: Estimation of the number of injecting drug users in the Toulouse conurbation in 1994 for different groups, using the most effective log-linear model

Population	Model	df**	X²	p	Missing	Total
Overall	AJ, AC*	1	0.03	0.87	437	930
Men	AJ, AC	1	0.00	1.00	333	700
Women	J, AC	1	0.24	0.62	114	240
Sex (S)	AJ, AC, AS	5	4.64	0.46	M=228 W=102	M=595 W=228
15-29 years	AJ, AC	1	0.12	0.73	429	429
30-44 years	AJ, AC	1	0.94	0.33	511	511
Age (V)	AJ, AC, AV	6	5.06	0.54	<30=216 >30=205	<30=483 >30=425

* = AC, AJ corresponds to a log-linear model comprising an interaction between A and C, and between A and J;
**= Degrees of freedom. Key; as for Table 1.

The population size was also estimated for each sex by means of the same procedure (Table 2). The same model was identified for men as for the general population. The best model for women contained a single interaction between the DAU and UHC.

A more complex analysis was also conducted with the inclusion of the sex variable in order to take account of possible interactions between sex and the various sources. The best model (see Table 2) contained an interaction between the UHC and DAU, between the JDSC and DAU, and between the sex variable and DAU. We can thus identify an interaction between sex and the DAU, indicating that the probability of being imprisoned differs according to sex.

The injecting drug user population was also divided into two age groups, the first being 15-29 years (267 persons) and the second 30-44 years (226). A further analysis covering the whole population was conducted incorporating the over-30s variable into the model, then separately for each age group. The best model (Table 3), both for the under-30s and for the over-30s, is identical to the one for the whole population. For the five-variable model, we identified an interaction between age and DAU, indicating an imprisonment probability differing according to age.

Table 3: Estimations of the prevalence of injecting drug use in the Toulouse conurbation in 1994 for the population aged from 15 to 54 years

	Estimation IDUs	95% CI	Population 15-54 years	Prevalence (per thousand)	95% CI (per thousand)
All	930	777-1,083	404.059	2.30	1.92-2.68
Men	700	558-842	200.834	3.49	2.78-4.19
Women	240	171-309	203.225	1.18	1.00-1.52
Men and Women	940		404.059	2.33	
15-29 years	429	270-588	205.529	2.09	1.31-2.86
Over 29 years	511	356-667	198.467	2.57	1.81-3.37
All ages	940		404.059	2.33	

Table 4: Estimations of the prevalence of opiate use in the Toulouse conurbation in 1994, for the population aged from 15 to 44 years

	Estimation opiate users	95% CI	Population 15-54 years	Prevalence (per thousand)	95% CI (per thousand)
All	1,156	962-1,350	332.654	3.48	2.89-4.06
Men	875	692-1,058	164.134	5.33	4.22-6.45
Women	301	213-389	168.520	1.79	1.26-2.39
Men and Women	1,176		332.654	3.54	
15-29 years	570	461-679	192.520	2.96	2.39-3.53
Over 29 years	574	400-748	140.134	4.10	2.83-5.34
All ages	1,144		332.654	3.44	

After calculating the variance of N for each model selected, we obtain an estimation of the size of the IDU population of the Toulouse conurbation, with its confidence interval. The estimation (Table 3) varies from 777 to 1,083 people for the whole population. Prevalence among the 15-54 years population is 2.30 per 1,000. It is 3.49 per 1,000 for men as against 1.18 per 1,000 for women.

The opiate user population

The most effective models for opiate users have the same interactions as for IDUs. These models were used in order to estimate the sizes of the various opiate user populations (Table 4). The number of opiate users is estimated to be 1,156 (CI 95 per cent 962-1,350). The overall prevalence is 3.48 per 1,000 (5.33 per 1,000 among men and 1.79 per 1,000 among women).

Discussion

The data collection phase of the study involved obtaining many authorisations and agreements. In strictly legal terms, it was the authorisation of the *Commission Nationale Informatique et Libertés (CNIL)* that allowed work to begin in earnest. The identification variables used were the same as for compulsory notifications of AIDS cases. They enabled a reliable search for overlaps to be made while respecting the ethical and legal requirements of confidentiality.

Obtaining the agreement of all potential data sources was a particularly long process because of the number of agencies. All the agency heads showed interest in the problems raised by the project and all gave their agreement in principle. However, collection was not possible in all agencies, either because of a lack of data (from the exchange bus and the narcotics squad) or because of the difficulty in choosing cases which could be recorded on a form (several clinical agencies). The institutional network for the care of drug addicts in the Toulouse conurbation offers an advantage for a study of this type. It provides all forms of care, but the number of agencies is low enough to allow personal contact as well as the adaptation of the collection method to each facility. Several facilities have already been working together for a long time, and this generates an excellent momentum for developing new therapeutic research and projects.

Although data were obtained, there were several problems, particularly with regard to the inter-agency consistency of the cases selected. The case selection procedure varied from one agency to another and this introduced some selection bias. In some agencies the procedure seemed effective in finding all the relevant cases, while in others it might have led to the loss of several cases suitable for inclusion in the study. Clinical agencies treating drug addicts for an organic problem often record little information about the characteristics of drug addiction, so it is not always easy to obtain relevant data. The only way of limiting this distortion is to have a wide selection of cases and a data registration form with exclusion factors.

Case definition proved to be a complex problem. We used a rather restricted definition in exploiting the data, in order to limit ourselves to a study of injectors and opiate users. It proved impossible to produce an estimate by this method for all individuals using only psychotropic substances. Interpretations of psychotropic dependence varied from one agency to another, and the inclusion base therefore varied too.

The identification variables authorised by the CNIL permitted high quality identification of overlaps between sources without prejudice to confidentiality. This is a particularly important factor for the relevance of the estimations obtained. In the Barcelona study (Domingo-Salvany *et al*, 1995) the weakness of the identifiers forced the investigators to develop a probabilistic model for identifying overlaps. Defective identification of overlaps involves overestimation and a widening of the confidence gap.

Perpetuating the feasibility of this type of data collection involves formalising the information network created. Facilitated access to data, which has usually already been collected, depends on the establishment of a permanent data storage system in each of the participating agencies. This information will be available when new estimations are needed. The initial phase for such a study will, in this way, be considerably shortened, and the data collected should be more relevant, hence improving the accuracy and quality of estimations.

Our calculations probably suffer from underestimation. Several sources did not make a fully exhaustive collection of data, and we lost some cases which theoretically could have been studied. Our 'survey base' was not as wide as we would have liked and thus our sample was not altogether representative. Several potentially significant data sources were unable to participate including the police, the methadone centres, the network of general practitioners and the neighbourhood services (exchange bus, low threshold agency). Though the drug addiction unit in a prison presented a negative dependence in comparison with the other sources, it is probable that police agencies are statistically independent of other services. In Glasgow, where this was found to be the case, the estimates including the police sample were considerably higher than when this sample was omitted.

The Toulouse estimates given here cover the population represented by our sample. Sub-groups of the addict population are probably not represented. Thus, socially integrated addicts, who seldom resort to health and social facilities, are probably underestimated. A stratification according to other variables, such as no fixed address, length of addiction and frequency of doses, would have been desirable. Unfortunately these variables were not sufficiently well indicated to permit such analyses. In order to find the most stable population possible, we confined ourselves to addicts having resided for at least three months in the Toulouse conurbation. Toulouse is a stopping point for people travelling to or from Spain; moreover, its care facilities treat people from the Midi-Pyrénées region and sometimes from the Parisian area. These cases, therefore, are not included in our estimation.

This is the first local estimation of the size of the addict population in France. It provides an assessment of the prevalence of addiction to opiates and injected drugs in the general population as well as offering useful denominators for all prevalence studies concerning the target population. It is possible, for example, to use a prevalence study to estimate the number of persons suffering from a disease (HIV infection) or having a specific problem. There are several estimations of this type, notably in Glasgow (Frischer et al, 1993), Bangkok (Mastro et al, 1994) and Barcelona (Domingo-Salvany et al, 1995). It may be noted that the estimated prevalences in the two European studies seem higher than in the Toulouse conurbation. In Glasgow in 1990, Frischer et al estimated the prevalence of injected drug use at 13.5 per 1,000 among people aged 15-54, i.e. six times greater than in Toulouse. In Barcelona in

1989, Domingo-Salvany *et al* estimated the prevalence of opiate use at 9.2 per 1,000 among people aged 15-44, i.e. almost two and a half times greater than the Toulouse estimation.

Estimations of the size of addict populations is a matter of concern for national authorities, for the *Observatoire Français des Drogues et des Toxicomanies* and local health and social action agencies, as well as for all practitioners in the Toulouse conurbation. A study of the prevalence of addiction to injected drugs by the capture-recapture method is feasible in France. This is a particularly useful method of studying populations which are difficult to reach. However, it involves close contact with a network of people professionally concerned with drug addiction, who are aware of the difficulties involved in collecting data and are keen to take part in research projects. Such people should, therefore, be regarded as full partners in the investigation. If the network is stable, it may very well serve as a basis for a local/regional system for the epidemiological surveillance of drug addiction.

Acknowledgements

This study was financially supported by *the Observatoire Français des Drogues et des Toxicomanies*. The authors would like to thank Isabelle Aptel, Catherine Arnaud, Frédéric Berthier, Jean-Claude Desenclos, Bruno Hubert, Roger Salamon and Véronique Vaillant, for their technical advice, and Christelle Andrieu, Anne Bertrand and Maité Delarue for their practical assistance in carrying out the study.

The authors would also like to thank: the GREATT (Groupe de Recherche en Épidémiologie Appliquée aux Toxicomanes de Toulouse); Lise Cuzin, Bruno Marchou, Jean-Charles Auvergnat (Infectious and Tropical Diseases Agency, Purpan Hospital); Christian Virenque, Laurence Dubost (General Intensive Care Agency, Rangueil Hospital); Bernard Cathala (General Intensive Care Agency, Purpan Hospital); Martine Lacoste, Kahlou Estrella, Serge Escot (Clémence Isaure Association); Chantal Thirion, Françoise Monterde (Association Anonyme Accueil Toxicomanes – Drug Addicts Anonymous); Alain Houette, Gérard Laurencin (Saint Michel Prison Drug Addiction Unit); Alain Lucido, Daniel Garipuy, Francis Saint Dizier (Joseph Ducuing Hospital); Roger Franc (Emergency Agency, Marchant Hospital); Anne-Marie Pezous, Laurent Schmit, Pierre Moron (Psychiatric Agency, Purpan – Casselardit Hospital); Pierre-Yves Bello, Françoise Cayla and Didier Fabre (Observatoire Régional de la Santé de Midi-Pyrénées (Midi-Pyrénées Regional Health Monitoring Centre).

References

Costes J.-M. (1995) 'Une estimation de prévalence', in: Carpentier C. and Costes J.-M. eds, *Drogues et toxicomanies: indicateurs et tendances*, Paris: DGLDT, OFDT, 44-45.

Domingo-Salvany A., Hartnoll R.L., Maguire A., Suelves J.M. and Anto J.M. (1995) 'Use of capture-recapture to estimate the prevalence of opiate addiction in Barcelona, Spain, 1989', *American Journal of Epidemiology*, 141 (6), 567-574.

Fisher N., Turner S., Pugh R. and Taylor C. (1994) 'Estimating numbers of homeless and homeless mentally ill people in north-east Westminster by using capture-recapture analysis', *British Medical Journal*, 308, 27-30.

Frischer M., Bloor M., Finlay A. *et al* (1991) 'A new method of estimating prevalence of injecting drug use in an urban population: results from a Scottish city', *International Journal of Epidemiology*, 20, 997-1000.

Frischer M., Leyland A., Cormack R. *et al* (1993) 'Estimating the population prevalence of injection drug use and infection with human immunodeficiency virus among injection drug users in Glasgow, Scotland', *American Journal of Epidemiology*, 138 (3), 170-181.

INSEE. (1991) *Recensement général de la population de 1990* (1990 General Population Census), 31 Haute Garonne, Paris INSEE.

Lert F. (1993) 'Épidemiologie de l'infection VIH parmi les toxicomanes', in: Rouault T. and Serryn D. eds, *SIDA, toxicomanie: une lecture documentaire*, Paris CRIPS, Toxibase 13-18.

Mastro T., Kitayaporn D., Weniger B. *et al* (1994) 'Estimating the number of HIV-infected drug users in Bangkok: a capture-recapture method', *American Journal of Public Health*, 84 (7), 1094-1099.

McKeganey N., Barnard M., Leyland A., Coote I. and Follet E. (1992) 'Female streetworking prostitution and HIV infection in Glasgow', *British Medical Journal*, 305, 801-804.

Wickens T. (1993) 'Quantitative methods for estimating the size of a drug-using population', *Journal of Drug Issues*, 23 (2), 185-216.

CHAPTER 11

MORE COMPLEX CAPTURE-RECAPTURE MODELS:
AN ILLUSTRATIVE CASE STUDY
USING DATA FROM GLASGOW, SCOTLAND

by Martin Frischer

While the previous chapters in this section have addressed theoretical issues involved in using the capture-recapture method (CRM), this chapter illustrates more complex models using three or more samples. It gives a practical illustration using data collected in Glasgow, Scotland, for a one year period (1990). The purpose of the study was to estimate the prevalence of drug injecting in the city in order to further determine the number of HIV positive injectors (Frischer *et al*, 1993).

The prevalence study began with multi-enumeration. Partial identifier information (gender, initials, date of birth, first part of postcode) was obtained from the sources shown in Table 1. Data collection varied from computerised records to manual searching through case reports. Many prevalence studies have ground to a halt at this early stage because agencies have refused to divulge, or to allow access to, identifier information. Although very few agencies in Glasgow took this view, there is concern that European directives will make future access to named data more difficult (Wald *et al*, 1994).

Table 1: Data sources used to estimate the prevalence of injecting drug use in Glasgow, 1990

Drug treatment agencies	1,476
- Non residential community projects	630
- Psychiatric hospital inpatients	231
- General hospital inpatients	194
- Addicts reported to the Home Office	264
Scottish HIV test register	507
Police (non-cannabis drug offences)	508
Needle and syringe exchanges	1,179
Total number of cases reported	3,670

The simplest scenario: two-sample capture-recapture

An example of a simple two-way CRM multiway table is shown in Table 2. The first sample consists of 1,276 individuals who received some form of treatment for drug use. The second sample consists of 507 people who had an HIV test and whose risk category was given as injecting drug use. Of these 169 were people who were also recorded in the first sample. Using the method described in Chapter 8 by Antònia Domingo-Salvany, the total population estimate is 3,238.

Table 2: Number of individuals recorded in two lists of drug users in Glasgow, 1990

Treatment sample (capture)	HIV sample	(recapture)	
	Present	Absent	Total
Present	169	1107	1276
Absent	338	unknown	
Total	507		

For this simple method to produce a reliable population estimate, the following criteria must be met: all individuals must have the same defining characteristics; identification of individuals must be accurate; detection of an individual in a sample cannot change the individual's behaviour with respect to another sample; all individuals must have the same probability of being sampled; and unobserved individuals must behave in a similar way to observed individuals. However, in the example shown in Table 2, it is unlikely that any of these criteria has been fully met, for the following reasons:

Defining characteristics

Treatment for drug use is heterogeneous, ranging from one-off attendance at a drug project to inpatient psychiatric care. Injecting drug use (IDU) as a risk factor for an HIV test does not specify any time period (i.e. a person could have an HIV test with risk factor 'IDU', although they stopped injecting several years ago).

Identification of individuals

Errors can be made in recording identifier information or people can give false information.

Individual behaviour

If somebody has treatment for drug use, they may be referred for an HIV test or might find out about testing facilities; thus people who received treatment for drug use may have been more likely to have taken an HIV test than those who were not in treatment.

Probability of being sampled

If there are many drug users who, for whatever reason, never come into contact with treatment agencies or HIV testing, the estimate of the drug-using population may well be wrong since it is entirely based on those who do.

More complex scenarios

As already discussed in previous chapters, simple models are easy to use, they do not require much data and it is easy to understand the effect of violating assumptions (e.g. if the samples are not independent). However, they are likely to misrepresent the population and introduce bias into population estimates. On the other hand, sophisticated models using more than two samples can provide a better representation of the population but they require more data. Such models can require a considerable degree of statistical expertise and population estimates can be unstable (i.e. slight changes in the model can result in large fluctuations in estimates).

As with the two-sample example shown in Table 2, there are definition problems for all samples shown in Table 1 with the exception of needle and syringe exchange. Discussion with drug treatment agencies provided further information, e.g. about 90 per cent of those seen were thought to be injectors. The police data were more problematic at this stage, although some checks were made during analysis (i.e. comparison of known injectors and overlaps between police and other samples). Checking for false identifiers was not feasible. The likelihood that the HIV test register may be contaminated by false identifying information was considered, but the high level of overlap between this source and the treatment sample provided some assurance on this issue.

Matching procedure

Where there is incomplete identifier information (e.g. initials rather than full name) it is probably best to use a 'probabilistic' matching strategy whereby a computer programme uses specified criteria to determine the probability of two cases being the same individual. In this study, probabilistic matching based on gender, date of birth, initials and the first part of the postcode was used to identify overlap cases. Clearly, matching on limited identification information may introduce error when identifying overlaps in two ways; 'false positives' could be recorded when two cases are thought to be the same individual while 'false negatives' could arise when overlaps are missed due to errors in recording identifier information. Careful checking of records at source and during the matching procedure was conducted to minimise these types of error. While the impact of errors in the present analysis is likely to be marginal, it is impossible to rule out the possibility that errors in the four samples could result in a different model being selected and consequently affect estimates of the number of unknown users.

Sample interaction

This term is used to describe a situation where detection of an individual in sample A alters the individual's behaviour with respect to sample B. For example if drug users arrested for drug offences then attend treatment agencies, the two samples will not be independent. In other words, drug users who are not arrested by the police may have a lower probability of being detected in the treatment sample than those who are. With only two samples there is insufficient information to detect interactions which could bias estimates. However, it is important to examine the range of two-sample estimates (see Table 3). In this case, the range is 3,828 to 8,642 and if the two extreme estimates are excluded the range reduces to 6,037 to 8,308. This relatively narrow range is not an inherent feature of the method – different sample sizes and overlaps could have resulted in widely discrepant two-sample estimates.

Table 3: Estimates of the number of drug injectors in Glasgow, 1990 based on information from two samples

Samples	n1	n2	Overlap	Total observed	Estimated unobserved	Total population	95 per cent CI
hiv & tr	507	1,276	169	1,783	1,428 - 2,323	3,828	3,211 - 4,106
hiv & ne-ex	507	1,179	99	1,686	4,252 - 5,294	6,037	4,896 - 6,980
ne-ex & tr	1,179	1,276	205	2,455	3,824 - 5,532	7,338	6,279 - 7,987
ne-ex & pol	1,179	508	75	1,687	4,576 - 7,871	7,985	6,263 - 9,588
hiv & police	507	508	31	1,015	4,460 - 10,064	8,308	5,475 - 11,079
tr & pol	1,276	508	75	1,784	4,996 - 8,571	8,642	6,810 - 10,355

hiv = Scottish HIV test register; ne-ex = Needle and syringe exchanges; tr = Drug treatment agencies; pol = Police - non-cannabis drug offences.

Where three (or more) samples are available, it is possible to assess if there are any interactions between samples using a more sophisticated form of CRM. The three-sample method does not require complicated statistics or computing (Bishop *et al*, 1975). With more than three samples, estimating population size requires the use of log-linear modelling. This is not a particularly complex procedure: Cormack (1992) describes how to perform the analysis using the statistical computer program GLIM (Payne, 1986) and how to calculate confidence intervals.

Table 4 gives key summary statistics for various models. Model 1, assuming independence between samples, does not fit the data well, judging from the X^2 statistic. Various combinations of sample interactions are then tested in order to see whether the model fit can be improved. The 'best' model, as judged from the X^2 statistic is model 3, with an estimate of 8,494 injectors.

**Table 4: Analyses of log-linear models used to estimate
the number of injecting drug users in Glasgow, 1990**

Model	Type of Model	X^2	DF	p Value	u	N
1	All samples independent	101.5	10	0.00	3,844	6,710
2A	Interaction between samples 1&2, 2&4	19.3	8	0.11	5,189	8,055
2B	Interaction between samples 1&2, 1&4	11.6	8	0.41	5,276	8,142
2C	Interaction between samples 1&2, 1&4, 2&4	6.8	7	0.56	6,000	8,866
3	Interaction between samples 1&2, 1&4, 2&4, 1&2&4	2.9	6	0.83	5,628	8,494

Samples: 1 = Scottish HIV test register; 2 = Drug treatment agencies; 3 = Police - non-cannabis drug offences; 4 = Needle and syringe exchange; u = Fitted value for missing cell (unknown injectors); N = Total number of injectors.

Although the model has acceptable statistical properties (i.e. low X^2), it does not necessarily follow that the estimate for the number of unknown injectors is correct, since this estimate is based on the behaviour of known injectors. One way to verify the model is to repeat the analysis for stratified sections of the population and summate the results. If the sum of the stratified estimates is approximately the same as the un-stratified estimate, it is reasonable to suppose that the latter is about right. If the stratified total is not similar this would indicate heterogeneity among sections of the population. Table 5 (overleaf) shows that, in this case, the stratified and un-stratified estimates are very similar.

Although stratification provides a form of 'internal' validation, external validation requires some independent measures. One possible method for external validation is to compare the predicted and actual number of HIV positive injectors. The HIV prevalence rate among 503 injectors tested in a multi-site survey (in and out of treatment) was 1.4 per cent (95 per cent CI 0.4-2.5 per cent). If there were 8,500 current injectors, there would be 119 HIV positive current injectors in Glasgow. Data to the end of December 1990 shows that there were 100 known HIV positive injectors from Glasgow, twelve of whom had died. As there are likely to have been several unknown HIV positive injectors (either to themselves or the register), the comparison provides some validation of the drug-injecting prevalence estimate.

Another form of external validation could be provided by the 1992 Drug Use and Drug Prevention Survey conducted in four UK cities including Glasgow (Leitner *et al*, 1993). The 1992 DUDP estimate of 2,000 current injectors is obviously much lower than the 1990 CRM estimate of 7,500-9,700. Apart from the observation that prevalence could have declined between 1990 and 1992, there are many reasons for exercising caution in comparing the two estimates. The DUDP estimates are based on the positive reports of three individuals, whereas the CRM estimates are based on 2,866 known drug users. It is easy to adduce reasons which would lead one in the direction of supposing that the DUDP estimates are too low; conversely it could be argued that the CRM figure is too high. As both methods depend on a large number of assumptions, it is largely a matter of personal preference. The authors of the DUDP note that drug professionals in Glasgow were more inclined to accept the higher estimate from the CRM study. However, this is a rather dubious form of validation since drug professionals might reasonably be expected to favour the higher estimate.

Table 5: Estimated prevalence of drug injecting in Glasgow, 1990

	Known injectors (N)	Known injectors (%)	Estimated no. of injectors	95 per cent CI	Population	Population prevalence (%)
All cases	2,866	34	8,494	7,491 - 9,721	628,000	1.2 - 1.5
Males	1,977	35	5,544	4,847 - 6,412	315,000	1.5 - 2.0
Females	889	28	3,238	2,364 - 4,689	313,000	0.8 - 1.5
Male/female			8,782			
Age-group						
15-19	264	29	904	634 - 1,384	88,000	0.7 - 1.6
20-24	1,137	41	2,750	2,287 - 3,317	104,000	2.2 - 3.2
25-29	878	33	2,602	2,043 - 3,438	96,000	2.1 - 3.6
30-34	342	30	1,138	792 - 1,762	81,000	1.0 - 2.2
35+	245	16	1,518	805 - 2,595	259,000	0.3 - 1.0
All ages			8,912			

References

Bishop Y., Fienberg S. and Holland P. (1975) *Discrete multivariate analysis: theory and practice,* MIT Press, Cambridge, MA.

Cormack R.M. (1992) 'Interval estimation for mark-recapture studies of closed populations', *Biometrics,* 48, 567-576.

Frischer M., Leyland A., Cormack R., Goldberg D., Bloor M., Green S., Taylor A., Covell R., McKeganey N. and Platt S. (1993) 'Estimating population prevalence of injection drug use and HIV infection among injection drug users in Glasgow', *American Journal of Epidemiology,* 138 (3), 170-181.

Leitner M., Shapland J. and Wiles P. (1993) *Drug usage and drug prevention: the views and habits of the general public,* Her Majesty's Stationery Office, London.

Payne C.D. (1986) The GLIM (Generalised Linear Model) System-Release 3.77, Oxford, Numerical Algorithms.

Wald N., Law M., Meade T., Miller G., Alberman E. and Dickson J. (1994) 'Use of personal medical records for research purposes', *British Medical Journal,* 309, 1422-1424.

MULTIPLIER METHODS

PART IV

INTRODUCTION

by Colin Taylor

*T*he opening chapter of this section is Martin Frischer's clear methodological description of the principles of prevalence estimation through the use of the Mortality Multiplier Method. Frischer identifies the two main components of the prevalence estimation procedure: the establishment of a mortality rate amongst drug abusers, and the establishment of the number of drug abusers who die. The combination of these two figures to calculate an overall estimate of the prevalence of drug abuse is explained, and his discussion brings out the assumptions that are required if this estimate is to be valid.

A range of studies are cited to show the various applications of the method and to highlight the interpretational difficulties that arise in different circumstances. In this first chapter, Frischer also takes the reader further afield and illustrates more advanced applications of the technique in the context of survey analysis. From the examples, he draws out a set of methodological guidelines for good practice in setting up such studies, with highly relevant and important caveats concerning departure from the assumptions that make the estimation procedure valid.

A very detailed contribution from Klaus Püschel subsequently focuses attention on the problems and difficulties in determining whether a death is drug-related or not. Citing the German experience and registration systems, he describes how a pathologist might identify such deaths. Whether a death ever reaches a post-mortem examination stage is clearly important in whether or not the death will be classified as drug-related, as are all the stages of administration and registration following the discovery or declaration of death. In that they affect the information that is gathered and produced, these issues are important in their own right, over and above the importance of any formal definitions of what constitutes a 'drug-related death' that may be subsequently applied to the findings. The implications for researchers using such data are discussed and a plea is made for more uniform procedures to be put in place across different countries.

Marina Davoli's contribution outlines the general procedures for a cohort mortality study and argues for their central usefulness in measuring mortality. The important distinction between studying the mortality of drug abusers and studying drug-related deaths is highlighted in this chapter. Drug abusers may die of causes unrelated, or not directly related, to their drug abuse and a drug-related death does not necessarily imply the dead person was abusing drugs - both 'therapeutic' drug users and innocent children may suffer deaths that are drug-related.

A cohort study - that is, the study of a carefully defined group of people over a period of time - is one of the most common ways of estimating the death rate amongst *drug abusers and Marina Davoli's chapter uses as an example the multi-city study in which she is involved. The discussion highlights the usefulness of standardising procedures and definitions in order to make the results comparable across different studies. Without this, the various types of cohort study that can be carried out may easily lead to differences in estimated mortality, induced simply by different methods of implementing the studies rather than by variation in mortality or drug abuse prevalence itself. The multi-city study that Davoli describes sought specifically to remove this additional and unwanted source of variation by using standardised definitions of cohort methods.*

Denmark possesses a long-running national register of all drug-related death nationwide. Henrik Sælan's thoughtful contribution uses these data to illustrate and illuminate many of the difficult issues that are pointed out in Martin Frischer's opening description that may affect the interpretation of the resulting prevalence estimates. His chapter complements that of Marina Davoli in only briefly referencing the cohort studies he uses to derive the death rates amongst drug abusers and concentrating instead on the second element of the prevalence estimation calculation, the number of deaths to drug abusers. His conclusion that the drug-related death register is very much over-inclusive in identifying deaths for use in the prevalence estimation exercise is, of course, particular to the Danish system but, nonetheless, indicates useful lessons for other countries.

Equally useful is his discussion of identifying trends over time, from at least two different points of view. Firstly, he points out the implications of needing to estimate prevalence by using death rates and numbers dying, both of which are calculated as averages over an extended period of time. Secondly, he emphasises and strongly demonstrates the usefulness of studying drug-related deaths in their own right as an indirect indicator of the prevalence of drug abuse.

Taken together, these four chapters, with Martin Frischer's as the methodological centrepiece, offer a wealth of detail and information on the application of the methods and principles in practice.

CHAPTER 12

ESTIMATING THE PREVALENCE OF DRUG ABUSE
USING THE MORTALITY MULTIPLIER METHOD:
AN OVERVIEW

by Martin Frischer

The addict deaths multiplier method for estimating the prevalence of drug use was developed in the United States during the 1970s. The method involved determining the annual number of drug-related deaths in New York City and assuming that these deaths represented a proportion (0.5 per cent) of active heroin users in the city (Baden 1971, 1972). The proportion was obtained from a follow-up study of addicts receiving treatment, and was crudely estimated by the death rate observed amongst those users. Clearly for this method to be accurate, two assumptions must be met: that the number of deaths due to all causes must be accurately ascertained, and that the mortality rate must apply to all active drug users, not simply to those who were followed up.

While in the case of New York it is plausible that these two assumptions were met, in practice, the use of multiplier techniques has become much more elastic. For example, the number of all-cause deaths in a city may be ascertained and an average mortality rate obtained from the literature may be used to derive a multiplier. Thus, a third assumption is introduced: that the mortality rate in the specified city is within the range reported in the literature. In more extreme cases, the number and rate of deaths among, for example, injectors, may be inappropriately used as a multiplier for the number of, for example, opiate users.

This paper describes the main features of Mortality Multiplier Methods (MMM) and provides guidelines on methodological standards.

From drug-related deaths to prevalence estimation

It is evident from the introductory remarks that this method could have wide applicability since, at first appearance, a relatively small amount of information is required. First, most countries have statistics on drug-related deaths. Second, it might plausibly be assumed that mortality rates vary within fairly narrow limits. However, in order to understand the method fully, it is necessary to consider issues relating to the definition of drug-related deaths and the determination of mortality rates.

Defining drug-related deaths

Most European countries have national and/or regional mortality registers where deaths are coded using the International Classification of Diseases (ICD). However, as Table 1 indicates, there are many types of deaths (and consequently ICD codes) which can be considered as 'drug-related'.

Table 1: Types of drug-related mortality

Drug refers to any substance (licit or illicit, excluding alcohol and tobacco) taken purely for psychic effects.

Related mortality refers to all direct and indirect fatalities, not necessarily pertaining to the person(s) using the drug. Interest is usually focused on drug abuse where abuse refers to use of illicit substances and, for licit substances, use without prescription and/or in contravention of the specified dose.

The main type of drug-related deaths are:

- overdoses (accidental, intentional or undetermined)
- deaths due to diseases connected with long-term abuse of drugs
- suicide related to dependence on drugs
- accidents influenced by drug use
- deaths due to behaviour associated with drug use e.g. violence or internal concealment.

Unfortunately this classification is only one of many, and even 'cause' of death is not always defined in the same way. For example, a death 'caused' by a drug overdose could be coded as such or, alternatively, as due to respiratory failure. Furthermore, without additional information, it is not possible to detect deaths among drug users where no ICD codes relating to drug or drug use are recorded. Thus, the number of deaths from a national or regional death register is likely to be an underestimate. A key factor in determining the extent of this problem will be the proportion of suspected drug-related deaths which are subject to pathological investigation. In areas where this is common or standard, it may be possible to get some idea of how drug-related deaths are coded. For deaths among drug users which are not directly drug-related, possible sources of information include legal/police departments and HIV registers.

The range of cause-specific deaths, and the environments in which these deaths occur, are considered in detail by Weiss (1993) who recommends that even if a common definition is not possible, there should at least be a common classification in order to distinguish 'direct' and 'indirect' causes of death. This could be achieved by adopting an American proposal whereby deaths are classified according to the *directness* of the drug's action (e.g. drug alone or in combination with other internal and external events) and the *mode* of administration; however this approach proved to be problematic in comparing nine American cities (Gottschalk *et al*, 1979). In cases where drugs are held to be directly responsible for death, there is also considerable debate regarding appropriate terminology. The term 'overdose', although widely used, can be misleading since, in many cases, it is not clearly established that death is a direct consequence of excessive drug dosage. Complicating factors include loss of tolerance (e.g. after treatment episodes or release from prison), environmental cues not previously associated with drug use and pre-existing medical conditions.

There are also reports of 'overdose' deaths where toxicological analyses indicate low drug levels not capable of inducing severe toxic phenomena (Tunving, 1988). In such cases, assuming that there are no other complicating factors, hypersensitivity (i.e. predisposition to respond abnormally to certain substances) might be the mechanism responsible for causing death. To complicate matters further, 'overdose' deaths may arise, not as a result of illicit substances *per se*, but because of diluents which increase the volume of a substance, additives added to enhance the effect of the primary substance or impurities which originate during the manufacturing processes in the case of synthetic substances. In addition to these factors, the administration of substances in combination may produce synergistic effects which, at the present time, are not well understood.

In the tenth revision of the *International Classification of Diseases*, overdoses can be classified, either in the 'poisoning' section for cases of accidental intake, or in the 'acute intoxication' section for cases of intentional drug-taking. However, given the foregoing remarks on overdoses, there will be many cases where this is not an easy distinction to make and the section chosen will depend on the information available to ICD coders.

Causal factors in drug-related deaths

Studies with differing perspectives on the relationship between HIV and mortality are summarised in Table 2.

Table 2: Impact of HIV on non-AIDS related mortality

Soellner *et al*, (1992)

Germany, 1991–92. An analysis of drug-related fatalities in forensic institutes found fewer HIV positive cases died of unintentional overdose compared to HIV negative cases. Possible explanation – HIV positive cases have more control over their drug use.

Barbarini *et al*, (1993)

Italy, 1986–91. Among injectors in treatment centres, the incidence of deaths from overdose among HIV positives (3.8 per cent) was significantly higher than among HIV negatives (2 per cent). Possible explanation – HIV infection may predispose to overdose-related death from the use of street heroin.

Mientjes *et al*, (1992)

Amsterdam, Netherlands, 1986–89. A prospective cohort study of injectors found that HIV status was not an independent risk factor for non-AIDS mortality.

Eskild *et al*, (1993)

Oslo, Norway , 1985–91. A prospective cohort study found that HIV positive cases were twice as likely as HIV negative cases to die from non-AIDS causes. Possible explanation – selection of high frequency injectors to HIV positive group. Important to examine non-AIDS mortality.

Taken in conjunction with the list in Table 3, which compares two studies with differing views on the relationship between methadone and mortality, this helps to illustrate further the dangers of generalising findings reported in particular environments to other settings.

Table 3: Impact of methadone on mortality

Gronbladh *et al*, (1990)

Sweden, 1990. Comparison of mortality among 115 'street' addicts and 166 receiving methadone maintenance therapy (MMT). The mortality rate for street addicts was 63 times that expected for comparable age/sex distribution compared to eight times for addicts receiving MMT. The authors conclude that MMT exerts a major improvement in survival rate of heroin addicts.

Harding-Pink, (1993)

Review of MMT, 1993. Reports from Melbourne (Australia) and Geneva (Switzerland) of an unexpectedly high level of mortality among people receiving MMT. Reports from the US in the early 1970s, when MMT was widely adopted, indicate high levels of methadone-related mortality – most victims were not receiving MMT but had obtained the drug illicitly. The author comments that methadone is highly toxic to anyone not tolerant to opioids. Death can occur when tolerance is incorrectly assessed and during maintenance when doses are combined. However, MMT programmes are often not in a position to monitor mortality.

Mortality rates

Research into mortality rates among drug users has been conducted almost exclusively among drug users receiving treatment (Perucci *et al*, 1991, 1992; Davoli *et al*, 1993). The reasons for this are straightforward: in order to calculate mortality rates, it is necessary to have identifier information on a group of people who are known drug users of a particular type; this information is then linked to a mortality register. Various types of mortality proportions and rates may then be calculated.

- annual mortality rate: percentage of deaths per year among groups of drug users;
- mortality rate per 100 years risk among a cohort of drug users (calculated from entry into the cohort or commencement of injecting): in international comparisons this rate may be adjusted to take account of age and gender variations;
- standardised mortality rate: ratio of cohort mortality rate to general population mortality rate adjusted for age and gender;
- cumulative hazard rate: probability that a case has survived a given number of years of injecting will die during the subsequent year (e.g. see Figure 1).

The first type of mortality rate has the advantage of being highly specific. However, the number of deaths in a particular year may, for example, be concentrated among a sub-group of drug users and it is, therefore, important to clearly define the population of drug users (e.g. heroin users). In many situations, this rate may be the most appropriate, although experience has shown that the annual mortality can vary considerably from year to year. For example, in Hamburg, the mortality rate among 'hard drug users registered by the police' was reported to be 1.32 per cent in 1983, 0.65 per cent in 1984 and 1.21 per cent in 1985 (IFT, 1994).

Figure 1: Kaplan-Meier hazard function for cohort of Glasgow injectors by age at cohort entry and HIV status

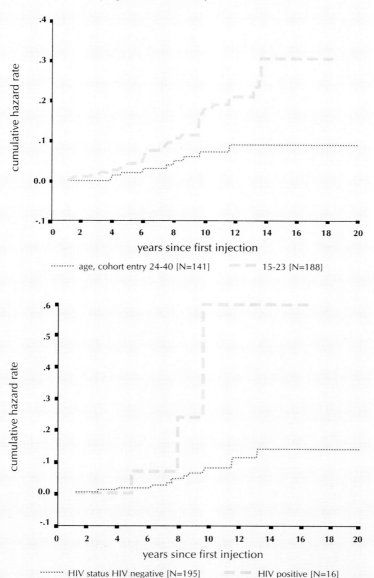

One way of avoiding fluctuations is to use a rate derived from many years of following up a group of drug users. However, an overall mortality rate for a cohort will take no account of changing patterns of mortality and, in some situations, it may be more appropriate to use an annual rate. In areas where annual data are available on an on-going basis, it may be advisable to use a moving average, e.g. over three years.

As indicated above, the rate in the New York study was 0.5 per cent. However, this rate was based on only one year of observation. A wide range of European studies conducted between 1970 and 1990 have reported annual mortality rates of between 1 and 2 per cent. It is possible that this rate will increase due to the impact of HIV on mortality among drug injectors. There is some evidence that a rate of about 3 per cent may be more appropriate in many locations (Frischer *et al*, ms.a).

Mortality rates have only been calculated for certain types of drug use and drug users, e.g. heroin users in New York, opioid injecting addicts attending hospitals or clinics in London (Oppenheimer *et al*, 1994). While there are case study reports of fatalities associated with particular drugs or drug users, these cannot be translated into rates. It is only meaningful to apply the Mortality Multiplier Method (MMM) to those types of drug use for which mortality rates have been calculated. Where it is not possible to ascertain the total number of all-cause deaths among drug users, it should be noted that the MMM will under-enumerate the population of drug users. The type and extent of under-notification of drug-related deaths will determine the degree of under-enumeration.

Applying the Mortality Multiplier Method

The best way of understanding MMM is to consider how the method has been used in practice.

Case Study A: District of Columbia, USA, 1971

Dupont and Piemme (1973) used the multiplier rate from the New York study to estimate the number of drug injectors in the District of Columbia (DC). They noted three reasons for caution: not all heroin-related deaths might be identified in DC; cultural patterns among addicts might influence the overdose rate; and the concentration of street heroin use outside NYC is likely to be different.

Ascertainment of mortality related only to heroin overdose. Other types of drug-related deaths were not included. After applying the New York mortality rate of 0.5 per cent to the 75 heroin-related deaths to obtain a figure of 15,000, they added the number of known heroin addicts receiving treatment to arrive at a figure of 17,700. The paper also reports two two-sample capture-recapture estimates of 19,900 and 20,400 which provide cross-validation for the MMM estimate.

Case Study B: Inner London, UK, 1982

This study differed from the previous study in two crucial respects (Hartnoll *et al*, 1985). First, deaths from *all* causes among drug users were ascertained. Second, a 1-2 per cent mortality rate, derived from previous UK studies of opioid-injecting addicts attending hospitals and clinics was used. With 22 deaths, the MMM resulted in an estimate of 1,100-2,200.

As in the American study, there were also two concurrent capture-recapture estimates: 2,148 and 2,435. There was a further estimate of 1,900 from the nomination technique. The similarity of these estimates suggests that the upper MMM estimate based on a mortality rate of 1 per cent produced a reliable estimate of the number of opioid injectors.

Case Study C: Greater Glasgow, UK, 1992/1993

The definition of drug-related death in this example was intermediate between that of New York and London: toxicological analyses in Glasgow of 52 deaths where 'drugs were implicated as a cause of death either through circumstance or toxicology' (Hammersley *et al*, 1995). Deaths of drug users from other causes such as infectious diseases and accidents while intoxicated were not included. MMM was applied assuming a 1 per cent mortality rate, suggesting 5,200 injectors/heroin users. In 1993, the number of drug-related deaths rose to 102 which yields an estimate of 10,200 injectors/heroin users.

It seems unlikely that prevalence would double in one year and other evidence indicates that incidence of injecting has remained fairly stable in the 1990s (Frischer *et al*, ms.b). Hammersley and colleagues rule out artefactual explanations, such as changing reporting procedures, and suggest that the rapid increase in drug-related deaths is due, not to increasing prevalence of drug use but to increasing poly-drug use involving heroin with benzodiazepines and alcohol. It is possible that the mortality rate did change between 1992 and 1993. Concurrent analyses of a cohort of injectors, followed since 1983, revealed a 1992 mortality rate of 1.67 per cent and a 1993 annual mortality rate of 1.98 per cent (Frischer *et al*, ms.c). Using these rates, the prevalence estimates are 3,113 and 5,151 for 1992 and 1993 respectively.

However, a four-sample capture-recapture study in Glasgow, 1990, indicated 7,500-9,700 current injectors, only 15 per cent of whom were in treatment at some point during the year in 1990 and only 47 per cent had ever received any form of treatment (Rhodes *et al*, 1993). Clearly, if non-treatment injectors have a lower mortality rate, the prevalence estimate might be very different.

Multiplier method and population surveys

Although the Mortality Multiplier Method can be used without reference to other methods, the previous section shows the value (and sometimes the complications) of cross-validation. Another use of the method is to supplement population surveys, where the prevalence of injecting and other forms of drug use is thought to be under-estimated.

This is well illustrated by the 1990 survey of drug use among people aged 12-39 in the former West Germany (IFT, 1994). In this survey, a representative sample of 31,363 people was drawn from the residents' register and sent a self-completion questionnaire. 19,208 (62 per cent) participated in the survey after several follow-ups. Various prevalence estimates were made; for current purposes we will focus on two groups: those who had taken opiates, amphetamines or cocaine at least 20 times in the last 12 months, and hard drug users who had also injected.

Whereas the proportion of respondents who took large quantities of alcohol or cannabis remained stable throughout the survey, the proportion of hard drug users increased with each additional follow-up. Detailed studies of non-responders in the USA (Turner et al, 1992) indicate that a proportion of non-responders do not differ from responders with respect to the use of cannabis or cocaine (neutral non-responders). However, some non-responders (18 per cent in the American study) were more likely to be taking these drugs. This group is referred to as critical non-responders. The 'true' prevalence is an additive function of the behaviour of three groups: responders (R_1), plus neutral non-responders (R_2) plus critical non-responders (R_3).

Prevalence rates among responders (P_1) of 'hard' and 'injecting' drug use were 0.18 per cent and 0.04 per cent respectively. These rates also apply to neutral non-responders (P_2). Prevalence among critical non-responders is:

$$P_3 = P_{1,2} * X$$

where X is a multiplicative factor derived from information about non-responders. The number of drug users (N) is therefore: $N = P_1*R_1 + P_2*R_2 + P_3*R_3$

Determining factor X is crucial to the prevalence estimation procedure. One way of estimating the magnitude of factor X is from mortality data. In 1991, there were 2,100 drug-related deaths in West Germany which is assumed to be a mortality rate of 2-3 per cent per year. Application of the MMM yields an estimate of 70,000-105,000 injectors which, in turn, yields an estimate of factor X = 35 to X = 57. For the hard drug users the plausible range of X is 23-36 (Table 4).

Table 4: Variation in number of estimated drug users in Germany, 1990

	X=1	X=23	X=36	X=57
Hard drug users	42,000	206,000	304,000	461,000
Injectors	10,000	47,000	70,000	105,000

The use of MMM to correct under-reporting in a population survey is a new departure and further work is required to assess the validity of this approach.

Other substances and modes of administration

While there is a range of mortality rates for categories of drug use such as injecting and addicts attending treatment agencies, there are no published rates for the large number of other drugs taken for psychic effect. This section provides a brief overview for selected substances taken from an unpublished 1994 review on *Substance Abuse Related Mortality: A Worldwide Review* (Frischer *et al*, ms.c.).

Volatile substances

In comparison to injecting drug use, there is very little surveillance or research on this topic and the activity, being largely confined to teenagers, is less well documented. In 'Fuel of the Forgotten Deaths', Russell (1993) suggests that solvents are mundane products lacking the glamour of drugs such as heroin or cocaine which are associated with more defined counter-cultures. However, the low cost and relative ease of obtaining solvents and fuels has led to their widespread abuse.

In the UK, more deaths have been attributed, in recent years, to butane and volatile substance abuse (VSA) than to heroin and cocaine overdoses. There are also reports of VSA deaths in many other countries, but as a monograph from the US National Institute on Drug Abuse indicates, there is very little comprehensive surveillance of VSA (Beauvais, 1992). Thus, it is very difficult to estimate the number of VSA-related deaths. If the British data are indicative of trends elsewhere, then VSA could be associated with as much mortality as heroin and cocaine overdose.

Cannabis

Although cannabis is generally thought to be one of the least harmful substances known to mankind (Gossop, 1993), recent studies indicate that cannabis use may be associated with an increased risk of certain types of cancer. A study in Sweden found that cannabis abuse may be more strongly associated with violent deaths than previously supposed (Rajs *et al*, 1993), while a longitudinal follow-up of Swedish conscripts, found higher levels of cannabis use were associated with higher levels of mortality (Andreasson and Allebeck, 1990). Overall, this type of drug abuse does not appear to have a marked impact on users' mortality, except perhaps in certain environments (e.g. violence associated with drug dealing, road traffic accidents).

Crack cocaine

The use of crack cocaine, although at present more localised in the American continent, is associated with high levels of (mainly indirect) mortality. With an estimated

314,000 regular crack users in the USA, there have been widespread media reports of violent deaths associated with crack dealing and research indicating elevated risks of Sudden Infant Death Syndrome among infants of crack-addicted mothers. In areas where there is an increasing trend towards crack injection, increasing mortality is a likely consequence, in view of the greater risks of injecting crack relative to opiates (Pickering et al, 1993).

Designer drugs

During the 1980s, new drugs were synthesised and, as with crack cocaine, the uptake of these drugs has been rapid in areas of availability. Drugs such as 3-methylfentanyl ('china white') are many times more potent than heroin and consequently their addictive capacity and potential for causing mortality is higher. This drug is already reported to have caused more than 100 deaths in California and there have been reports from north-eastern USA of deaths related to china white (Hibbs et al, 1991). In the UK, 3,4-methylenedioxymethamphetamine ('ecstasy'), taken mainly in recreational settings associated with youth culture has been implicated in a number of deaths (Henry et al, 1992).

Using the Mortality Multiplier Method with other indices

Given the limitations of mortality data, it might seem plausible to apply a multiplier to some other indicator such as the number of arrests for drug offences. However, extension of the MMM is probably ill-advised for the simple reason than any multiplier is likely to be arbitrary. The MMM is plausible because of the wide range of studies which have reported similar mortality rates. Rates for activities such as drug arrests are likely to vary within and between locations, and these rates are likely to change over time due to changing policies.

Conclusions

Although MMM is a simple method of prevalence estimation, its use is appropriate in situations where the basic assumptions outlined above are met. Guidelines are summarised in Table 5.

Unlike other methods which require extensive fieldwork or statistical analyses, MMM is simple to conduct and should be a rapid and inexpensive method for prevalence estimation. However, unlike, for example, capture-recapture analysis, it is not possible to provide statistical confidence intervals; the plausibility of MMM estimates depends on the context in which the method is applied.

Currently, there are two main difficulties in applying MMM. The first relates to ascertaining all-cause deaths among drug users. Unless a special study is conducted, it is likely that the all-cause ascertainment will be underestimated.

Furthermore, there is also the probability that, in many cases, even drug overdoses will be coded under some other category (e.g. respiratory illness), which will not normally be detected as drug related, unless for example, drug dependence is recorded as a secondary cause of death.

The second difficulty is in deciding what mortality rate to apply. For drug injectors, a rate of 2-3 per cent per annum will probably provide a reasonable estimate, although the World Health Organisation collaborative cohort study shows considerable variation over time and between centres (Perucci *et al*, ms.a). The East European centres in particular reported rates of 3 per cent and upwards from 1990 onwards.

Table 5: Guidelines for conducting mortality multiplier studies

Establish *the number of all-cause deaths among population of interest, e.g. drug injectors, opiate addicts.*

- The usual starting point for this will be a national or regional mortality register; understand how the register operates i.e. who completes death certificates (pathologist or other medical practitioner); find out customary practices for coding primary and secondary causes of fatalities associated with drug overdoses. If it is not feasible to establish the number of all-cause deaths, clearly define some subset, e.g. drug overdoses.

Establish *the most suitable mortality rate from which to derive the multiplier.*

- This rate could be from a variety of sources, e.g. the mortality rate among registered addicts, a cohort study, literature from previous studies, or a discussion with local experts.

Derive *the multiplier from the mortality rate.*

Multiply *the number of drug-related deaths by the multiplier.*

- It would be prudent to use an appropriate range. There are variations of the basic MMM whereby the results of the multiplication may be added to, for example, the total number of addicts in treatment.

Compare *MMM results to other studies, e.g. population survey, capture-recapture analysis.*

State *all the parameters of the study when presenting the results.*

- Although this may seem obvious, many MMM estimates are presented in documents which do not describe how the estimates were obtained nor do they clearly specify the group of drug users to whom the estimates relate.

To summarise, the Mortality Multiplier Method is probably the simplest way of esti-mating the prevalence of drug use. The method does not require statistical expertise and, in some situations, requires only routine data. Where more extensive data collection is required, there may be resource implications. However, if the number of drug-related deaths can be accurately determined, careful attention to simple guide-lines should ensure a reasonable prevalence estimate.

References

Andreasson S. and Allebeck P. (1990) 'Cannabis and mortality among young men: a longitudinal study of Swedish conscripts', *Scandinavian Journal of Social Medicine*, 18 (1), 9-15.

Baden M. (1972) 'Investigation of deaths from drug abuse', in W.I. Spitz and R.S. Fisher (eds) *Medico-legal investigations of death*, Springfield, C.C. Thomas.

Baden M. (1971) 'Narcotic abuse: a medical examiner's view', in C.H. Wecht (ed) *Legal Medicine Annual*, New York, Appleton Century Crofts.

Barbarini G., Griscorio B., Edo S. *et al* (1993) 'Death for overdose and HIV positivity in Italy: can we suppose a pathogenic correlation?' *IX International AIDS Conference* (Abstract PO-C15-2927), Berlin.

Beauvais F. (1992) 'Volatile substance abuse: trends and patterns', in C. Sharp, F. Beauvais and R. Spence (eds) *Inhalant abuse: a volatile research agenda*, NIDA Research Monograph 129, US Department of Health and Human Services, Rockville, Maryland.

Beebe D.K. and Walley E. (1991) 'Substance abuse: the designer drugs', *American Family Physician*, 43 (5), 1689-1698.

Davoli M., Perucci C.A., Forastiere F. *et al* (1993) 'Risk factors for overdose mortality: a case-control study within a cohort of intravenous drug users', *International Journal of Epidemiology*, 22 (2), 273-277.

Dupont R.L. and Piemme T.E. (1973) 'Estimation of the number of narcotic addicts in an urban area', *Medical Annals of the District of Columbia*, 42 (7), 323-326.

Eskild A., Magnus P., Samuelsen S.O. *et al* (1993) 'Differences in mortality rates and causes of death between HIV positive and HIV negative intravenous drug users', *International Journal of Epidemiology*, 22 (2), 315-320.

Frischer M., Green S.T. and Goldberg D. *Substance abuse related mortality: a worldwide review,* Geneva, United Nations Drugs Control Program (ms.a).

Frischer M., Taylor A., Goldberg D. *et al* 'Incidence of injecting drug use in Glasgow' (ms.b).

Frischer M., Goldberg D., Berney L. *et al* 'Survival and mortality among a cohort of Glasgow drug injectors' (ms.c).

Gossop M. (1993) *Living with drugs* (third edition) Cambridge, Cambridge University Press.

Gottschalk L.A., McGuire F.L., Heiser J.F. *et al* (1979) 'Drug abuse deaths in nine cities: a survey report', *NIDA Research Monograph 29*, US Department of Health and Human Services: Rockville, Maryland.

Gronbladh L., Ohlund L.S. and Gunne L.M. (1990) 'Mortality in heroin addiction: impact of methadone maintenance', *Acta Psychiatrica Scandinavica*, 82 (3), 223-227.

Hammersley R., Cassidy M. and Oliver J. (1995) 'Drugs associated with drug-related deaths in Edinburgh and Glasgow, November 1990 to October 1992', *Addiction*, 90, 959-965.

Harding-Pink D. (1993) 'Methadone: one person's maintenance dose is another's poison', *Lancet*, 341, 665-666.

Hartnoll R., Lewis R., Mitcheson M. *et al* (1985) 'Estimating the prevalence of opioid dependence', *Lancet*, 203-205.

Henry J.A., Jeffreys K.J. and Dawling S. (1992) 'Toxicity and deaths from 3,4-methylene-dioxymetamphetamine ('ecstasy')', *Lancet*, 340, 384-397.

Hibbs J., Perper J. and Winek C.L. (1991) 'An outbreak of designer drug-related deaths in Pennsylvania', *Journal of the American Medical Association*, 265 (8), 1011-1013.

Institut für Therapieforschung (1994) *Report on the methods of estimating the extent of the drug problems in Germany*, IFT, Munich.

Mientjes G.H., Van Ameijden E.J., Van den Hoek A.F. *et al* (1992) 'Increasing morbidity without rise in non-AIDS mortality among HIV-infected intravenous drug users in Amsterdam', *AIDS*, 6 (2), 207-212.

Oppenheimer E., Tobutt C., Taylor C. *et al* (1994) 'Death and survival in a cohort of heroin addicts from London clinics: a 22-year follow-up study', *Addiction*, 89, 1299-1308.

Perucci C.A., Forastiere F., Rapiti E. *et al* (1992) 'The impact of intravenous drug use on mortality of young adults in Rome, Italy', *British Journal of Addiction*, 87 (12), 1637-1641.

Perucci C.A., Davoli M., Rapiti E. *et al* (1991) 'Mortality of intravenous drug users in Rome: a cohort study', *American Journal of Public Health*, 307-1310.

Perucci C.A., Davoli M., Rapiti E. *et al* 'An international comparative analysis of mortality among injecting drug users' (ms.a).

Pickering H., Donoghoe M., Green A. *et al* (1993) 'Crack injection', *Druglink*, 8 (1), 12.

Rajs J., Fugelstad A. and Jonsson J. (1993) 'Cannabis associated deaths in medico-legal post-mortem studies', in CRC Press (edited by CRC Press Inc.) *Cannabis*, 123-134.

Rhodes T., Bloor M., Donoghoe M. *et al* (1993) 'HIV prevalence and HIV risk behaviour among injecting drug users in London and Glasgow', *AIDS Care*, 5, 413-426.

Russell J. (1993) 'Fuel of the forgotten deaths', *New Scientist*, 137, 21-23.

Soellner R., Castrup U., Heckmann W. *et al* (1992) 'Does an HIV infection increase the probability of dying by a drug overdose?' *VIII International AIDS Conference* (Abstract PoD 5092), Amsterdam.

Tunving K. (1988) 'Fatal outcome in drug addiction', *Acta Psychiatrica Scandinavica*, 77 (5), 551-566.

Turner C.F., Lessler J.T. and Gfroerer J.C. (eds) (1992) *Survey measurement of drug use: methodological studies,* US Department of Health and Human Studies, Maryland.

Weiss G.M. (1993) 'Causes of deaths related to drug abuse: an overview', *Consultation document for WHO Programme on Substance Abuse,* WHO, Geneva.

CHAPTER 13

DETERMINING THE NUMBER
OF DRUG-RELATED DEATHS

by Klaus Püschel

Experts in this field know about the long-standing and seemingly never-ending debate about regional, national and international statistics and trends concerning drug-related fatalities, which relates particularly to the standardisation, validation and comparability of data. There is no generally accepted definition of the terms 'drug', 'drug-related' and 'drug-related death', so there is some confusion concerning terminology and classification systems. Different terms (such as drug-related death, drug abuse-related death, drug-induced death, poisoning, overdose, intoxication) have been introduced (WHO, 1994). In reviewing drug-related mortality, the lack of common terminology or classification systems is revealed as a major problem when making international comparisons of data. Even within Europe, countries use different definitions. Moreover, they have established different registration strategies and the list of the substances associated with drug-related death includes a wide variety of legal and illegal substances with regional idiosyncrasies.

Drug-related death is a rather heterogeneous concept. It occurs under varying circumstances and covers different patho-anatomical and toxicological characteristics. In some cases, there is no hint or clue at all that a death is drug-related, in others, it is quite obvious. The thoroughness of police investigations at the scene of death, the quality of post-mortem external and internal medical investigations and the incidence of toxicological analyses varies considerably. A full list of factors and activities influencing the determination of drug-related deaths would need to include:

- anamnestic information;
- death scene investigation;
- external investigation of the dead body;
- validity of death certification;
- frequency and intensity of toxicological and morphological investigations and autopsy rate;
- specialist discipline of the investigator (e.g. concerning hair analysis);
- socio-demographic, forensic and medical data exchange between institutions;
- validity of registration and documentation procedures;
- representativeness and long-term stability of the data sampling, handling and retrieval strategies.

The consequence seems to be that the identification, classification and registration of drug-related deaths are open to manipulation. Moreover, it sometimes appears that politicians, police, health care institutions and drug aid organisations present and interpret statistics, not according to a realistic scientific approach, but largely according to lobbying interests.

For about two decades, our own strategy as forensic-medical scientists in Hamburg has been to acquire facts concerning the drug scene through long-term, reproducible and scientifically-orientated investigations, based mainly on morphological and toxicological findings and using constant definitions.

Definitions and statistics

In Germany, a drug is defined by the Narcotics Act (the so-called 'Betäubungsmittelgesetz'). The term 'narcotic' is purely a nomen juris. It is not identical with pharmacological or medical terminology and can be changed by decrees to bring it up to date. The main headings of substances and derivatives coming within the legal meaning of the term narcotic in the Betäubungsmittelgesetz are:

- illegal narcotics – e.g. cannabis, heroin, LSD;
- legal, but not prescribable narcotics – e.g. codeine, dihydrocodeine (except in divided doses in antitussive medicaments);
- legal and prescribable narcotics – e.g. cocaine (for local analgesia), methadone, morphine, opium.

In addition, many drugs which are used as alternative or substitute drugs for those listed are registered.

In Hamburg, we have a very close co-operation between the police and the Institute for Forensic Medicine. Every unexpected sudden death and every unnatural death is brought to our morgue and submitted at least to a thorough external investigation. It is a routine procedure that blood, urine and hair of all fatalities aged between 15 and 50 years are screened for drugs. Autopsies with intensive chemical-toxicological analyses are common.

Since 1979 in Germany, a death is registered as drug-related if it satisfies the following criteria, which were developed by the police (definition of the Bundeskriminalamt, IFT, 1994):

- death due to intentional or accidental overdose;
- death due to long-term abuse of drugs;
- suicides connected with drug dependence;
- fatal accidents influenced by drugs.

A death is registered as drug-related if a causal connection to the use of illegal drugs or substitutes is evident. Group 1 represents about 70 to 90 per cent of all drug-related deaths. Groups 2, 3 and 4 are extremely heterogeneous in their related morphological and toxicological findings, and, in particular, differentiation between accidental and suicidal overdose or even homicides may be rather difficult. Generally the combined effects of internal disease and relative overdose can be responsible for the fatality, although in our experience adverse drug effects play no important role. Homicides and internal concealment fatalities are not registered as drug-related deaths in Germany.

During the early 1980s, the number of drug-related deaths in Hamburg lay between 30 and 50 cases yearly; from 1988 it increased dramatically until 1991; it is now decreasing slightly (Figure 1). The situation is the same as in the Federal Republic of Germany as a whole where we had about 1,500 to 2,000 drug-related fatalities in recent years. A comparison between different regions in Germany shows that the rate of drug-related deaths per 100,000 people differs widely.

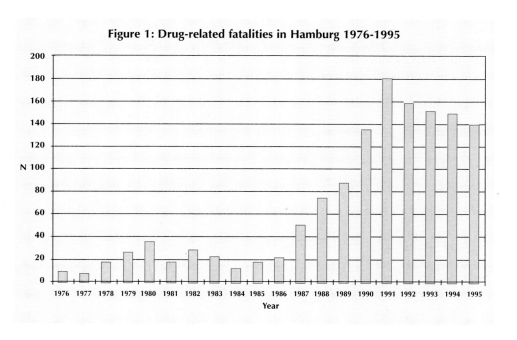

Figure 1: Drug-related fatalities in Hamburg 1976-1995

High mortality rates can be found in the city states of Hamburg (about ten drug-related deaths per 100,000 inhabitants), Bremen and Berlin. As is found almost everywhere, male drug abusers predominate, the sex ratio being about five to one. The average age of the drug victims has increased during the last two decades from 25 to approximately 30.

Phenomenology, morphological findings, internal diseases

Drug deaths mostly occur in city centre areas. However, a decentralisation of drug dealing and drug use and a movement to the suburbs has occurred. Most drug addicts die in an apartment; others are found in hospitals, toilets, public places and hotel rooms.

The attendant circumstances of the death can sometimes be clear, e.g. a syringe in a vein and injecting paraphernalia near the corpse. On the other hand, there might be no hint of preceding drug abuse at all. For example, ex-users may die in hospital after long-term abuse because of an acquired internal disease. The scene of death when a drug-related death is involved may not always be as straightforward as it appears: the paraphernalia of drug abuse may have been cleared away by the deceased's associates and death made to appear 'natural' (Vanezis and Busuttil, 1996).

Injection marks are the most important indications of intravenous drug addiction and must be recognised during the external examination of the corpse. Injection tracks are mostly found in the cubital area and on the forearm. Sometimes drug abusers inject themselves in places which make recognition difficult, e.g. in the mouth, neck, feet, or lower legs. Dissection of the cubital veins shows cribriform scars of the vascular wall and adjacent bleeding. In about 10 to 20 per cent of cases, no injection marks are found, since many users nowadays use very small insulin syringes. And, of course, some abusers die after sniffing or inhaling the drugs.

Sometimes tattoos, the design of which give a clue to drug addiction, e.g. a syringe, are found. The tattoos often reflect the existential views of the drug abuser: impending danger of death connected with the use of heroin. Sometimes the tattoos are broadly coloured, spiritual and very expressive and the clue to intravenous drug abuse may be hidden. Tattoos are also a common means of concealing needle tracks.

With long-term narcotic abuse and progressive social collapse, a lack of dental hygiene leads to vigorous caries, dental defects and periodontal lesions. Infections, dermatological diseases, signs of neglected nutrition and hygiene are common (Janssen et al, 1989; Karch, 1993; Robin and Michelson, 1988). However, reliance on stereotyped ideas concerning the outward appearance, nutritional status and obvious morphological signs of a drug user should be avoided because fatalities do not necessarily fit into schematic classifications.

Histological investigations have to be carried out in every case to determine the severity of the accompanying diseases and their importance in causing death (Heckmann et al, 1993; Karch, 1993; Kringsholm, 1993; Püschel, 1993). The most important organs for histological investigation in drug deaths are the liver, the lungs, the heart and the brain. The findings can relate either to the direct effects of the drugs or to concomitant infections, hypoxias or bleeding. The finding of foreign-body granulomas at the site of injection marks and in the lung is of special diagnostic importance in indicating intravenous drug abuse. Multiple pulmonary foreign-body granulomas can lead to lung fibrosis and lethal pulmonary hypertension. With the help of electron microscopy and X-ray micro-analysis, we were able to identify the foreign body material such as talc and cornstarch which are auxiliary substances used in the production of tablets and which are sometimes used for 'cutting' the drugs.

Accompanying inflammatory diseases play an important role in the health status (Levine and Sobel, 1991; Püschel, 1993). They are mostly due to non-sterile injection practices and needle sharing among drug addicts. Tetanus and other anaerobic infections with septic complications are not frequent in our material, but endocarditis, myocarditis, meningitis and encephalitis are occasionally found. Pneumonia may be caused by respirative disorders, coma, aspiration and depression of the immunological system, and it is a common finding in about 15 per cent of all drug-related fatalities. About 20 per cent of the fatalities are accompanied by an inhalation of vomit, which is then found in the lungs.

About 70 to 80 per cent of the drug victims exhibit inflammatory liver changes. These are mostly unspecific reactive or chronic types of hepatitis. Chronic aggressive hepatitis, liver cirrhosis and acute viral hepatitis make up about 10 per cent of all cases. Co-infections with hepatitis B and C are often detected and post-mortem serological investigations demonstrate high prevalence rates for both types of hepatitis. Calculating the high prevalence rate of 50 per cent or more and the malignant clinical course of hepatitis C, it can be predicted that this infection will turn out to be a severe medical problem for intravenous drug abusers. Currently the prevalence rates in Germany are about ten times higher for hepatitis C than for HIV (Lockemann et al, 1995).

The myocardium sometimes shows degenerative and inflammatory changes and this is found in about 5 to 10 per cent of cases in our experience, mostly with non-specific scattered mononuclear infiltrates and focal myocardial fibrosis (the so-called 'borderline' myocarditis, according to the Dallas classification). Active myocarditis is rare; and active infectious endocarditis, especially right-sided valve vegetations, is scarcely found in our material.

The impact of HIV and AIDS

Special attention is paid to the spread of HIV infections and AIDS among the high risk group of injecting drug users (Frischer et al, 1993; Pompidou Group, 1994; Korf, 1995; Püschel et al, 1995). The morphological alterations found in drug deaths have broadened enormously in scope because of the HIV infections. Kaposi sarcomas and opportunistic infections are characteristic findings. It should be mentioned, however, that only very few HIV-infected drug addicts in Germany have died from full blown AIDS up to now – these cases have a higher risk of dying from unnatural causes, especially intoxication. In our experience, the route of infection can be through sexual intercourse as well as through needle sharing.

The WHO reports on AIDS cases clearly show that, in some countries, a great proportion of the cases derive from this group, particularly in Southern European countries – for instance, Italy and Spain – where the percentage of intravenous drug addicts among the AIDS cases is very high. Previous epidemiological research has pointed to an explosive spread of the disease. We tried to develop a monitoring system for HIV-1 prevalence among intravenous drug addicts by HIV screening of the drug-related deaths (Püschel *et al*, 1995) – to a certain extent, these drug-related deaths may be considered a random sample of the intravenous drug addicts in any particular region. It should be pointed out that post-mortem serological investigations have proved to be a safe and reproducible procedure even in cases with advanced autolysis.

HIV-1 prevalence has decreased and now seems to be stabilising in German cities (Figure 2). In Hamburg the prevalence rate is the lowest among the big cities in Germany, about 5 to 10 per cent, but regional differences are obvious and prevalence generally lies between 0 per cent and a maximum of 20 per cent. The figures for drug-related fatalities are similar to our figures from living users who have been investigated during clinical therapy.

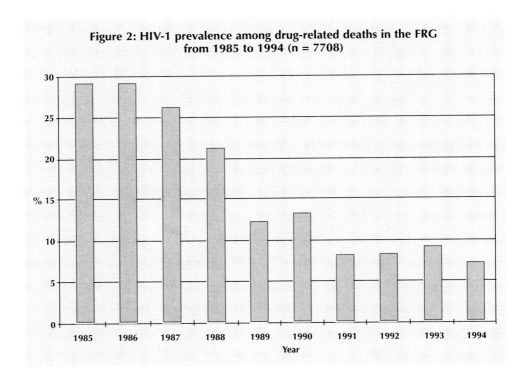

Figure 2: HIV-1 prevalence among drug-related deaths in the FRG from 1985 to 1994 (n = 7708)

Fatalities caused by diseases acquired from drug addiction (like AIDS or chronic hepatitis B or C) are underestimated categories of drug-related deaths. The responsibility can be directed at the physicians performing the necroscopy who fill out the death certificates inadequately. In comparisons with the official data from the AIDS centre, we found some AIDS deaths not registered as drug-related in Hamburg, even though the infection had been acquired by intravenous drug abuse.

Toxicological findings

Toxicological investigation is indispensable in all questionably drug-related deaths and it mostly determines the diagnosis of cause of death.

The spectrum of morphine concentration in the blood of the corpse is quite wide. The lethal concentration depends on the actual individual disposition of the injecting drug user. Relatively low doses are frequently found in the blood. The extremes for morphine and morphine conjugate levels in blood lay between 0.003 and 10.0 µg/ml. Suicidal overdose is characterised by extraordinary high concentrations (Heckmann et al, 1993; Püschel, 1993).

The term 'overdose' is highly relative and depends on actual susceptibility (Püschel et al, 1993a). Accidental death cases sometimes occur after periods of abstinence (e.g. after abstinence therapy or withdrawal, or in prison) or by combined action of different substances, e.g. alcohol, pills and drugs. The percentage of acute intoxications by heroin in Hamburg is rather high; about 70 to 90 per cent of the drug victims had monoacetylmorphine in their body fluids and tissues. Combined intoxication, especially with alcohol, barbiturates and benzodiazepines, is common. The situation in Hamburg is not representative of Germany in general. Some other substitute drugs predominate in other cities. Deaths from cocaine – mostly after intravenous injections and in combination with heroin – are relatively rare.

About 20 per cent of the drug-related deaths showed a blood alcohol concentration (BAC) of 1 per cent or more (including 6.4 per cent with 2 per cent or more) and about 20 per cent had a BAC of less than 1 per cent. Our medical and sociological investigations showed that a group of older opiate consumers – about 5 to 10 per cent – are primarily alcohol addicts using heroin additionally after long-time alcohol abuse (Püschel et al, 1993b).

Special investigations and observation are required for proof of opiates and cocaine in the nose – in cases of sniffing. Hair samples undergo toxicological investigation for narcotics from root to tip. By sectioning the hair, conclusions as to the drug career and the drugs consumed can be drawn. These hair analyses are of special value in the diagnosis of former drug consumption and pathogenic aspects of internal diseases. Nowadays methadone maintenance treatment is very widespread in Germany. Consequently, methadone was – not unexpectedly – found in the body fluids and tissues of about 20 per cent of all drug-related fatalities in 1995, mostly in combination with other drugs.

Violent deaths

Finally, the definition of drug-related death includes accidents and suicides under the influence of drugs. With reference to external force as cause of death, the morphological findings may also be present as injuries after traffic accidents, strangulation, drowning, burning, etc. The category of accidental and suicidal traumatic deaths does not normally undergo forensic investigation for the exact mechanism of death. Drug screening of all of the cases which were brought to the mortuary of our institute revealed narcotics in the blood and hair of a considerable number of cases without any hint of drug use in the police files. Especially after periods in hospital, where a clinical toxicological investigation is unusual, there is no chance to discover the involvement of narcotics at the time of the accident or suicide attempt. This is why we cannot estimate the whole number of accidents and suicides under the influence of narcotics (Schulz-Schaeffer *et al*, 1993).

Conclusions

Our experiences with morphological, toxicological and serological investigations of drug-related deaths over a period of years lead us to the following recommendations.

Drug-related death is a very broad concept. Many cases are obvious, others may be revealed only by extensive investigations. Every questionably drug-related death should be subjected to an autopsy and detailed micro-morphological, toxicological and serological investigations.

The epi-critical analyses should be carried out by morphologists and toxicologists – not by police officers or epidemiologists.

Although a high morbidity is associated generally with intravenous drug abuse, the fatalities are mostly caused by heroin overdose, at least in our region. The supply of heroin has increased hugely, and the changing purity of the drug appears to be a danger with respect to accidental or unexpected overdoses.

Detecting every case of drug-related death helps to determine the extent of drug abuse, the effectiveness of social and medical treatment programmes and changes in the drug scene. However, the quality of statistical calculations and conclusions cannot be more accurate than the standard of the underlying case work and analytical findings.

Serological screening can be useful in the epidemiology of infectious diseases. To the extent that drug-related fatalities may serve as an unbiased sample, continuous monitoring of the HIV prevalence gives a representative impression of HIV spread among living intravenous drug addicts. Regional variations are obvious, and hepatitis C has turned out to be a considerable medical problem for intravenous drug addicts.

What we try to do is to convince the authorities that post-mortem investigations are an important reference for all kinds of medical, social and juridical interventions in the fields of drug abuse and drug deaths.

Detailed examination of the deceased and the life-threatening conditions of abuse helps the living addicts to survive. One can obtain much objective information from a dead body, sometimes even more than from living addicts.

There is no doubt that it is difficult to distinguish between drug-induced deaths and deaths among drug addicts, therefore an international agreement about a definition for drug-induced (or drug-related) death and standardised investigation protocols are absolutely necessary for international analyses.

So far we are not convinced that drug abuse fatalities are a rational basis for a multiplier estimation method: a prerequisite should be a set of established guidelines for conducting such multiplier studies in order to allow comparability.

References

Frischer M., Leyland A., Cormack R., Goldberg D.J., Bloor M., Green S.T., Taylor A., Covell R., McKeganey N. and Platt S. (1993) 'Estimating the population prevalence of injection drug use and infection with human immunodeficiency virus among injection drug users in Glasgow, Scotland', *American Journal of Epidemiology*, 138 (3), 170-181.

Heckmann W., Püschel K., Schmoldt A., Schneider V., Schulz-Schaeffer W., Soellner R., Zenker C. and Zenker J. (1993) *Drogennot- und -todesfälle*, Nomos Verlagsgesellschaft, Baden-Baden.

IFT-Research Report Series, Vol. 71E (1994) *Report on the methods of estimating the extent of the drug problem in Germany*, Institut für Therapieforschung, Munich.

Janssen W., Trübner K. and Püschel K. (1989) 'Death caused by drug addiction: A review of the experiences in Hamburg and the situation in the Federal Republic of Germany in comparison with the literature', *Forensic Science International*, 43, 223-237.

Karch S.B. (1993) *The pathology of drug abuse*, CRC Press, Boca Raton.

Korf D.J. (1995) *Dutch treat; formal control and illicit drug use in the Netherlands*, Thesis Publishers, Amsterdam.

Kringsholm B. (1993) 'Histological evidence in fatal drug addiction', *Med Leg Quad Cam*, 5, 2, 175-192.

Levine D.P. and Sobel D.J. (1991) *Infections in intravenous drug abusers*, Oxford University Press, New York.

Lockemann U., Püschel K., Fehlauer F., Laufs R., Polywka S., Sánchez-Hanke M., Heinemann A. and Schulz-Schaeffer W (1995) 'Development of hepatitis B-, hepatitis C- and HIV prevalence among drug-related fatalities (Hamburg 1984–1993)', *Acta Med Leg Soc*, 44, 188-189.

Pompidou Group (Co-operation Group to Combat Drug Abuse and Illicit Trafficking in Drugs) (1994) *Multi-city study: drug misuse trends in thirteen European cities*, Council of Europe Press, Strasbourg.

Püschel K. (1993) 'Drug-related death – an update', *Forensic Sci Int*, 62 (1, 2), 121-128.

Püschel K., Lockemann U., Klostermann P. and Schneider V. (1995) 'HIV-1 prevalence among drug related deaths. Suggestion for a European monitoring system', *Rom J Leg Med*, 3 (3), 259-264.

Püschel K., Teschke F. and Castrup U. (1993a) 'Etiology of accidental/unexpected overdose in drug-induced deaths', *Forensic Sci Int*, 62 (1, 2), 129-134.

Püschel K., Teschke F., Castrup U., Schulz-Schaeffer W. and Heckmann W. (1993b) 'Typology of drug abuse deaths in Hamburg', *Forensic Sci Int*, 62 (1, 2), 151-155.

Robin H.S. and Michelson J.B. (1988) *Illustrated handbook of drug abuse, recognition and diagnosis*, Year Book Medical Publishers, Chicago.

Schulz-Schaeffer W., Elwers W. and Schmoldt A. (1993) 'Undetected drug addict fatalities', *Forensic Sci Int*, 62, 157-159.

Vanezis P. and Busuttil A. (1996) *Suspicious death scene investigation*, Arnold, London.

WHO (1994) *Deaths related to drug abuse. WHO PSA 93.14*, Geneva.

ESTABLISHING MORTALITY RATES
FROM COHORT DATA

by Marina Davoli

Measures of mortality in the general population are easily available in most countries; in a mortality rate, the denominator is an estimate of the size of a specific population for a defined period and place, and the numerator is the number of deaths generated by this population during that period. This mortality rate can be made specific to a given time, place, age, sex, and so forth, depending on the availability of information for the relevant specified sub-groups. The requirements for measuring mortality rates in the general population are:

* the availability of an estimate of average size of the study population during the study period;
* a comprehensive ascertainment of the number of deaths in this population for the corresponding period, and;
* the coding of causes of death, in particular circumstances, such as requiring cause-specific death rates.

Most countries worldwide currently produce estimates of total and cause-specific mortality in the general population (WHO, 1992); nevertheless, the validity of the data varies, especially where cause-specific mortality is concerned (United Nations, 1991). Routine estimates of the size of the population of drug abusers and comprehensive ascertainment of both deaths and cause of death are generally unavailable.

Drug-related deaths data

As far as the issue of the number of deaths of drug abusers is concerned, figures are often derived from data on drug-related deaths. There is no specific code in the International Classification of Diseases for injecting drugs use and, therefore, it is only possible to measure deaths classified as relating to drug dependence (ICD-9: 309) or relating to injury and poisoning (ICD-9: 965) (Frischer *et al*, 1993). Other sources of data for overdose deaths are sometimes available, but their validity is unknown. In Italy, information on overdose deaths derives from the National Mortality Register (under the ICD-9 code 304) and from the Ministry of Interior Affairs (deaths attributed to overdose found by the police). These two sources of data not only produce different figures but, more importantly, they often do not refer to the same persons. The agreement between these data sets was examined for the

Lazio region between 1987 and 1992. Linkage was possible for between 60 per cent and just under 80 per cent of cases, and agreement of diagnosis of death ranged from just over 40 per cent to 90 per cent.

A second limitation in using 'drug-related' deaths to approximate mortality of drug abusers, comes from the fact that drug abusers also die from other causes. The proportion of 'drug-related' deaths (ICD-9: 304; 965) out of the total number of deaths, estimated in the World Health Organisation (WHO) Multi City Study of Mortality of Injecting Drug Users, ranged from 0 in New Haven to 46.7 per cent in Liverpool during the period 1980-1992 (Injecting Drug Users Mortality Study Group, undated).

As a result, an alternative method is often chosen to establish mortality among drug abusers: a mortality cohort study of this population.

Defining a mortality cohort study

Definition of case

The exact definition of 'drug user' for enrolment in the cohort needs to be clearly stated. The definition of drug user requires a specification of:

- the type of drug (cannabis, alcohol, amphetamines, heroin, cocaine, etc.);
- the route of administration (intravenous, inhaling, smoking, etc.);
- the frequency and recency of use.

Most of the studies available to date relate to injecting drug users for at least two reasons. Firstly, drug injection is currently the most risky drug-using behaviour; and secondly, the more feasible way to enrol drug users to be followed up for a mortality study is through treatment centre records, and a majority of drug users attending treatment centres in Europe are drug injectors. As a result of using treatment centres as contact points for enrolment, there is almost certainly a selection bias in the populations usually studied in relation to the population of drug abusers as a whole, since entering treatment is probably less likely for non-injecting drug abusers than for injecting drug users. Even if inferences are restricted to injecting drug abusers only and there is no attempt to make inferences about the whole drug-abusing population, additional biases might well still occur. The likelihood of a drug injector entering treatment is a function of choice of study time – the longer the enrolment period, the more likely it is that an injecting drug user entered treatment at least once and so the more likely it is that at least some infrequently treated injecting drug users will be enrolled. It is clearly also a function of choice of place – the proportion of injecting drug users reporting having ever entered any treatment programme during their lifetime of injection varies from 47.7 per cent in Glasgow to 77.1 per cent in Rome.

Definition of cohort

Longitudinal studies can be defined according to the timing (as well as the length) of the period of follow-up, the time period of enrolment and the criteria for enrolment.

According to timing of follow-up it is possible to design:

- retrospective cohort studies, with follow-up of subjects from the past to the present, and determination of disease rates (or mortality) during the time period;
- prospective cohort studies, with follow-up of population from the present into the future and determination of disease rates during the time period.

According to timing of enrolment, there are two main cohort study designs:

- fixed cohort, with a study population that includes individuals enrolled only at a single point in time or during some specified brief time interval;
- dynamic cohort, with a study population that includes individuals who were enrolled, terminated or died at variable points in time.

Regarding criteria for enrolment into a cohort study of injecting drug users, several different study designs might be identified:

- 'prevalence' cohort in respect of injecting behaviour: the subjects enrolled in the cohort are already injecting drugs;
- 'incidence' cohort in respect of injecting behaviour: the subjects are enrolled in the cohort at the time of their first injection;
- 'prevalence' cohort in respect of treatment: the subjects enrolled in the cohort are already in treatment;
- 'incidence' cohort in respect of treatment: the subjects enrolled in the cohort are those entering treatment for the first time.

These different types of study are often combined with one another. In cohort studies of drug abusers, the most likely combination is to use a retrospective/prospective dynamic cohort, 'prevalent' in respect to injecting behaviour, with both a 'prevalent' and 'incident' component in respect to treatment. Note that it is not usually feasible to enrol an 'incident' cohort in respect to injecting behaviour.

With reference to using a combination of types, the mortality rate derived from a study of a cohort including both drug users already in treatment and drug users entering treatment for the first time represents a weighted average of the two different mortality rates, one for those previously treated and one for first-timers. If the mix of types is 'natural', that is, no over- or under-weighting of the two groups is purposively included in the design, this should not create problems of interpretation generally, provided this enlarged definition is consistent throughout the study. Otherwise, and specifically when comparing results with other cohort studies that may be different in this respect, this weighted nature of the mortality rate should be taken into account in the interpretations of the results. In this context, it should be noted that any rate is an average of different sub-groups: different treatment histories, different injection careers, and so forth; interpretation of results should always be made bearing this in mind.

An example: the WHO Multi City Study of Mortality of Injecting Drug Users

In 1990, a WHO Multi City Study of Mortality of Injecting Drug Users (Injecting Drug Users Mortality Study Group, undated) was conducted in Liverpool, Glasgow, Warsaw, Moscow, Rome, Turin, Naples, Barcelona and New Haven. A standardised protocol was developed to enrol and follow up different cohorts of drug injectors. This study illustrates the steps that need to be taken to ensure consistency in the design of a multi-site study.

Inclusion and exclusion criteria

Inclusion rules must be clear and explicit. For each individual, the date on which observation begins must be well defined; after that date the individual contributes person-years of observation and is at risk for contributing events of interest to the study (e.g. death). An individual does not enter the cohort and does not contribute person-years at risk until all entry criteria have been satisfied. The date of exit from the study is the last date on which an individual could contribute observable person-years at risk. In every study, a date has to be specified as the end of the follow-up period for the analysis to begin. It is important to note that date of entry into the study and date of first exposure to risk are not necessarily the same and will often be different; it is the number of years of exposure to risk while in the study that is required in the final analysis. Inclusion criteria for the Multi City cohort were the following:

- ever injecting drugs;
- entering treatment during the defined recruitment period (different periods across cities);
- availability of personal identifiers.

Table 1 shows the size and the characteristics of the study populations enrolled in each city along with the corresponding recruitment period.

Follow-up procedures

The follow-up process needed to be able to detect the disease or death events that are the defined endpoints of the study for an individual; that is, to determine the numerator information for the rate calculation. It also had to detect which cohort members were currently under observation and how many person-years at risk they contribute, by recording when deaths and losses due to migration occur; that is, to determine the denominator information for the calculation of the mortality rate. Further information required on the cohort members included cause of death.

Table 1: Multi city study of mortality of injecting drug users - study population

City	Recruitment period	Number of IDUs	Male to female ratio	Mean age at first injection (years)	Mean age at entry (years)	Injection of opiates (%)
Liverpool	1984-92	815	2.6	20.5	25.3	94
Glasgow	1983-92	367	1.8	16.3	23.6	59
Barcelona	1987-91	4,201	2.9	19.4	26.5	80
Turin	1978-92	6,975	4.4	na	23.4	95
Rome	1980-91	4,660	4.2	20.2	24.3	95
Naples	1980-92	3,785	11.9	19.5	23.1	100
Moscow	1980-92	505	2.6	22.1	28.6	52
Warsaw	1983-92	656	2.9	18.2	25.6	100
New Haven	1985-90	1,588	1.7	na	30.4	46*

* = Information available only for 30% of the subjects; na = not available

Sources of vital status data in cohort studies

Several different sources can act as the potential source of vital status data (record-ing of death). In particular, for the Multi City Study, vital status as of 31 December 1992 was ascertained at the last municipality of residence or through record linkage with national or local mortality registries. In using the latter source, it was assumed that all subjects not found in the mortality registry were alive.

Migrants might have a mortality different from that of stable residents in the area. For example the overall mortality rates (per 100,000) for the general population in Italy during the period 1981-84 were 1,026 among males stable in the areas as opposed to 1,139 among males who migrated between areas; the corresponding figures for females were 872 and 928 respectively. Major efforts should therefore be invested in tracing migrants in a cohort study, especially since it is possible that migration might be a more serious problem among drug users, with an even bigger effect on mortality.

Calculating years at risk in the study

The validity of a cohort study depends on both the complete ascertainment of the events of interest (i.e. deaths, migration, etc.) and on the correct computation of the population at risk (or, more accurately, the person-years at risk). Individuals leave the population at risk either through death or through migration to a country or region where follow-up mechanisms of the study cannot be made (or are not) operative.

There are different options for dealing with losses to follow-up in the analysis. For the purpose of the analysis of the Multi City Study, we applied the most conservative approach, which consisted in assuming that losses to follow-up were alive at the end of the study period and in taking the full study period as contributing years at risk for these people. The opposite approach, giving a higher death rate, would be to assume that losses to follow-up were dead at the end of the study period. This option would normally lead to unnaturally high rates and is unsuitable when losses to follow-up are high, as they often are. A more acceptable alternative to the Multi City approach would be to curtail the number of years at risk contributed by individuals who are lost to follow-up at the point of loss and to count their vital status as that which obtained at the point of loss. This, in effect, assumes that mortality after being lost to follow-up is the same as for similar individuals who are not lost.

Another problem arising in the computation of person-years at risk in a cohort of drug users is the assumption that drug injectors entering the cohort never stop injecting; this would inflate the amount of person-years of injecting risk that is estimated. For this reason, the interpretation of mortality rates for drug injectors should be to consider it as applying to their drug-injecting 'career' rather than to the precise number of years (or even months or days) during which they actually injected.

Determination of cause of death

Cause of death information for an identified death can be obtained in Italy by requesting copies of death certificates from state or municipal vital statistics offices. A 90-95 per cent or higher cause of death determination rate is a desirable target. Coding the causes of death reported on the certificates should be done by a nosologist trained in the rules specified by the International Classification of Diseases (ICD) volumes compiled by the WHO. Revisions to the ICD are made roughly every ten years and changes in coding for some causes may influence the mortality findings of the study. In the Multi City Study, causes of death were coded routinely according to the ninth revision of ICD in all countries, except Russia, where a local coding system was used and then adapted into ICD-9.

Problems in making comparisons of mortality rates over time and between countries

Although a large number of different mortality studies have been published, the lack of a standardised methodology impairs the interpretation of the possible comparisons among these studies. Despite many limitations, the Multi City Study, using a standardised methodology, allowed for temporal and geographical comparisons of mortality among injecting drug users. For making such geographical and temporal comparisons, it is clearly advisable to use age-specific or age-standardised rates. The age-standardised overall mortality rates in the Multi City Study showed marked temporal and geographical differences as shown in Figure 1. Problems still existed when cause-specific mortality was considered (see Table 2).

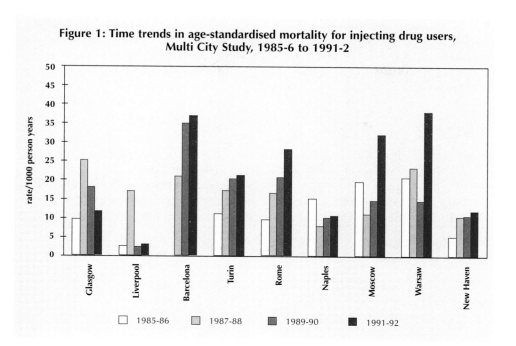

Figure 1: Time trends in age-standardised mortality for injecting drug users, Multi City Study, 1985-6 to 1991-2

Table 2: Proportional mortality for major categories of cause of death among injecting drug users

City	AIDS (042-044; 279)*		Mental disorders (290-319)		Diseases of circulatory system (390-459)		Injury and poisoning (800-999)		Ill defined conditions (780-799)		Other causes of death		Total number of deaths
	N	%	N	%	N	%	N	%	N	%	N	%	N
Liverpool	1	0.0	3	20.0	0	0.0	8	53.3	0	0.0	4	26.7	15
Glasgow	1	3.4	4	13.8	0	0.0	19	65.5	0	0.0	5	17.3	29
Barcelona	121	26.3	6	1.3	21	4.6	239	51.9	2	0.4	71	15.5	460
Turin	99	17.6	66	11.7	14	2.5	274	48.7	26	4.6	84	14.9	563
Rome	188	29.4	177	27.8	38	5.9	94	14.7	13	2.0	129	20.2	639
Naples	35	7.5	32	16.0	6	3.0	50	25.0	41	20.5	36	18.0	200
Moscow	0	0.0	1	2.0	14	28.6	20	40.8	0	0.0	14	28.6	49
Warsaw	0	0.0	4	4.9	4	4.9	26	31.7	35	42.7	13	15.8	82
New Haven	16	27.6	0	0.0	4	6.9	11	19.0	15	25.9	12	20.6	58

* = ICD 9 coding of cause of death.

There is, in fact, a wide variation in ascertainment of causes of death across different cities; problems resulting from varying validity of cause of death ascertainment and classification cannot be ruled out. This should be considered both in the interpretation of results and in the potential use of cause-specific mortality rates as addict death multipliers.

Conclusions

In conclusion, cohort studies are a frequently chosen method to estimate mortality among drug users and so to derive addict death multipliers for estimating the prevalence of drug abuse. A standardised methodology should be applied for the method to be used across different countries. In summary, the main issues to be addressed and clearly stated in a protocol of a cohort study of mortality among drug users are:

- definition of case;
- cohort definition;
- effective follow-up procedures;
- determination and coding of cause of death;
- computation of person-years at risk;
- computation of mortality rates.

References

Frischer M., Bloor M., Goldberg D., Clark J., Green S. and McKeganey N. (1993) 'Mortality among injecting drug users: critical reappraisal', *Journal of Epidemiology and Community Medicine*, 47, 59-63.

Injecting Drug Users Mortality Study Group (nd) Mortality of injecting drug users: a longitudinal international study (submitted for publication).

United Nations (1991) *Demographic Yearbook*, United Nations.

World Health Organisation (1992) *World Health Statistics Annual*, WHO, Geneva.

CHAPTER 15

DRUG-RELATED DEATHS
AS AN INDIRECT INDICATOR,
BASED ON THE DANISH EXPERIENCE

by Henrik Sælan

This chapter gives a practical example of the use of drug-related deaths to estimate prevalence, using a case study from Denmark. Comparison and validation of different data sources suggests that the rising mortality among 25-49 year olds indicates an increasing prevalence of problem drug use.

Case counting exercises

In 1976, the first effort was made to count the number of drug addicts in 1975 in Greater Copenhagen by case-finding (Council on Alcohol and Narcotics, 1977). Greater Copenhagen consists of the County of Copenhagen and the municipalities of Copenhagen and Frederiksberg, which together have a population of about 1.2 million inhabitants.

The following institutions and registers with information about contacts with a drug abuser were approached in 1975 in Greater Copenhagen:

- social service offices, 31 in all (15 responses);
- hospital wards, 7 in all (5 responses);
- general practitioners, about 1,000 in all (665 responses);
- the National Board of Health Register regarding prescription of methadone and other opiates;
- the National Register on Psychiatric Admissions;
- the Copenhagen Prison;
- the Prison Service;
- the Social Treatment Services for drug addicts, 6 in all (all responded).

This gave a total of 2,981 different persons known as drug abusers or drug addicts under 30 years of age with a registered address in the area. In the study questionnaire there was no definition of the concept of drug abuse or drug addiction. It was concluded that there was a minimum of 3,000 drug abusers in Greater Copenhagen in 1975.

As drug-related deaths until then had always shown an even distribution between the capital and the provinces (see Figure 1), and as there was no better estimate regarding the provinces, an estimate of the total number of drug addicts in Denmark was calculated by doubling the Copenhagen number, giving a figure of between 5,000 and 10,000 drug addicts, allowing for methodological uncertainty. With a total of 2.7 million 15-49 year olds, the estimate amounts to 0.19 per cent to 0.38 per cent of the population at risk.

In 1982, a similar case-finding study was carried out in the County of Vejle in Jutland (Misfeldt and Byskov, 1983). The prevalence estimate was 0.18 per cent of the 15-34 year olds in the county.

Drug-related deaths

In 1970, the Minister of Justice decided that in all cases where there was a medico-legal inquest following a death suspected to be connected with drug abuse, there should also be a medico-legal autopsy and toxicological analysis. This means that almost all unnatural and unexpected deaths in Denmark suspected to be connected with drugs are submitted for forensic investigation. In the case of natural deaths, mostly in hospitals, this happens less frequently. Every year, in a meeting between the police authorities and representatives of the forensic institutes, difficult cases are discussed and the number of drug-related deaths is decided upon. The number is the published in a Yearbook by the police. In 1982, a study was undertaken (Kringsholm, 1982) where the proportion of undetected drug-related deaths was estimated, and it appeared to be 5 per cent of the official number.

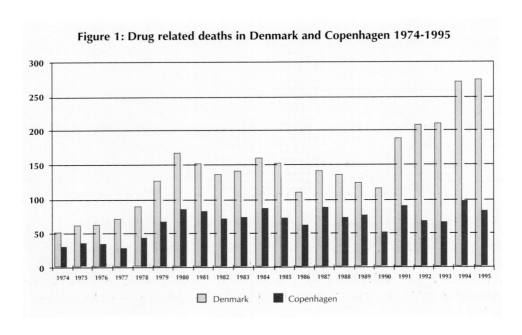

Figure 1: Drug related deaths in Denmark and Copenhagen 1974-1995

Figure 1 shows the number of deaths which have occurred in Denmark, including Copenhagen, since 1974. There was a rising tendency in the 1970s, a stable period in the 1980s and then again increasing numbers in the 1990s. Note that the number of deaths in Copenhagen, the capital, has not increased since 1980. The recent changes have mainly taken place in the provinces.

As drug-related deaths had been used as a key indicator together with other measures in estimating changes in the size of the drug-abusing population since the early count in 1976, the question arose of how the mortality experienced in the 1990s should be interpreted. There was a sudden rise in drug-related deaths, from about 140 deaths per annum in the 1980s to about 240 per annum since 1992.

Was this an indication of rising prevalence of abuse or of rising lethality? The question could not be easily answered because, at that time, there had been major changes in treatment services and it was generally believed that the social conditions for drug addicts had been deteriorating. The treatment had changed from stationary to ambulatory care and there had also been severe budget cuts. To add to this, the numbers of people in methadone treatment had tripled to about 3,000. The methadone was mainly prescribed by general practitioners and delivered from pharmacies and was not taken under controlled conditions. As a result, there were large amounts of illegal methadone on the drug market and the proportion of methadone poisonings rose to about 30 per cent of all drug-related deaths (Steentoft, 1994).

Mortality rates

In 1995, there was a review of Danish follow-up studies on drug addicts giving information on deaths (Sælan, 1995). Of ten reports reviewed, three were found to give valid information. Of the three, one was very old and the study material consisted of persons addicted in the earlier contexts preceding the present wave of addiction.

A 1972 study, on a cohort which had been followed for six years, found an annual death rate of 2.5 per cent (Green, 1986). In a second study which started in 1973, the figure was 2.4 per cent at the eleven year follow-up (Haastrup and Jepson, 1988) and 1.9 per cent after 20 years (Sørensen, Jepsen and Haastrup, 1966). But even if we regard the annual rate as more or less constant at about 2 per cent over the years, the causes of death changed over time. Poisoning was the cause of death in 90 per cent of the cases in the first five year period, but only 40 per cent in the last. AIDS was the cause attributed to 10 to 30 per cent of annual deaths between 1989 and 1993. In general, various infectious diseases and violent injuries replaced the poisonings in later periods of observation.

It is clear that, when using cohort studies, these should be undertaken at suitable time intervals in order to monitor any changes in lethality and pattern of causes of death among drug abusers, both as a source of information in itself and as a means to validate the use of death registers in this field.

Prevalence estimation

Using the deaths multiplier method, the 2 per cent annual death rate suggested by the cohort studies in the 1980s, taken together with about 140 drug-related deaths (see Figure 1), produced a central estimate of 7,000 addicts, which was in accord with the estimate resulting from the early case-finding study. In a very recent study (not yet published) from the County of Vejle in Jutland, 175 addicts were followed up for 15 years, and the annual death rate was 1.6 per cent. This result and the 20 year follow-up data give no reason for believing that mortality rate among drug addicts has been rising in any significant way in the last ten to twenty years in Denmark. This means that a new central estimate of the prevalence of drug abusers in Denmark, using the multiplier method, would be 12,000.

Further information and analysis of drug-related deaths

A detailed study of data in the Danish Death Register was carried out with regard to further information on drug-related deaths (Juel and Helweg-Larsen, 1996). In

Table 1: Drug-related deaths in Denmark 1970-1993

	Manner of death	Underlying cause ICD codes, 8th edition	Addiction indicated **	Number of deaths
A	Poisoning	E853-E854	Yes	845
A	Suicide by poisoning	E950	Yes	483
A	Accident, suicide or homicide by poisoning	E980, N965, N978	Yes	338
B	Poisoning	E853, E854	No	362
B	Accident, suicide or homicide by poisoning	E980, N965, N978	No	124
C	Other accident	E800-E852, E855-E949	Yes	755
C	Other suicide	E951-E959	Yes	342
C	Homicide	E960-E969	Yes	38
C	Accident, suicide or homicide	E980-E989	Yes	873
D	Natural	303.8, 304	No	298
D	Natural	000-303.7, 303.9, 305-796	Yes	1,771
	Total			6,229

A = poisoning with addictive substances with addiction indicated as contributing cause (303.8, 304); B = poisoning with addictive substances, addiction not indicated as contributing cause; C = violent deaths among addicts (addiction contributing cause, 303.8, 304); D = natural deaths among addicts. ** Addiction indicated as contributing cause with codes 303.8 or 304. Source: Juel and Helweg Larsen, 1996.

the Danish Death Register, three codes from the death certificate are recorded, but only the underlying cause of death is published in the routine statistics. The codes for contributing causes and different manners of death can be analysed separately if required. Table 1 summarises the 6,229 deaths found by each sub-category of cause and manner of death in the period 1970 to 1993. This was the last year that Denmark used the 8 Edition of ICD codes; from January 1994, ICD 10 Edition has been used.

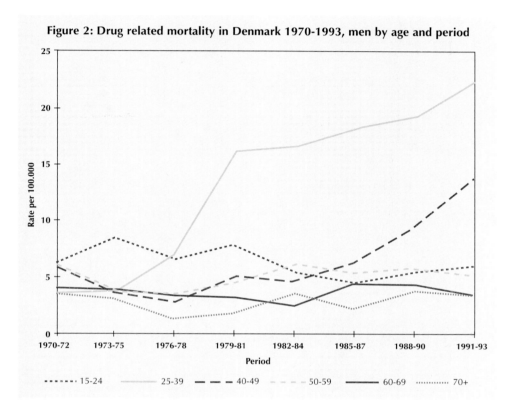

Figure 2: Drug related mortality in Denmark 1970-1993, men by age and period

Figures 2 and 3 show the age-specific mortality per 100,000 in the age-group for males and females from 1970 to 1993. The picture is somewhat different for males and females but the 25-49 age group shows rising rates for both sexes. Among females, the older age group, over 50 years, also have high rates. When the birth cohorts were analysed, a rising mortality rate was observed for younger birth cohorts. At the same time there seemed to be a stagnation in the trend as the youngest birth cohorts had lower mortality rates. This was clearly seen for males but not as evident for females.

In Figure 4, the development over time in different categories of causes is shown for 25-39 year old males. The causal categories are those summarised in Table 1. The figure shows rising rates in all except category C, mainly comprising violent deaths.

Figure 3: Drug related mortality in Denmark 1970-1993, women by age and period

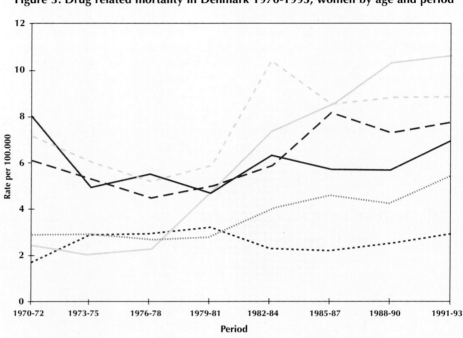

Figure 4: Drug related mortality in Denmark 1970-1993, men 25-39 by cause of death

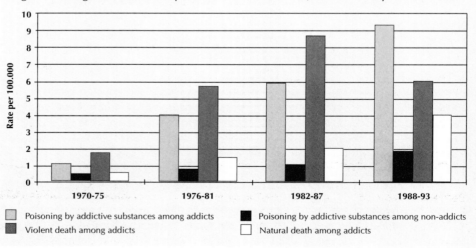

Validation of the drug-related deaths data

The Death Register data were validated by comparisons with two other sets of data, using the same codes as previously described and shown in Table 1. In the first case, Death Register data for 1992 were compared with police statistics for the same year. There were 393 deaths in all; of these 169 (43 per cent) were common to the two registers whereas 185 (47 per cent) appeared only in the Death Register. After examination of the original death certificates only 34 of these 185 (18.4 per cent) deaths were found to be drug-related, in the sense that these persons belonged to an addicted population using illicit drugs. The remaining 151 deaths (185-34) consisted of older persons, with a majority of females, suffering from chronic conditions and having addictive use of legally prescribed addictive painkillers. These deaths were almost all excluded when only deaths of people up to 39 years of age were considered.

In the second comparison, the cohort of 300 addicts described earlier (Haastrup and Jepson, 1988; Sørensen, Jepsen and Haastrup, 1966) was searched for in the Death Register by their personal identification number. Of the 119 deaths known to have occurred among this cohort, 102 (85.7 per cent) appeared in the register under the codes listed in Table 1.

On the basis of these two studies, the Death Register in Denmark appears to have an acceptable coverage of drug-related deaths when contributing causes of death are also included.

Conclusions

In conclusion, cohort studies do not show significant rises in annual death rates. However, mortality among 25-49 year olds in the Death Register is rising (and incidentally so is the number of drug-related deaths in police statistics). Consequently, in the face of non-increasing death rates, there is evidence of rising prevalence of drug abuse in Denmark when drug-related deaths are used as an indirect indicator.

References

Council on Alcohol and Narcotics (1977) *Young drug addicts in Greater Copenhagen in 1975,* Copenhagen.

Green J. (1986) 'Deaths among adolescents referred to institutions', *Ugeskrift for Læger,* 148, 1359-64.

Haastrup S. and Jepsen P.W. (1988) 'Eleven year follow-up of 300 young opioid addicts', *Acta Psychiatrica Scandinavica,* 77, 22-6.

Juel K. and Helweg-Larsen K. (1966) 'Drug-related mortality in Denmark 1970-1993', In: Dadsfald blaudt stofmisbrugere, 1970-1995. National Board of Health (Denmark).

Kringsholm B. (1982) 'Hidden deaths in drug addicts in Denmark in 1968-1979', *Ugeskrift for Læger,* 144, 341-4.

Misfeldt J. and Byskov J. (1983) 'Drug addicts using injections in the County of Vejle. I. Prevalence, incidence and mortality', *Ugeskr Læger,* 145, 2041-4.

Sælan H. (1995) *Deaths among drug addicts,* National Board of Health (Denmark).

Sørensen H.J., Jepsen P.W. and Haastrup S. (1996) 'Mortality in 300 drug addicts. 20 year follow-up', In: Dadsfald blaudt stofmisbrugere, 1970-1995. National Board of Health (Denmark).

Steentoft A., Kaa E., Simonsen K.W., Kringsholm B., Worm K., Hansen A.C., Toft J. and Dragsholt C. (1996) 'Deaths among drug addicts in Denmark', *Ugeskrift for Læger,* 156, 6215-9.

NOMINATION METHODS

PART V

INTRODUCTION

by Martin Frischer

Nomination techniques involve direct contact with samples of drug users who provide access to and/or information on their peers. This section considers the use of such information in estimating the prevalence of drug use.

Colin Taylor's chapter begins by noting that nomination estimation is a form of the multiplier method (which has been described earlier in Part IV). The chapter contains a detailed theoretical overview of the statistical basis for nomination estimation and considers the various ways in which access to samples may be gained. Critical to the success of nomination methods is the randomness of the samples.

This issue is further developed in the subsequent chapter by Dirk Korf. He notes that, in practice, snowball methodology is often employed to gain access to drug users and considers the advantages and disadvantages of this particular method. His argument is supported by evidence from a wide range of field studies. The chapter raises-important methodological issues for any study which relies on recruiting drug users in the community.

ESTIMATING THE PREVALENCE OF DRUG USE USING NOMINATION TECHNIQUES: AN OVERVIEW

by Colin Taylor

The use of nomination methods as a means of obtaining information about difficult-to-reach populations dates back many years having enjoyed a certain amount of fame and notoriety in the 1970s. Interest in these methods is now developing again in drug use epidemiology, its main virtue being its usefulness in dealing with relatively rare events. This paper considers the use of nomination methods specifically in estimating the size of a drug-using population which, in many instances, is a relatively small proportion of the general population. The term 'nomination techniques' refers to sampling methods which attempt to gather data not just from the respondent to the initial sample, but also from individuals nominated by these respondents. This includes methods in which data about nominees are gathered not simply from the respondents, but from these nominees directly.

Principles of population estimation using nomination estimation

The principles involved in using nomination techniques specifically to estimate prevalence of drug use are the same as those described elsewhere for the multiplier method. This procedure is characterised by:

- a benchmark – the total number of the drug-using population who were in treatment at some point during the year in question, e.g. 3,000;
- a multiplier – an estimate from some sample survey of the proportion of the drug-using population who were in treatment that year, e.g. 20 per cent (one fifth).

By applying the same benchmark-multiplier calculation to these figures, the overall drug-using population size would be: 3,000 / (1/5) = 3,000 x 5 = 15,000.

The variety of ways in which the sample estimate of the treatment ratio of 20 per cent may possibly be obtained will constitute the body of this chapter. Even without specifying these for the moment, there are clearly many other definitions in the above procedure that need to be tightened and various compromises that must be made. For instance, we need to specify exactly what sort of treatment we mean: perhaps 'in methadone treatment' is a precise enough definition, or perhaps a list of specific treatment agencies would be preferable, depending upon how the data are to be collected. Note again that the definition of this sub-group – those in treatment – is primarily for the convenience of the researcher, and it is simply a stepping stone to the answer we want to calculate. *Any* clear and precise definition will do, provided it is the *same* definition that is used in both the enumeration of the benchmark sub-group and in the sample data collection. Note too that this definition should include specification of the geographical extent of the locality or region being considered, as well as the precise time-slot to which the data apply.

Estimating the multiplier value

Obtaining a core sample

Ideally, to estimate the ratio we need a random sample of drug users of the type we are interested in – all drug users, opiate users, injectors and so on. The practical consideration of obtaining a full sampling frame – a list of all drug users from which to draw the sample – in advance of the sample being drawn makes it a complete impossibility. Indeed, if it were possible it would clearly make the exercise of estimating the population size a waste of time. Alternative methods of sampling are also available. For instance, various 'capture lists' can be used, although care and ingenuity is often required in using them correctly (by capture list we mean one of the data sources of names or other identifiers discussed in the capture-recapture section). 'Site sampling' can be used, and perhaps an extended network sampling procedure (by site sampling we mean a procedure that selects drug users at one or more geographical locations, where they are likely to be found). Random samples can be generated from sample surveys of the general population, although with reservations (by population sample survey we mean a full probability sample drawn in the traditional manner from a sampling frame covering the general population).

These sampling procedures are discussed later with specific reference to their usefulness in nomination procedures. To begin, however, in order to focus on the nomination procedures themselves, we will assume that we have generated a random sample of drug users by some means or other, for instance, by simple site sampling. Note that because we have not used traditional methods of statistical sampling, we do not know what fraction of the total drug-using population our sample comprises. This random sample is, in many contexts, referred to as the 'core sample' of respondents.

Nomination ratio methods

'Nomination methods' are generally thought of as estimation methods based on information which individuals in a sample provide about their network of acquaintances. We are using the term 'nomination ratio methods' to apply specifically to prevalence estimation by benchmark/ratio methods that estimate the required ratio from nominee information.

Broadly put, sample members are asked to name or nominate drug-using acquaintances and to say whether these acquaintances have been in touch with drug treatment centres, health services or any other similar body, within a stipulated time period. The proportion of treatment attenders nominated by the sample is then used as a multiplier (as described above) to give an estimate of the total number of drug users in conjunction with the benchmark known attendance figures at the drug treatment agencies.

Given a core random sample of drug users, typically we ask two questions of our core sample respondents, broadly of the following sort: 'How many of your acquaintances have used drugs regularly in the last year?' and 'How many of these have been for treatment in the last year?' From these two answers the proportion of drug users in treatment can be calculated. Of course the questions will need rather more precise definitions of 'drug user' and 'treatment'. Respectively these will vary according to: the aim of the study and the target population, and the type of benchmark data source available. Whether one year or another time span is more appropriate also needs to be determined, as do the geographical limits of the study.

It is evident that we are making a trade-off here: the greater number of drug users that the nomination technique uses in its calculations is bought at the expense of information accuracy. The respondent's personal impression of the drug-using population and their treatment is actually what is being recorded in the survey, and accuracy will depend upon how well the respondent answers, or can be encouraged to answer, the two questions. It is important, therefore, that the definitions used (for 'drug user') and the benchmark choice ('treatment' in this example) are elements that a respondent is likely to know about their nominees. Whether they are injectors or not, whether they have had an overdose episode, and so forth, are all relatively 'knowable' characteristics; precise frequency of use or polydrug use, being tested for HIV and many others would probably not be as reliably known by respondents about anyone other than themselves. Note too that since we are effectively asking each respondent for their estimate of the 'in treatment ratio', whether there is some double-counting of particular nominees across respondents or not is not critical; the respondents' estimate of the ratio is all that is used.

A direct question technique

An adaptation is to ask a direct question such as 'What proportion of your drug-using acquaintances have been for treatment?' This is almost certainly less useful. It is likely to be a more difficult question to answer, and the answer may be subject to more rounding off than when it is asked in two stages; secondly, it would be usual to weight each respondent's answer by its statistical reliability, namely the number of drug users on which the respondent's estimate was based, and this we would not know. In effect, a weighted estimate of this sort is simply the total number of treated drug users nominated in ratio to the total number of users nominated.

Errors in reporting nominees' status

Note that in the first of the two questions, the respondent may not know that a number of his/her acquaintances were taking drugs regularly that year. This omission is not actually important, since what we wish to know is the proportion of those who have been for treatment that year. If this is known accurately then the answer will be good enough for our purposes, but it is important that the respondent does know the treatment status of their nominated acquaintances. Failing to know that a drug-using acquaintance has been for treatment will distort downwards the proportion of those reported as having had treatment; and following through the calculation procedure, this will lead to too large a multiplier value and a final over-estimation of the size of the total drug-using population. The reverse reporting error is also quite possible. If the respondent has the drug use of an acquaintance brought to their attention only because of an overdose or treatment episode, this is likely to distort their estimation of the proportion in treatment upwards, with a corresponding downward error in the final estimate of the population size. In this ratio estimation procedure, there is clearly considerable room for error, but it is difficult to say that there would be a consistent upwards or downwards bias.

Reliability of nomination methods

Verification of nominee information

Although the term 'nominee' has been used in describing the preceding method of estimating the ratio we want to know, it is evident that no *identification* of these nominees is required. All we need to know are the numbers of acquaintances in response to the two questions, not who they are. When we consider the possibility of the respondent identifying the nominee, either by full name and address, or by some code-matching label such as initials and date of birth, or Soundex code (a coding method for scrambling the name of an individual to preserve confidentiality but still to allow cross-matching), then the possibility arises of verifying the information given by the respondent about the nominees. There are three obvious methods of acquiring the relevant nominee information:

- without identification: nominee counts – take report of respondents in sample;
- with identification: nominee record checking – check treatment status directly with treatment records;
- with identification: nominee tracing and interview – check both treatment status and drug-using status directly with nominee.

The pros and cons of requesting identifier information on nominees from the respondents can be debated at length. But the main objections are that asking for potential breaking of confidentiality by asking for identification of the nominees can lead to disruption of the sampling and the sample information provided, with the possibility of a refusal to co-operate; and partial identification, such as initials or Soundex coding, can be difficult to match against other information and may give a misleading impression of accuracy. The main points in favour are that there can be verification to some extent or other of information supplied about nominees, and that interviewing identified nominees opens the way to chain referral sampling with a relatively easy access to many more drug users.

Bias in reporting

When, for example, the numbers of users in treatment is the benchmark, it is clearly important in estimating the treatment proportion/multiplier that there should be no general preference for treated drug users as opposed to untreated drug users to be reported as nominees by the respondents. It is possible that such a preference exists in some subset of respondents, for instance, amongst treated drug users themselves there may be a tendency to know a higher proportion of treated acquaintances. Other similar biases can be present in the reporting: males may be more likely than females to know other males, and drug users will be more likely than will non-users to know other users. The estimation procedure is, perhaps surprisingly, robust to many such biases, provided that the core sample is a random representation of the drug-using population. The resulting estimates may be more variable — that is, have a high sampling variability — than otherwise, but no necessary bias arises from this in the result provided the sample is representative.

One bias that will disrupt the estimation procedure is the first of those listed: a possible tendency for those in treatment or who have been in treatment, to nominate preferentially others who have been in treatment. The central assumption that this will not be so is a reflection of similar assumptions in the other methods of prevalence estimation which have been discussed in other papers and, in that sense, is common to all estimation methods. In using the number of drug user deaths, for example, in conjunction with a multiplier estimated from drug user death rates, it was shown to be necessary to assume that the estimated death rates apply appropriately to the overall number of deaths — that is, that the number of deaths in the observed sample cohort is neither over nor under-stated. Similarly, in capture-recapture studies, it was necessary to assume that the two sources were independent capture points — that is, that the proportion of people captured at the second source, who were also first-source captures (i.e. in the 'overlap' of the two sources), represented fairly the overall proportion of the overall total population who were first-source captures.

It should be noted that, even when reporting is unbiased, there is a small technical bias present in all standard ratio estimation methods. It is, however, only apparent in small samples, and is correctable by a slight amendment to the multiplier/benchmark calculation. Therefore, it will be disregarded in what follows.

Multiple benchmark methods

An immediate and useful generalisation of the benchmark-multiplier techniques is to employ multiple benchmarks, if overall data are available. Thus, besides using those in treatment as a benchmark group, it would be possible to use those arrested by the police as well, for example. Both questions would then need to be asked of the respondents about their nominees, giving two chances of calculating a multiplier. This calculation becomes a little more complicated under these circumstances, since it is necessary to ensure consistency between the results of the two calculations. (In fact, technically, the calculation mirrors the analysis of a multi-source capture-recapture study.)

It is also possible to extend this further to more benchmarks, giving a 'profile' of drug users categorised by many characteristics rather than a single benchmark. Furthermore, it is possible to include in this 'profile' demographic breakdowns such as the number of females in treatment, the number of young males arrested, and so forth. Any information which can be collected in the sample from the respondents about the nominees, or by any other means, can be used in this way, greatly strengthening the power and potential accuracy of the procedure.

An example: the Wirral study

A study in four towns in the Wirral area of England in 1986 (Parker *et al*, 1988) used a variety of these techniques to estimate the size of the opiate-using population and remains one of the few comparative studies of these methods. These techniques were used on a focused sample of 60 drug users. The way the sample was obtained is not our main concern here at the moment – in fact it was obtained by snowball sampling, with a sketchily-documented selection of the zero-stage sample members. We will consider the base sample of 60 referrals as a core sample that is used to generate further nominees. Of particular interest are the nomination methods and the methods of calculation that were used.

A benchmark of 237 drug users who were known to various stipulated agencies in the region – including treatment registers and drug-related arrest lists – in a stipulated year was established. The multiplier was established by sample several techniques from the (same) core sample of 60 people.

A. Respondents only: direct question (n-dq)

The 60 members of the core sample of drug users were asked whether they had been in treatment during the study period. The self-report was that 19 had done so in the stipulated period. A simple variant of the basic procedure was also used, in which it was possible to verify that the respondents, who were identifiable (either by name or by an initials/age/sex combination) were in fact recorded as having been to the agencies. In this particular study, it appears that there were no discrepancies in the self-reported status of the respondents. The 19 identified as being part of the benchmark group give a proportion of 19/60 and an overall multiplier of 3.2. This technique has been described above and does not use nomination methods in the sense that the sample has been described here – it uses only the core sample respondents.

B. Reported nominee proportion (n-pr)

The 60 core referrals were asked to nominate their five closest acquaintances who regularly used heroin during the year. They were confined to acquaintances of the same sex as the respondent themselves, to provide a narrower focus for the potential nominee list. Of these 300 nominees, the respondents were asked to report how many had been in contact with stipulated agencies, in order to compute the appropriate multiplier. The final reported figures were adjusted for double-counting in both the number of nominees and the number of those reported known to agencies, using a crude form of the simple identifier information that was available. The final figures were overall 170 nominees of whom 55 were known in the benchmark group, giving a multiplier of 3.1.

C. Nominees with identification for verification (n-id)

The 60 core sample members were asked to name up to ten nominees who were regular drug users, and to supply identifying information on them. This resulted in a proportion of refusals (seven of the 60 sample members). The remaining 53 nominated 297 drug-using acquaintances. This was reduced to 163 unique users by making use of the identifier information. Further checking of the identifiers against the benchmark lists showed 66 were known in the benchmark sub-group, yielding a multiplier of 163/66 or 2.5. It should be noted that an additional check was introduced in this method, namely that a nominee had to be nominated by at least two respondents to give greater certainty that they were in fact a drug user.

The different types of benchmark/multiplier calculations given above (n-dq, n-pr, n-id) were computed separately within each of the four townships that comprised the study. The results for the separate townships are given in Figure 1, where towns are ranked by level of drug use (Town A = high, Town D = low).

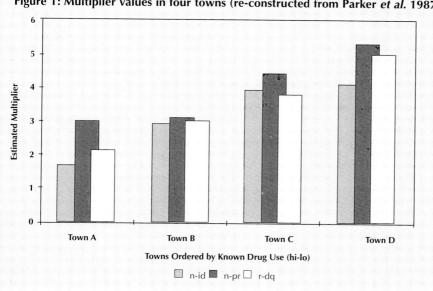

Figure 1: Multiplier values in four towns (re-constructed from Parker *et al.* 1987)

The evident trend for towns with higher known drug use to have lower multiplier values may have many explanations. The simplest is probably a selection bias: namely, that, if a town is selected because it has a low number of known drug users there is a greater chance that it reflects a low ratio of known drug users than a high ratio. Hence the multiplier might well tend to be greater in these areas where drug use is least.

When looking at the different estimates of the multiplier supplied by the different methods within each town, it can be seen that a certain amount of consistency in the answers has been achieved. Moreover, the different methods give a similar pattern of answers across the four towns, suggesting that distinctive properties and possible minor biases pertain to the three methods. The smallest multiplier generally occurs when method C ('Nominate up to ten drug-using acquaintances ...') is used, whereas the tighter question of method B ('Nominate five closest same-sex drug-using acquaintances ...') is consistently the largest. Many explanations can be postulated for this; it is worth noting that the results certainly agree with the theory that respondents who have a wider choice of potential nominees might tend to name more in-treatment nominees – these perhaps being higher-profile drug users and more readily brought to mind.

Some limitations of the methods

With specific reference to some drugs such as cocaine, there are difficulties in using drug treatment programmes, other health service agencies and police and court records to provide a benchmark figure for these users. People who use only cocaine often do not readily figure in these sources, and there is a danger that the estimation would be inadvertently directed too much towards multiple drug users. The technique, therefore, can provide only a rough estimate of cocaine use prevalence, with a considerably large sampling error. In general, the principal limitations of the technique will arise from: (a) the core sample that provides the nomination data for estimating the multiplier needs to be representative; (b) the method requires a fairly accurate benchmark figure for numbers in treatment over the time period in question. These may be incorrect if the same set of treatment agencies is not used in the nomination question and in the benchmark, or if there is serious tendency for some drug users to register at more than one treatment agency in the same period, or if drug treatment agency records are not fully accurate; (c) the proportion of nominees attending treatment programmes can be erroneous because respondents may not know with any great degree of reliability whether their nominees have attended a treatment programme or not. There is also a danger of people deliberately providing wrong information about their acquaintances.

The potential double counting of nominees (that is, the same person being nominated by more than one respondent) does not, in itself, influence the total of those in treatment in proportion to all nominees. This proportion is effectively calculated for each respondent individually and then averaged (with weights) across all respondents, successfully avoiding such complications (Hartnoll *et al*, 1985).

Focused core samples

Sampling issues

We now turn to issues in drawing a sample by which to estimate the multiplier through nomination methods, assuming it is impossible or inefficient or otherwise inadvisable to launch a general population survey as a basis. Note that all we require is a random sample of drug users, and this can be obtained by filtering them off a general population survey or by more direct methods. The term 'focused core sample' indicates that the aim is to sample drug users directly, rather than simply identify them amongst a general population sample, and to indicate that this sample can be the initial wave (sometimes called the zero stage) to be used in a multi-wave chain referral procedure (snowball sampling). The sample should be such that it is efficient at finding as many (drug-using) nominees as possible; and it gives no preference to finding nominees who are treated users over those who are non-treated, and vice versa (or whatever benchmark group is being used, if it is not treatment figures).

Bias in focused sample selection

The main problem in drawing a focused sample will be the need to find a mechanism by which to draw the sample in the absence of the complete sampling frame required by classical statistical survey methods. Two options arise. The first is to use any lists of drug users which are available, knowing that these are partial and often self-selected lists of drug users; these are the 'capture lists' used in capture-recapture studies discussed in previous sessions. The second is to use some form of 'binomial sampling' (Goodman, 1961) or 'site sampling' (TenHouten, 1971).

Capture lists

To supply the core sample, it is possible to use, as a sampling frame, lists of drug users who are in treatment and to use their nominees to provide the information on the treatment ratio. In this case, the treatment proportion amongst respondents is not useful (being 100 per cent) and the multiplier calculation must be confined to the nominees only. However, lists of drug users who are in treatment, or who have been in treatment recently, might well not satisfy the bias criterion of no treatment preference with respect to their nominees.

One option is to use a 'site sampling' (or 'binomial sampling') method. Such samples have difficulties of their own in practice, which we will not discuss in detail here, but we simply note that such a sample is not *a priori* going to have a bias in preferentially yielding nominees who are treated as opposed to untreated. Again, if one of the sites chosen is the treatment clinics themselves, some bias may arise.

Crossed capture lists

An ingenious elaboration which tries to safeguard against this possibility of bias is to do a double-study, one using the treatment subset as its benchmark and the other using police arrests as its benchmark subset. It then becomes possible, records permitting, to use the police records as a sampling frame to provide a sample ratio for the 'treatment benchmark' calculation. Hopefully, this reduces to a minimum any potential tendency for sample respondents to have any obvious bias in nominating treated users. Then, by using the treatment lists for the 'arrests benchmark' calculation, the obverse is also true. Hopefully, the potential bias in each is considerably reduced by this cross-over technique, and each should provide an improved estimate of their respective ratios.

Selection control in site sampling

Stratification has often been discussed as a potential way of controlling the sample selection. Stratification of the population under study is the easiest and surest way to improve representativeness of the sample. Multi-site sampling offers an opportunity to stratify the sample if the researcher has, or can collect, information on the population numbers in the intended strata. Such strata might be different physical locations, such as clubs, pubs and so forth, or they might be circles of social cohesion, such as students, musicians and golf club members. The difficulty is not in devising strata – these usually spring readily to mind – but in defining strata that can be enumerated during the data collection or have been enumerated beforehand. TenHouten discusses the idea of extending such site samples to a plurality of sites, in order to sample more effectively from the whole population under study. Hendricks *et al* (1992) describe using the principle by sketching out a map of the city's likely centres of cocaine use in order to draw a multi-site sample from these centres.

The heavy reliance on random (binomial) selection to obtain a core (or zero-wave) sample throws up several aspects of the procedure which need to be considered in relation to site sampling. These relate to the implications for assessing the sampling probabilities of any population member. Apart from the need for careful procedures in the sampling process to ensure that no immediate interviewer preference causes individuals to be sampled differentially, there are questions concerning the 'coverage' of the sites – how far do they encompass the entire target population – and questions concerning frequency of attendance – how often do different individuals attend the site or sites. The final line is that everyone in the population is assumed to attend the sample points and, if the sample is intended to be drawn by a simple random sampling (SRS) procedure, to attend with the same frequency.

Clustering and its effects

Clustering normally implies the congregating together – at least from the point of view of selecting sample members – of groups of similar people and, as such, is an inefficiency factor. When they are clusters of similar people, they reduce the effective spread of the sample across the variety of people in the population. Clustering is clearly of particular importance in snowball sampling, where chaining from one sample member to the next implies the inclusion of several possibly similar people as a result of including any one of them. Clustering in itself does not of itself produce a biased sample, it produces an inefficient sample; inefficiency from the point of view of keeping sampling error variance to a minimum.

Chain referral (snowball sampling) procedures

Once we accept the possibility of obtaining identification of the respondents' nominees, it becomes possible to follow up these nominees personally and to obtain from them a second wave of nominees. The multiplier calculations can make use of all such nominees in the second wave as well as those in the first. Any number of waves may be added in a similar way, with the intention of obtaining as many drug users as possible on which to base the estimate of the required ratio.

The statistical analysis of a snowball sample requires careful consideration and is fraught with many potential pitfalls generated by the sampling procedure. These have a considerable literature relating to them, grounded in the theories of sampling on a network of individuals. Requirements of calculating sampling probabilities and of analysing weighted non-independent observations make the procedures potentially complex. However, we note here that the simple overall calculation of the required proportion of people in the benchmark group (e.g., treatment during the year) is adequate for our immediate purposes, if we are prepared to assume that there is no reason for nominees in the chain referral procedure to nominate people in the benchmark group at a greater rate than is their natural frequency of occurrence. Whereas this assumption can be violated in many ways, it may, nonetheless, not be an unreasonable approximation to the truth in many circumstances.

Defining the snowball procedure

The snowball procedure is defined statistically by the number of nominations (links) the zero-wave respondent is asked to give and by the number of waves (stages) that the link-tracing procedure completes. This method of definition of the snowball procedure will hold whatever the actual nature of the link, that is, whatever the question by which the respondent is asked to make nominations, and whether or not the link relationship is necessarily mutual (e.g. 'Who have you used cocaine with, ever?') or is potentially uni-directional ('Who are the people you most often use cocaine with?').

There is a variety of different ways of treating the number of links and the number of stages in a snowball procedure, the first and foremost being whether they are fixed to be the same for everyone in the sample or whether they are allowed to vary naturally as the sample waves progress. In spite of ground-breaking work by Goodman

(1961), in practical terms for a study wanting to make even approximate statistical inferences about population parameters, it is not at all clear what the theoretical consequences are in terms of efficient use of a given sample size or collection effort, or in terms of the bias of the resulting estimates. There are no theoretical statistical guidelines on what type of snowball procedure to adopt, except to make the core (zero-stage) sample as large as possible.

Apart from the lack of any theoretical statistical considerations, for most purposes it would seem inefficient to fix in advance the number of nominees or the number of stages. Usually, the primary consideration is to obtain enough people by the procedure to allow reasonable numbers for analysis/description. It seems preferable for efficiency of effort and for administrative ease to let the nomination process proceed without imposing constraints on its format. The procedure could be terminated either by reaching a predetermined number of sample members or, more likely, a predetermined financial resources limit, or by sampling to extinction – that is, until the last wave adds no further new nominees.

In practical terms, the reporting of the proportion (or number) of acquaintances who have used drugs and who have been treated for drug use is probably best kept as focused and directed as possible. The more leeway allowed to a respondent in the phrasing of the appropriate questions, the more opportunity there is for the respondent to answer in a loaded or selective way. This is probably a principal source of potential bias in the procedures and, therefore, limiting or controlling it is desirable. Strictly speaking, there is no need for the nominee linking question in the chain referral procedure (e.g. 'Who are the people you regularly use drugs with?') to be the same as the question used as the base in the ratio calculation ('Who are your five closest drug-using acquaintances? How many have been in treatment this year?'). The ability to trace, interview and verify information given about the nominees is compromised, however, when the two sets of people differ.

Alternative nomination strategies

In order to determine the number of stages in a snowball sample, the decision can be made *ad hoc* as the sampling procedure progresses or until no further stages can be made. In order to determine the number of links for selecting nominees, the options are: (a) tracing all links nominated by the respondent; (b1) tracing a selection made at random which is a fixed proportion of the respondent's nominees; (b2) tracing a selection made at random which is a fixed number of the respondent's nominees (a method studied in Goodman's original 1961 paper); (c) tracing links in a predetermined importance order from the list of the respondent's nominees, taking either a fixed number from or a proportion of the list, for example 'first best friend' and 'second best friend'; (d) tracing links in a predetermined reverse importance order from the list of the respondent's nominees, taking either a fixed number from or a proportion of the list; for example taking the list in the order the respondent nominates, but bottom first.

Hendricks *et al* (1992) list these alternatives and have noted that the theoretical implications of these different alternative strategies is still unclear and that it is perhaps best for the choice to depend upon the goal of the study. For different purposes, each of these alternatives has advantages and disadvantages in terms of rate of growth of the sample, the risks of a restricted (biased) sample, etc. Hendricks *et al* (op. cit.) speculate tentatively on some guidelines. If the purpose of 'snowballing' is to obtain a snowball sample that is closest to a simple random sample (in terms of the equiprobability of subjects selected from a defined population), then option (b) or (d) may be good choices. Option (b) introduced a strong randomisation factor in each nomination step, as is necessary for the application of Goodman and Rapoport's formulae (1980) for estimating population parameters. Option (d) may also produce a relatively unbiased sample, given Rapoport's observation that a tracing through 'loose ties' ('eighth best friend') between nominators and nominees will yield a sample that is very similar to that derived from the completely randomised model.

With respect to predetermination of the number of stages, only one-stage snowball samples seem to offer any useful results. Since all snowballs will contain this stage, any results can be applied to this subset of the overall sample, ignoring later stages. It would suggest that, if these estimation procedures are important to the study, then the initial zero-stage sample should be as large as possible (something which is always and in all conditions a good idea) and all available links should be traced at stage one.

Nomination ratio techniques in multi-wave snowball samples

As we have seen, it is possible to ask the relevant questions about how many drug-using associates a respondent has within the snowball nomination structure as a matter of course, and to then use the benchmark-multiplier calculations described above to estimate population size. An elaboration of the procedure which is available in snowball samples is as follows. For each respondent, both in the zero-stage sample and in the subsequent stages snowball sample, the proportion of nominees attending drug abuse treatment centres is calculated and these proportions averaged (pooled) across all respondents. These proportions can then be compared for each successive wave of the snowball, to chart any tendency to decrease as the sample spreads further from the core zero wave. This tracking might be particularly useful if the initial sample was not an attempt at being randomly drawn, or even representative, but was, for example, a treatment site-sample.

It may be hoped that the better estimate is provided by the later, more remote waves of the sample but, in fact, the hope is not justified. To the extent that these later waves differ, they unquantifiably play down the contribution those members near the core zero-wave sample would make to the overall average.

Rigour in fieldwork versus rigour in sampling

Many authors have stressed the need for rigour in fieldwork when constructing a snowball sample. The following much quoted problem areas were originally put forward by

Biernacki and Waldorf (1981, p. 144): finding respondents and starting referral chains; verifying the eligibility of potential respondents; engaging respondents as research assistants; controlling the types of chains and number of cases in any chain; pacing and monitoring referral chains and data quality.

It is salutary to note that only two of these are concerned with the statistical-theoretical aspects of snowball sampling and that the remainder deal with practical ground-level considerations.

References

Bieleman B., Diaz A., Merlo G., Kaplan Ch. D. (1993) *Lines across Europe: nature and extent of cocaine use in Barcelona, Rotterdam and Turin.*

Goodman L.A. (1961) 'Snowball sampling', *Annals of Mathematical Statistics*, 32, 148–170.

Hartnoll R.L., Mitcheson M., Lewis R. and Bryer S. (1985) 'Estimating the prevalence of opioid dependence', *The Lancet*, 203-205.

Hendricks V.M., Blanken P. and Adriaans N.F.P. (1992) *Snowball Sampling: a pilot study on cocaine use*, (IVO).

Parker H., Newcombe R. and Bakx K. (1987) 'The new heroin users: prevalence and characteristics in Wirral, Merseyside', *British Journal of Addiction*, 82, 47-57.

Rapoport A. (1980) 'A probabilistic approach to networks', *Social Networks*, 2, 1-18.

TenHouten W.D., Stern J. and TenHouten D. (1971) 'Political Leadership in Poor Communities: applications of Two Sampling Methodologies', in: Orleans and Ellis Jr., *Race, change and urban society*, Vol 5, Urban Affairs Annual Review, Beverly Hills, Ca, Sage Publications.

CHAPTER 17

THE TIP OF THE ICEBERG: SNOWBALL SAMPLING AND NOMINATION TECHNIQUES, THE EXPERIENCE OF DUTCH STUDIES

by Dirk J. Korf

It is not easy to obtain a representative picture of developments in heroin use by consulting general household or school surveys. The prevalence of heroin use is normally too low to permit any reliable conclusions to be drawn on trends in the size and composition of heroin-using populations. As an alternative, researchers sometimes opt for 'captive' samples of institutionalised heroin users, such as prisoners, probationers, methadone patients or addicts undergoing inpatient treatment.

Heroin users are also studied by qualitatively oriented researchers, mostly ethnographers. A common method in the latter studies is snowball sampling, but methodological problems are often ignored and ethnographic field studies of heroin users are mostly limited to street samples. From an epidemiological viewpoint, it is often questionable whether findings from either institutionalised or snowball samples are representative of the total population of heroin users. Sometimes institutionalised populations of heroin users are compared to street populations. Data on HIV prevalence among Amsterdam methadone clients have been compared to findings from street samples. When the rates turned out more or less the same, the researchers concluded that methadone clients can be taken to be a representative sample of the Amsterdam heroin-using population (van Ameijden, 1994). Such a conclusion is, of course, far too hasty. The most visible sub-group may be in no way representative of the population. The tip of the iceberg does not, by definition, resemble the part under water.

What matters in typological and ethnographic studies is usually the theoretical generalisability of the findings rather than statistical representativeness. Most respondents are drawn from institutionalised populations or street scenes, although theoretically they could also come from other environments. One benefit of these types of studies is that they have helped to systematise snowball methodologies. In principle, the combining of institutional and street samples makes it possible to reduce selection bias in studying the entire population of heroin users. But both types of studies generally fail to make clear to what degree their samples are statistically representative of that overall population. They find similarities between two, possibly overlapping, segments of the tip of the iceberg. The underwater part could prove altogether different in nature.

Nomination techniques in practice

Since nomination techniques are discussed in Chapter 16 by Colin Taylor, this chapter focuses on field experiences. In several field studies we applied nomination techniques, for instance by asking respondents whether they had received methadone through a standard provision programme and/or at a police station following arrest. However, we did not actually estimate prevalence using a multiplier.

Application of nomination techniques has to fulfil at least three criteria, namely statistical representativeness of the field sample, reliable self-reported data and an unambiguous definition of the target population.

Sampling bias must also be reckoned with in applying nomination techniques. Although we endeavoured to eliminate it, it will always be a factor to some degree. Table 1 summarises schematically the effects sampling bias can have on estimations derived using nomination techniques. As snowball sampling is one of the most widely applied methods for collecting nominee data, we focus on this method in more detail.

Table 1: Effects of sampling bias in nomination estimates

	Sampling bias	Denominator	Effect on estimate of population size
Over-representation	Over-inclusion	Enlarged	Under-estimation
Under-representation	Over-exclusion	Reduced	Over-estimation

A four-stage model of snowball sampling

Snowball sampling involves researchers first orientating themselves in the target population, then making contacts and interviewing respondents. At the end of each interview, respondents are asked to assist in finding new respondents. Chains of respondents are thus generated through referrals from earlier respondents. The sample can be extended on and on by interviewing new referrals. Theoretically, the snowball sampling method is well suited for research within hidden populations of heroin users. It may even make it feasible to recruit a sample that is statistically representative of the entire heroin-using population.

In practice, many so-called 'snowball' studies appear to be site surveys, i.e. surveys among small networks of friends, colleagues, etc. Whilst snowball sampling has been widely used in the social sciences, Biernacki and Waldorf have warned that 'the procedures and problems entailed in its use have received only cursory attention' (Biernacki and Waldorf, 1981). These researchers applied snowball sampling methodology in studying the process of 'natural recovery' from heroin dependence, in order to construct a theoretical model for this phenomenon. They distinguished five different problems in the application of snowball sampling. A later publication by Watters and Biernacki devoted more attention to statistical representativeness

(Watters and Biernacki, 1989). This study is more quantitative and epidemiological in nature. In an outreach experiment on harm reduction, intravenous drug users were issued with bleach which they could use to disinfect used needles. To ensure that no gaps would fall in their field knowledge about the population of users, Watters and Biernacki developed a five-stage strategy they call *targeted sampling.*

I have integrated the various steps of snowball sampling which appear in the works cited above into a model consisting, ideally, of four successive stages: *preparation of the fieldwork; initiating snowballs; chain referrals* and *controlling quality.* These four stages are outlined in Table 2. The model contains all the elements referred to in the above publications as well as some additional components of my own.

Table 2: Structure and analysis of snowball sampling

Preparation of the fieldwork	Initiating snowballs	Chain referrals	Controlling quality
Defining target population			
Initial mapping			
Finding and training field research assistants*			
Ethnographic mapping			
Initial plan by neighbourhood			
	Finding respondents		
	Verifying potential respondents		
		Engaging respondents as referral assistants	
		Starting referral chains	
			Controlling chains and number of cases
			Pacing and monitoring referral chains
			Interim findings shaping questions and instruments
	Revision of of target plans	Revision of target plans	
			Monitoring data quality
			Testing self-report reliability *

* Elements not explicitly mentioned by Biernacki *et al* which have been added by the author.

Preparation of the fieldwork

Preparation begins by tentatively defining the target population. The researcher determines which people are to be studied, in what geographical area and with what objective. Then the whole area to be studied (a city, for example) is divided into appropriate smaller areas (neighbourhoods), and these are charted in more detail *(initial mapping)*. Next, potential research sites are explored more thoroughly by means of field observations and other qualitative methods *(ethnographic mapping)*. The preparatory stage is finished off by deciding at which sites and with which respondents the snowball sample will be initiated *(initial plan)*.

Both preparation and execution of the study demand that the researchers be familiar with the geographical area (city or neighbourhood) and the population to be studied. The recruiting and training of competent field research assistants is therefore a critical element of the preparatory stage. They are of the utmost importance for adequate ethnographic mapping.

Initiating snowballs

The key issue in achieving a statistically representative sample using the snowball method is: where, and with what, potential respondents will the snowballs be started? Potential respondents must be checked for membership in the population – whether they really are frequent heroin users, for example.

Chain referrals

The practicability of snowballing stands or falls with the co-operation of respondents in their role as 'referral assistants'. They must be willing to provide names of potential new respondents and they must be prepared to assist in finding them. This makes extra demands on field research assistants. It is important, too, to verify that the new respondent is indeed the person to whom the researcher has been referred.

Controlling quality

This phase involves the monitoring of the process of chain referrals. On the basis of regular intermediate analyses, it is decided whether or not to extend chains, and ideas are developed about other networks which may be thought to exist within the population, but have not yet been located. Strategies are worked out to establish contacts with them.

> *'Control is exercised in an attempt to ensure that the sample includes an array of respondents that, in qualitative terms, if not rigorous statistical ones, reflect what are thought to be the general characteristics of the population in question.' (Biernacki and Waldorf, 1981, p. 155).*

Besides quality control of the sampling procedure – the focus of Biernacki and his colleagues – monitoring the quality of the *data* reported by respondents is also a must. One way we do this is by testing the consistency of their self-reporting.

My classification into four successive stages is, as I noted, an ideal model. In reality, snowball sampling is a dynamic process, in which findings in later stages can have retroactive consequences for an earlier stage. In this way, for instance, the original definition of the target population (early in Stage 1) may later be adjusted on the basis of information gained during the ethnographic mapping (later in Stage 1). Or interim findings (Stage 4) can give cause to revise target plans (Stages 2 and 3). This feedback mechanism is shown in Table 2 by arrows drawn between stages.

Preparing the fieldwork

Having defined the target population, the next problem was to find it. Our first step was to map the research terrain and explore it ethnographically. We ensured the quality of this geographic and ethnographic mapping by recruiting and deploying field research assistants at an early stage. They were selected on grounds of famil-iarity with sites and networks of the targeted groups. During this first stage of field orientation, we spoke informally with individuals from the target population. We soon learned that both researchers and field assistants must be more than just skilled interviewers. They must also be well known to the drug users or at least well informed about their social worlds, and they must be prepared to hang about exten-sively day and night no matter what the weather. In putting together the field teams, we paid special attention to team members' familiarity with specific categories of potential respondents (gender, age, ethnic background and nationality) and with local sites in order to ensure that the scope of the investigation would be as broad as possible. Some field assistants worked on more than one of the studies. All field teams included at least one experienced current or former heroin user.

Initiating snowballs

Researchers who employ snowball sampling must first and foremost establish a rela-tionship of mutual trust and respect with their initial respondents (at the zero stage of the snowball chain). These initial contacts are often key people such as experi-enced drug users who will go on to vouch for the researcher to their friends and acquaintances, guiding the newcomer safely through the social group under study (Morrison, 1988). Key contacts can also help dispel worries of respondents about the confidentiality of the information given (Hammersley and Morrison, 1987; Morrison, 1988; True and True, 1977). Such worries are not always easily allayed. Ultimately the burden is on the researcher to come across to the respondent as trustworthy. Familiarity with the research population, patience and tact are crucial.

Our goal of statistical representativeness posed specific problems for us in initiating snowballs. Some of them related to the size of the research populations. Especially in dealing with large populations of heroin users, as in Amsterdam, we had to take a whole variety of sub-populations into account. The less these sub-populations overlapped with one another, the smaller the chance that a snowball started in one of them would lead us through referrals into another sub-population. The danger was always present that we would get stranded on top of the iceberg and fail to access hidden users. If we only started snowballs with visible users, we would not automatically wind up meeting hidden ones. The problem is even trickier in places where scarcely any visible users are present. The researcher must then rely entirely on hidden users for initiating snowballs. This type of predicament arises especially in rural areas.

Chain referrals

Respondents were asked to nominate by name or nickname the other users they knew who satisfied our criteria, such as using heroin several days a week. From this list of nominees, we chose the next respondent-to-be and asked the 'referral assistant' to help us find him or her, thereby lengthening our chains of respondents.

The advantage of chain referrals, either randomised or non-random, is that the researcher is introduced to new respondents by someone they know, or at least that the previous respondent can be used as a reference. Such an introduction, of course, is no watertight guarantee of the co-operation of the new respondent.

An important point in the lengthening of chains is which nominee(s) the researcher will choose. If you pick the first person the respondent names, you run the risk of getting stranded in a small sub-group. I have noted above that random selection of respondents at the zero stage of snowball sampling is feasible in theory and sometimes in practice. Why not apply random sampling, we reasoned, at later stages of the chain as well? We worked out this idea into a procedure which was easy to apply in the field. At the close of the interview the respondent was asked, 'What other foreign heroin users do you know personally?' The respondent was to make a numbered list of their names or nicknames, up to a rather arbitrary maximum of 25. The next potential respondent was then chosen on the principle of chance. As the number of nominees per referral assistant could vary, and the random selection had to be performed in a wide range of places, we adopted a flexible procedure. From a pack of playing cards we counted out cards equalling the number of nominees. For the first ten nominees, hearts were used (ace of hearts = nominee 1, two of hearts = nominee 2 etc.). For nominees 11 to 20 clubs were used, and for nominees 21 to 25 diamonds. The next step was to shuffle these cards and draw two of them randomly, corresponding to two of the nominees. We then asked the interviewee to help us find the two randomly selected potential respondents. The first one located was asked to take part.

Since 1985, we have applied the same technique of random chain referral in several field studies. The only variation was that nominees from the appropriate target group were asked for. Obviously the chain referral technique takes a good deal of time, not so much for the interviews (approximately one hour) but for finding the new respondents once drawn. This involves hanging around, making and sustaining contacts with respondents and key informants in the scene, and the targeted search for the new respondents.

Quality of sampling

The main quality criteria are: (i) the extent to which snowballs actually develop from initial contacts through successful referrals; (ii) the length of the chains. I compare the outcomes with those of two other studies of hard-drug users which also applied randomised chain referral.

The degree to which snowballs are actually generated from initial contacts is reflected by the percentage of *loners* within the samples. Loners are zero stage respondents who failed to refer us successfully to another respondent in a chain. As shown in Table 3, almost a quarter (22 per cent) of the respondents in the Heroin Tourist (HT) study were loners. Fewer loners were encountered in the Gooi study (13 per cent), and only 5 per cent in the Conson and the Homeless Youth (HY) studies. The large majority of respondents in all four studies belonged to snowballs.

Table 3: Length of snowballs in four field studies compared to two Dutch cocaine studies

Study	N	Zero stages	Loners	Number of chains	Respondents in chains	Average chain length (loners excluded)
Heroin tourists	382	162	22%	78	78%	3.8
Conson	202	46	5%	35	95%	5.5
Het Gooi	119	34	13%	18	87%	5.7
Homeless youth	137	30	5%	23	95%	5.7
Cocaine Amsterdam (Cohen, 1989)	160	81	27%	39	73%	3.0
Cocaine Rotterdam (Bieleman and De Bie, 1992)	110	84	76%	15	24%	1.7

The snowballs in the four field studies ranged in *length*, i.e. number of cases in the snowball, from two ('two-stage snowball sample') to 14 cases ('14-stage snowball'). Leaving the loners aside, we found that the *total number* of snowball chains in the four studies varied from 18 (Het Gooi) to 78 (HT). The average length of the chains was shortest in the HT study (3.8 respondents) and longest in the Gooi and HY studies (5.7).

Why, then, did proportionally fewer heroin tourists belong to snowball chains (78 per cent), and why were their chains shorter than in the other studies? It would stand to reason that network formation among the foreigners was less extensive (fewer and/or smaller networks of users) than amongst the resident populations in the other three studies. A large proportion of the heroin tourists had not been in Amsterdam for long. It is worth noting, however, that the Italian respondents, whose average stay was comparatively short, were the group most likely to be found in longer chains.

Our four studies with randomised chain referrals are also compared in Table 3 with two other Dutch studies in which similar methodology was applied. In one of them, on non-deviant cocaine use in Amsterdam, 73 per cent of the 160 respondents belonged to chains of referral (Cohen, 1989). In the other, on the nature and extent of cocaine use in Rotterdam, only 24 per cent of the 110 respondents belonged to chains (Bieleman and De Bie, 1992).

In our studies, from 78 per cent to 95 per cent of respondents were in chains, and the chains in our studies are also longer. The Rotterdam cocaine study had an average chain length of 1.7 (loners excluded) and the Amsterdam cocaine study 3.0, compared to 3.8 to 5.7 in our studies. (Calculated for Rotterdam from Bieleman and De Bie (1992, p. 21) and for Amsterdam from Cohen (1989, p. 66).)

In principle, two kinds of explanation can be offered for the fact that we were more successful in building snowballs than the cocaine researchers. One involves possible differences between populations of cocaine users, on the one hand, and the drug-using populations in our studies, which in most cases consisted exclusively or predominantly of heroin users. Differences in chain length could be a consequence of a lower degree of network formation among the former, as we also saw among the heroin tourists.

It would seem plausible that recreational cocaine users are not integrated into networks of other users to the same extent that heroin users are, and furthermore that they would be more reluctant to label themselves as cocaine users in the presence of strangers such as researchers. These factors, of course, would impede the building of snowball chains. Our own experience with cocaine users in the Alkmaar study would seem to confirm this explanation: it took longer to gain access to their network and to induce them to be interviewed than it did with the heroin users (see the 'pub scene' in Figure 1).

The second type of explanation for our more successful snowball chains relates to the quality of the work of the field assistants, for instance their ability to gain the confidence of respondents, or their perseverance when candidate respondents are hard to trace. The fact that in the Amsterdam cocaine study more and longer chains were generated than in the Rotterdam study may imply the influence of such factors. Within the Amsterdam study, interviewers with more experience in drug research succeeded in building more and longer chains than their less experienced colleagues.

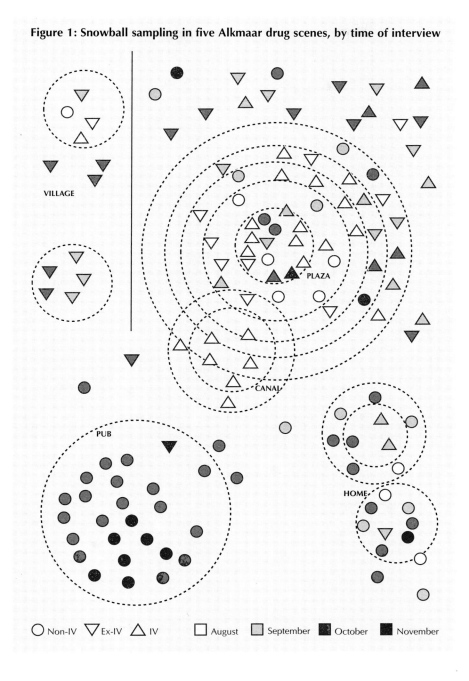

Figure 1: Snowball sampling in five Alkmaar drug scenes, by time of interview

○ Non-IV ▽ Ex-IV △ IV ☐ August ☐ September ■ October ■ November

Statistical representativeness

The key problem in the representativeness of snowball samples of heroin users is that even the best models will always express relationships in terms of probabilities rather than of certainties (Edwards, Arif and Hodgson, 1981). We can therefore never be completely sure that a statistically representative sample has been achieved. As each study progressed, we asked ourselves repeatedly whether we had overlooked potentially existing sub-populations and, if so, how we could still gain access to them.

Here we were heedful of Glaser and Strauss (1967) and later elaboration by Biernacki and Waldorf (1981), Biernacki (1986), and Watters and Biernacki (1989). Researchers and field assistants met at least once a week to discuss how the research was progressing. We also used these meetings to check whether anyone had been interviewed twice. If that was the case, no snowballs were allowed to originate from the second interview. Also, no new snowball was to be started within networks or scenes where we knew one already existed.

One way of testing whether a sample of heroin users is statistically representative is to compare it to another sample. Towards the beginning of this paper, I cited an Amsterdam study in which institutionalised heroin users were compared with a street sample of users and I aired my reservations that both types of sample may have tapped the same part of the iceberg and failed to consider hidden users. In our Alkmaar study we tested this supposition.

As previously noted, our goal there was to reach the entire target population. We started with the most visible and accessible members and only gradually came into contact with the hidden users. This progression can clearly be seen in Figure 1. The most visible users in the Plaza Scene could be interviewed at a relatively early stage (light shading), while the more peripheral users tended to be interviewed later (dark shading).

Figure 2 reveals further that members of the Plaza Scene in particular can be characterised as institutionalised users. In this illustration, the dark-shaded respondents had taken part in the local methadone dispensing programme, Brijder, within the past six months. The black symbols represent users who had been involved both in the methadone programme and in other local drug care activities. The light-shaded ones took part in the latter activities but not in the methadone programme, while the white symbols refer to respondents who made no use at all of local drug care programmes during the period in question. The distinctive character of the Pub Scene is revealed here once again: no respondents from this scene had been in touch with local drug care during the six-month period. The same applied to the Village Scene members, who were from smaller communities in the vicinity of Alkmaar.

Comparison of Figures 1 and 2 shows that the most publicly visible users are largely identical to the institutionalised users, whereas the hidden users are institutionalised to a very limited extent.

Figure 2: Contacts with Alkmaar drug care services in past 6 months, by scenes

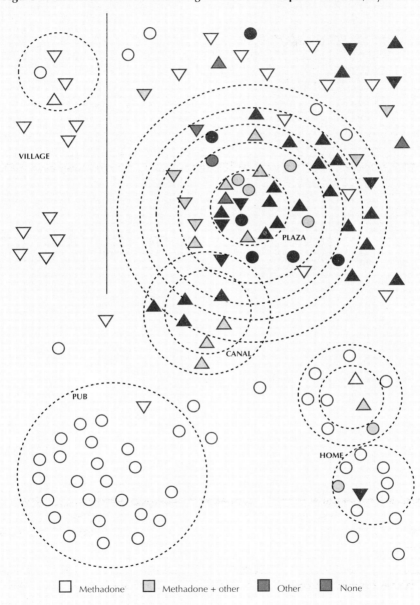

Social structures of snowballs

As we have known since the classic studies of Becker and Zinberg, patterns of drug use depend heavily on the *settings* in which the drug use occurs (Becker, 1963; Zinberg, 1984). Social actors such as friends play a crucial role in these settings. The evolution of drug careers is also strongly dependent on users' social environment.

In employing snowball samples we cannot rule out that certain sub-groups will be over- or under-represented. To assess better how representative our field studies were of the target populations, I have analysed the structure of the snowball chains on the basis of the variables 'age', 'gender' and 'nationality/ethnicity' and compared the respondents in long chains (5 or more respondents) with other respondents who were 'loners' or members of short chains (2 to 4 respondents). These findings are illustrated in Table 4, which depicts typical examples of chains of referral.

Table 4: Chain referral structure of longer snowballs

Age-1	46 → 34 → 23 → 44 → 25 → 28
Age-2	21 → 21 → 21 → 20 → 28 → 23 → 26 → 24 → 21 → 23 → 31
Age-3	34 → 35 → 36 → 36 → 42
Gender-1	M → M → F → M → M → F → M → M → M → M
Gender-2	M → M → M → M → M → M → M → M → M
Gender-3	F → F → F → F → F
Ethnicity-1	NL → NL → NL → NL → NL → NL → NL → NL → NL
Ethnicity-2	NL → NL → Sur → NL → Oth → NL
Ethnicity-3	NL → Mor → Mor → Sur → NL → NL → NL → Ind → NL → NL → Ind
Nationality-1	Ger → Ger → Ger → Ger → Ger → Ger → Ger
Nationality-2	Ger → US → Ger → Ger → Ö → Ö → Ger
Nationality-3	It → It → It → It → It → It → It → It → It
Nationality-4	It → It → SA → Por → It → It

The analysis of the snowballs suggests that the social networks of most heroin users are mixed in age and gender. Age differences have no evident determining influence on their social structure. Loners and short-chain respondents do not appear to be over- or under-represented in the field samples. This would seem to favour the statistical representativeness of the samples.

As for gender, networks of street prostitutes could be a source of disproportionate representation of women or certain types of women in samples, thereby threatening statistical representativeness. This problem arises especially in urban areas where street prostitution is practised. In those urban areas with bigger populations of heroin users, such as Amsterdam, there is a stronger tendency towards homogeneous social networks based on ethnicity and language. This is also an obvious threat to representativeness.

Networks and friends

Analysis of social networks directly on the basis of our snowball chains would have the limitation that we imposed certain restrictions on referrals. Therefore, we also asked respondents to tell us about some characteristics of the nationality or ethnic background of the five persons they were in closest contact with (Table 5).

Table 5: Networks of friends: ethnic background and nationality in five field studies

Study	No. of friends	Ethnic Dutch	Resident ethnic minorities*	Other nationalities		Hard drug user	Non user
				Own	Other		
Heroin Tourists**	885	24%	5%	45%	26%	78%	22%
Conson	1002	59%	30%	3%	7%	63%	37%
- Dutch	588	79%	13%	-	8%	60%	40%
- Surinamese	279	22%	76%	-	2%	67%	33%
- Moroccan	45	29%	71%	-	-	71%	29%
- Other	90	60%	21%	19%		70%	30%
Homeless Youth	543	76%	6%	14%	4%	n.a.	n.a.
- Dutch	413	88%	6%	7%			
- Surinamese	34	68%	32%	-	-		
- Moroccan	75	33%	62%	5%			
- Other	21	29%	10%	62%			
Het Gooi	530	79%	17%	4%		60%	40%
Alkmaar	642	85%	15%	-	-	51%	49%

* chiefly Surinamese and Moroccan ** recorded only in 1986.

We may conclude that the social networks of frequent heroin users are composed in large part of fellow heroin users. Degree of urbanisation has no significant influence on the proportion of users in networks: more or less the same network composition obtains among local Amsterdam users (Conson) as among users in Het Gooi and Alkmaar. We can interpret this, at least in some measure, as the same strong orientation to one's fellows that we encounter among other citizens (work mates, professional colleagues). However, a further explanation is that frequent users of heroin find themselves isolated from the rest of society. This can account for why the heroin tourists are the most strongly isolated. Their stay in Amsterdam is comparatively short and they are unlikely to have contacts there from their pre-heroin days.

Like the snowballs analysed above, the friendship networks of most drug users and homeless youth, especially in Amsterdam, are based heavily on their own national or ethnic background. The populations studied constitute relatively closed networks. Within them we find sub-populations which are ethnically rather homogeneous and which overlap one another only slightly.

Conclusions

When applying a nomination technique, snowball sampling will frequently be used to collect data. However, snowball sampling itself requires more than just interviewing a sample of persons which is easy to catch. Since populations of heroin users (and users of other drugs as well) are often hidden, a well-structured sampling procedure is a prerequisite. It is advised to stratify the nomination data (e.g. by ethnicity or gender).

References

van Ameijden E.J.C. (1994) *Evaluation of AIDS-prevention measures among drug users: the Amsterdam experience,* Wageningen, Posen and Looijen.

Becker H.S. (1963) *Outsiders. Studies in the sociology of deviance,* New York, The Free Press.

Bieleman B. and De Bie E. (1992) *Between the lines. A study of the nature and extent of cocaine use in Rotterdam,* Groningen, Intraval.

Biernacki P. (1986) *Pathways from heroin addiction; recovery without treatment,* Philadelphia, Temple University Press.

Biernacki P. and Waldorf D. (1981) 'Snowball sampling: problems and techniques of chain referral sampling', *Sociological Methods and Research,* 10 (2), 141-163.

Cohen P.D.A. (1989) *Cocaine use in non-deviant subcultures,* Amsterdam, University of Amsterdam, Institute for Social Geography.

Edwards G., Arif A. and Hodgson R. (1981) 'Nomenclature and classification of drug- and alcohol-related problems. A WHO Memorandum', *Bulletin WHO,* 59, 225-242.

Glaser B. and Strauss A. (1967) *The discovery of grounded theory. Strategies for qualitative research,* Chicago, Aldline.

Hammersley R.H. and Morrison V.L. (1987) 'Effects of polydrug use on the criminal activities of heroin users', *British Journal of Addiction,* 82 (8), 899-906.

Morrison V.L. (1988) 'Observations and snowballing. Useful tools for research into illicit drug use?' *Social Pharmacology,* 2 (3), 247-271.

True W.R. and True J.H. (1977) 'Network analysis as methodological approach in a Latin city', in: R.S. Weppner (ed) *Street ethnography. Selected studies of crime and drug use in natural setting,* Beverly Hills, Sage.

Watters J.K. and Biernacki P. (1989) 'Targeted sampling: options for the study of hidden populations', *Social Problems,* 36 (4), 416-430.

Zinberg N.E. (1984) *Drug, set and setting. The basis for controlled intoxicant use,* New Haven, Yale University Press.

COMBINING AND COMPARING DIFFERENT ESTIMATION METHODS

PART VI

INTRODUCTION

by Alan Quirk

T he previous sections of this monograph have focused on elaborating the strengths and weaknesses of particular estimation techniques. The chapters comprising this section examine the use of two or more estimation methods combined, in order to compare the results obtained by different methods and to improve the estimation of drug problems within a city or country. Drug use is not a static phenomenon. The history of drug use across Europe shows major changes, with some periods experiencing a rapid rise of problem drug use and others a levelling of new cases.

Ludwig Kraus examines the applicability of 'classical' statistical estimation approaches, which generally provide a cross-sectional estimate of prevalence at a point in time, and 'system dynamics' models which attempt to show changes in the extent of drug use over time. He uses examples drawn from studies of heroin and 'hard' drug users in Germany. Kraus also describes how system dynamics models, by integrating various sources of data, simulate the time-related processes of drug use. It is argued that this approach is particularly useful in that it provides estimates of both the incidence and prevalence of drug use in different periods.

Dirk Korf provides a useful summary of the range of methods which can be used to estimate the number of heroin users in a country. These are household and school surveys, extrapolations from drug seizures, drug deaths and other indirect parameters, ethnographic mapping, case counting, capture-recapture (CRC) and nomination techniques.

The relative utility of each method is discussed using data from various European countries. In particular, he highlights the limitations of trying to draw conclusions from a correlation of trends in an indicator such as drug seizures and a measure of harm from drug use – drug-related deaths. In some countries there is a positive correlation between these indices, in others, the correlation is absent. Korf goes on to compare CRC with nomination techniques. While it is acknowledged that no exact estimate can be reached, CRC nonetheless seems to offer a reasonable estimate of the numbers of resident problem drug users.

Findings from a more localised study in Germany are presented by Wolf Kirschner. Kirschner presents a Berlin study which compared the results obtained by CRC with those obtained from a system of anonymous monitoring undertaken by a sample of physicians (ANOMO). The statistical requirements and assumptions are discussed, and the findings derived from them are presented. Methodological problems associated with ANOMO are examined, particularly those of documentation bias and double- or multiple-reporting of cases.

Kirschner concludes that such a combined approach can improve our understanding of local populations of injecting drug users.

The success of estimation projects will depend not just on the technical competence of the investigators and the appropriateness of the estimation techniques, but also on the quality of the data available and the co-operation of agencies and subjects from whom data are collected.

Estimations made under conditions of limited resources for epidemiological research, a comparative lack of prior knowledge about the phenomenon, or an inhospitable socio-economic environment, are described in the final three chapters.

Zsuzsanna Elekes gives an honest account of the practical difficulties she encountered in estimating the prevalence of illicit drug use in Budapest. The quality of data available from the police, health institutions and foster homes was found to be poor, which casts doubt on the validity of estimates derived from these sources.

Elekes describes the considerable mistrust which the researchers encountered when dealing with institutional staff. Similar suspicions characterised key informants in the snowball study, making it difficult for it to be carried out. Elekes concludes that, in such a context, snowballing may be an ineffective way of mapping non-registered opiate users. It is argued that the greatest problem facing epidemiological research on drug use in Hungary is the widespread tendency for negative attitudes towards illicit drug users.

Janusz Sierosławski and Antoni Zieliński describe the methods they used to estimate the prevalence of opiate injection and addiction in Poland. The authors describe how, in a changing political environment, their scientific estimations have had to compete with those from advocates and an alarmist media.

The authors discuss the three types of estimation undertaken: a snowball study in two regions; estimates derived from in-patient drug treatment data; and CRC. Their estimates strongly suggest that those presented in the media overestimated the extent of opiate addiction. The authors argue that the increasing sophistication of epidemiological techniques is making it hard for politicians to ignore their findings.

The importance of producing good quality epidemiological information is also stressed by Dušan Nolimal. He describes the methods of secondary data analysis, key informant estimation and snowballing which were used to estimate the prevalence of heroin use in Slovenia.

Although the primary goal of the three studies was to identify high risk groups for the purposes of targeting appropriate interventions, the data nonetheless allow for prevalence estimations to be made. The problems encountered in the studies are discussed. It is argued that, in light of an economic and political environment which may be conducive to further increases in the prevalence of heroin injection, it is essential that the intervention response be based on sound epidemiological data rather than anecdotal evidence.

In the final chapter, Richard Hartnoll concentrates on how to assess the validity of prevalence estimates, especially when the prevalence drug use patterns are changing, and how to interpret what the resulting prevalence rates mean within the context where they may be used. These questions are addressed through examples from the author's research on drug indicators and prevalence estimation methods in London in the 1980s, supplemented by more recent experience.

The first question is approached by comparing different estimation methods over successive years to reach a 'best estimate' of 'real' prevalence levels and trends in opiate dependence based on an analysis of the probable direction of error of each estimate.

The second question is approached by comparing the prevalence estimates for the years concerned with a 'package' of other indirect opiate indicators (treatment, police arrests, seizures of heroin, mortality, morbidity) over a longer period of time spanning the years for which prevalence estimates were obtained. This analysis indicates that although the combined package of indirect indicators do not add information about absolute prevalence, they are very useful for validating the trends observed over time. This analysis also provides valuable insight into how indicators behave with respect to the time-lag between changes in 'real' prevalence and the point when these changes are reflected in the different indicators.

The inclusion of the results of simultaneous sociological research on local drug use patterns was essential for interpreting the figures and trends reflected in the estimates and indicators.

The chapter concludes that prevalence estimation is not just a scientific procedure of applying formulae, but one that also involves a creative process of fitting together different types and levels of information and testing if they are consistent so as to achieve a coherent picture of the whole that best accounts for the diversity of the available data.

CHAPTER 18

STATISTICAL ESTIMATION METHODS AND SYSTEM DYNAMICS MODELS

by Ludwig Kraus

Only a minority of drug users will establish contact with a drug surveillance system. The majority will remain undetected, never using available counselling services, treatment centres or making contact with law enforcement agencies. These users form a 'hidden' population.

In this chapter, I will discuss two methods used to estimate the size and composition of the hidden population of heroin injectors and hard drug users (all drugs except cannabis) in Germany: 'classical' statistical estimation methods, which generally provide a 'snapshot' of prevalence at a point in time, and system dynamics models, which attempt to show changes in the extent of drug use over time.

A taxonomy of methods

We can make three general distinctions between statistical estimation methods and system dynamics models which are helpful in establishing which is the most appropriate method to use.

Firstly, the dynamic nature of the population has to be considered. System dynamics models produce estimates by simulating the interaction of multiple data indicators over a specified period of time in an 'open' study population. Here, the possible departure and entry of individuals into a drug-using population is modelled within the estimation process. Statistical estimation methods, by contrast, commonly assess the size of a population by extrapolating a single data indicator at a single point in time. These do not usually allow for significant changes within the study population, such as death or rehabilitation, and are best used in estimating 'closed' populations.

Secondly, the type of data used in each estimation method will often be different. The aim of system dynamics models is to construct an interrelated network of indicators which will estimate or describe changes in the study population. Often, if such indicators are not available as either direct or indirect data, 'unobserved' variables will be used. These are assumed values, usually based on educated insights, which are used to carry out the estimation. Statistical estimation methods, however, are normally based upon direct and indirect data.

Thirdly, an awareness of the integration and ease with which data from different reporting systems can be compared should be maintained. If such data contain explicit identifier information and if it is possible to gain access to this information across a number of reporting systems, then CRC methods can be used. However, if political and ethical reasons dictate that such a direct exchange of identifier information is not possible, system dynamics models can accommodate for this by again using unobserved variables.

In short, the main difference between the two approaches is that statistical estimation methods extrapolate their assessments from the observable properties of individual drug users at a single point in time, whereas system dynamics models build up an interrelated network of data indicators whose interaction over a period of time is simulated through a series of calculations (Wickens, 1993).

National prevalence estimations

In Germany, a variety of national data sources is available for estimating the number of drug users. These sources are outlined below in Table 1.

Table 1: National prevalence estimations in Germany

Method	Data	Assumption	Target Population	Estimation
Population survey and Mortality Multiplier Method	Sample	Dark-field	Injecting heroin users	70,000 - 105,000
	Drug-related deaths	Mortality		
Multiplier benchmark method	Drug-related deaths	Dark-field	Hard drug users	91,000 - 143,000 Hard drug users
	Register of drug use	Duration of drug use		
System dynamics model	Register of drug use by age	Age at onset of drug use	Heroin users	100,000 Heroin users
		Termination of drug use		
		Registration in surveillance system		

Statistical estimation methods

Population surveys and the Mortality Multiplier Method

Although we could have estimated the number of heroin injectors using drug-related deaths statistics and a multiplier alone, we decided to combine such estimates with data from the German population survey of 1990 in an attempt to calculate to what degree the survey underestimated the total number of injecting heroin users.

The 1990 German population survey used self-completion postal questionnaires in a sample of 19,208 individuals representatively drawn from the German population. These individuals, aged between 12 and 39, were asked about their drug use. Although the survey achieved a satisfactory response rate (62 per cent), only eight respondents reported having injected heroin in the last twelve months. This represented only 0.042 per cent of the total sample and, consequently, could not be used to generate accurate estimations of the total heroin-using population (IFT et al, 1994).

To calculate the factor by which this population survey underestimated the total number of injecting heroin users, that is the 'hidden' population, a series of assumptions were made about those individuals who had not responded to the survey and the probability of their using heroin (Table 2). On the basis of a previous study in America (Caspar, 1992), it was assumed that a small proportion of the non-respondents would display the same prevalence of drug use as those who responded to the survey. However, it was also assumed that the substantial proportion of non-respondents would have a higher prevalence of drug use.

These assumptions were then related to estimates derived from the drug-related death multiplier and a series of possible values were calculated (IFT et al, 1994).

Table 2: Estimation based on a population survey

M:	Population of size N
Z:	Subset of injecting drug users
S:	Representative sample
S_1:	Respondents (proportion of responders Q_1 = 0.62)
S_2:	Neutral non-respondents with the same prevalence as the responders (proportion Q_2 is assumed to be 0.2)
S_3:	Critical non-respondents with a higher prevalence (proportion Q_3 is assumed to be 0.18)
S_3:	Estimated probability of a positive case of S_1 or S_2 (0.00042)
$P_{1,2}$:	= X * $P_{1,2}$: Estimated probability of a positive case of S_3
	Estimated size of Z: N * [$P_{1,2}$ * ($Q_1 + Q_2$) + P_3 * Q_3]

Given that the number of drug-related deaths in 1991 equalled 2,100 and assuming a mortality rate between 2 to 3 per cent each year, it was estimated that there were between 70,000 to 105,000 German drug users. At X = 1 the number of injecting users yielded an estimate of 10,000 people.

These estimates indicate that the German population survey underestimated the number of injecting heroin users by a factor of between seven and ten.

Estimates based on police drug register and drug-related deaths statistics: multiplier benchmark method

In Germany, law enforcement data collected on the number of drug offenders include information on the substances consumed by an individual (excluding cannabis). However, drug offenders are only included in the data the first time they are charged and no distinction is made between drug-dependent and episodic users. Additionally, the regular comparison of national drug-related deaths statistics and the registered drug user data allows the German police to keep a record of previously unknown individuals. In the last ten years, this disparity has ranged from 30 per cent to 55 per cent.

To estimate the number of first registered hard drug users, the number of cases known to the police between 1982 and 1991 (n = 65,000) were counted. This ten-year period was chosen to reflect the findings of studies based on treated drug users which suggest this to be the mean duration of an individual's drug use (Robins, 1979; Bschor, 1987; Marks, 1990). A multiplier was then estimated using a ratio of the total number of drug-related deaths to the number of these deceased individuals previously registered by the police as hard drug users. Again, this comparison was made over a ten-year period.

The resulting figures ranged from 70 per cent to 45 per cent, which related to a factor of between 1.4 to 2.2. From this we were able to estimate that the number of hard drug users in Germany was between 91,000 and 143,000 individuals (Table 3).

Table 3: Estimation based on police drug register and drug-related death statistics

K:	Number of current users of hard drugs
E:	Number of first registered drug users in past 10 years
F:	Dt/Dn, ratio of total number of drug users in the population and the number known to the police
Dt:	Number of all drug-related deaths in a given year
Dn:	Number of drug-related deaths registered by the police in a given year

The total number of hard drug users registered by the police for the years 1982-1991 was E = 65,000.

$K = E*F$

With E = 65,000 and F = 1.4, K = 91,000
F = 2.2, K = 143,000

System dynamics model estimations

To derive an estimate of the annual incidence of heroin use, a system dynamics model originally used to investigate the changing age distribution of initial drug use over the last two decades was employed (Herbst and Kraus, 1995). In order to simulate the annual number of first registered heroin users who are classified by age according to their incidence of first registration, the number of users who started using heroin in each year had to be calculated. If the annual number of new heroin users is known, the prevalence can be calculated.

Assumptions

Although data on the number of registered heroin users in Germany did exist, a system dynamics model required any unobserved variables to be given assumed values. In this case, these unobserved variables related to the onset and termination of heroin use, the registration of heroin use and the age distribution of the onset of heroin use. The resulting assumptions are summarised below:

- the age at onset of heroin use is log-normal distributed with a peak at age 18-20;
- heroin consumption started in the late 1960s and initially affected younger age groups;
- the time period in which heroin is taken is Weibull distributed, beginning with the onset of heroin use, includes any registration of the user into police drug offence records and finishes with the termination of heroin use;
- process parameters remain constant over time.

Three other assumptions were also integrated into the system dynamics model. These, however, were taken from previous academic research which arguably improves the validity of the model and its resulting estimates:

- the average duration of drug dependency reported in the literature was estimated at ten years (Robins, 1979; Bschor, 1987; Marks, 1990);
- only 45 per cent to 70 per cent of drug-related deaths are recorded in the police register of drug offenders (Bundeskriminalamt, 1994);
- the age distribution of the onset of drug use has a risk function which is positively skewed with a long tail and a maximum at age 18 to 20 (Herbst *et al*, 1994; Chen and Kandel, 1995).

Data

The annual number of registered heroin users was split into five age groups. To allow for any changes in the age distribution of the population, the incidence of registration was divided by the population size in each calendar year. Those users younger than 14 years of age and older than 39 years of age were excluded from the simulation because of missing lower and upper limits. However, heroin incidence rates in both age groups were small and no significant bias was encountered.

Simulation process

The final estimation was accomplished in three steps:

Firstly, the initial values for the parameters of the termination and registration functions were chosen. Given the total number of registered heroin users in each calendar year, the total incidence of heroin users at time *t* was calculated.

Secondly, parameters relating to the age distribution of the onset of heroin use were chosen. From this, the number of heroin users in each age group over successive years was determined. Additionally, the registration process of those starting heroin use was simulated and those heroin users who were assumed to have terminated their drug consumption were subtracted from the population.

Thirdly, the estimated incidence values for each age group in each year were compared with the observed data. In an iterative procedure, the model parameters were systematically varied with the aim of minimising any differences between predicted and observed data.

Results

Figure 1 shows the best results for the simulation. There is a peak incidence in 1976 followed by a peak prevalence between 1978 and 1980. There was a further peak incidence between 1989 and 1991, with a corresponding peak prevalence in 1992.

Figure 1: Number of registered heroin users, estimated incidence of heroin users and estimate prevalence of heroin users

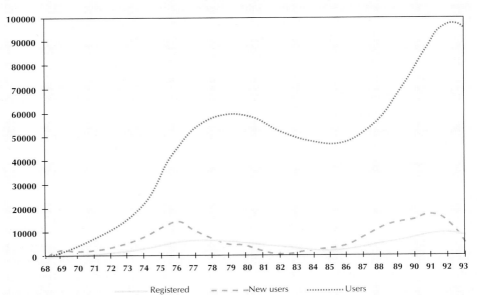

The mean duration of heroin consumption was found to be twelve years and the mean duration period until the user was registered was seven years. This corresponds to the respective mean duration of drug use stated in the literature. The decline in the number of estimated drug users between 1980 and 1986 is corroborated both by treatment statistics (Simon *et al*, 1994) and drug-related deaths statistics (Bundeskriminalamt, 1994).

Conclusions

This chapter has examined the applicability of statistical estimation and system dynamics models in estimating the total population of heroin and hard drug users in Germany. Although no single method is perfect, and although a multiple-method and multiple-data approach are recommended at all times, the use of system dynamics models appears to be particularly promising in a country such as Germany.

Dynamics models simulate the time-related processes connected to drug use by integrating different sources of data and other available information. Consequently, a system dynamics model can only be as good as the data it utilises. The variety of direct and indirect data available on a national level in Germany from law enforcement, health, education and social service agencies makes such an approach particularly suitable for national prevalence estimates.

References

Bschor, F. (1987) 'Erfahrungen mit Drogenabhängigen', *Der Kriminalist*, 323-325.

Bundeskriminalamt (1994) *Rauschgift Jahresbericht 1993*, Wiesbaden.

Caspar, R. P. (1992) 'Follow-up of respondents in 1990', in F. Turner, J.T. Lessler and J.C. Gfroerer (eds), *Survey measurement of drug use. Methodological studies*, 155-173, DHSS Pub. No. (ADM) 92-1929, Washington, DC: U.S. Government Printing Office.

Chen, K. and Kandel, D.K. (1995) 'The natural history of drug use from adolescence to the mid-thirties in a general population sample', *American Journal of Public Health*, 85 (1), 41-47.

Herbst, K. and Kraus, L. (1995) 'Die "Verschiebung" des Einstiegsalters bei Heroinkonsumenten: Eine Studie zur Epidemiologie des Drogenkonsums', *Zeitschrift für Klinische Psychologie*, 24, 90-97.

Herbst, K., Schumann, J. and Kraus, L. (1994) 'Zusatz- und Kontrolluntersuchung im Rahmen der Bundesstudie des Bundesministeriums für Gesundheit: "Repräsentativerhebung zum Konsum und Mißbrauch von illegalen Drogen, alkoholischen Getränken, Medikamenten und Tabakwaren", IFT-Berichte Bd. 73, München: IFT Institut für Therapieforschung.

IFT Institut für Therapieforschung, München, Institut für Rechtsmedizin, Universität Hamburg und Bundeskriminalamt, Wiesbaden (1994) *Report on the methods of estimating the extent of the drug problem in Germany*, IFT-Research Report Series, Vol. 71 E, München: Institut für Therapieforschung.

Marks, J. A. (1990) 'Staatlich abgegebene Drogen: Eine absurde Politik?' in D. Ladewig (Hrsg.), *Drogen und Alkohol*, 108-128, Lausanne: ISPA-Press.

Robins, L. N. (1979) 'Addict careers', in R. Dupont, A. Goldstein and J. O'Donell (eds), *Handbook on drug abuse*, 325-326, Washington D.C.: National Institute on Drug Abuse.

Simon, R., Strobl, M., Hüllinghorst, R., Bühringer, G., Helas, I. and Schmidtobreick, B. (1994) *Jahresstatistik 1993 der ambulanten Beratungs- und Behandlungsstellen für Suchtkranke in der Bundesrepublik Deutschland*, Freiburg: EBIS-Bericht Bd. 19, München: Institut für Therapieforschung.

Wickens, Th.D. (1993) 'Quantitative methods for estimating the size of a drug-using population', *Journal of Drug Issues*, 23 (2), 185-216.

COMPARISON OF DIFFERENT ESTIMATION METHODS IN THE NETHERLANDS

by Dirk J. Korf

Statistics on trends in heroin use are of general interest for the planning of socio-medical and legal control facilities and for evaluating the effects of formal control strategies. Is it possible to estimate how the number of heroin users has evolved in a country? To answer this question, I will discuss several methods that can be used to estimate the numbers of heroin users:

- household and school surveys;
- extrapolations from drug seizures;
- extrapolations from drug deaths;
- extrapolations from other indirect parameters;
- ethnographic mapping, case counting and nomination;
- capture/recapture.

Household and school surveys

Household and school surveys and censuses are the most common ways of measuring the prevalence of licit and illicit drug use. However, especially when it comes to heroin use, population surveys are mainly studies of non-users (Hartnoll, 1993). Self-reported lifetime prevalence of heroin use in school and household surveys is commonly around or below one per cent, and the rate of recent use is far lower (Table 1). Such a low rate reflects the low prevalence heroin use in the general public. But because heroin users are so rare in general populations, probability sampling methods can seldom yield accurate approximations of the prevalence of heroin use. These are extremely costly, with huge samples needed, and hence are rarely feasible. The validity of estimates of heroin use based on population surveys is further undermined by high non-response and denial rates within the target population.

Sometimes prevalence rates within certain age groups or geographical areas may still be high enough to allow estimates to be made. In the 1994 Amsterdam household survey, the highest lifetime prevalence rates for heroin (3.1 per cent) were found among 30-39 year-olds (Sandwijk *et al*, 1995). By the end of the 1970s, young males in five health districts in Harlem (New York) were reporting opiate use seven to ten

Table 1: Self-reported heroin use in nine surveys in the Netherlands

Authors	Year	Survey method	Population	Ages	N.	Sometime use	Current use	Recent use	Current use
Sijlbing (1984)	1983	Household	National	15-24	1,306	1.0%	—	—	—
Plomp, Kuipers & Van Oers (1990)	1988/89	School	National	12-18	5,596	0.5%	0.3%	—	0.3%
Korf et al (1990)	1989	Household	Suburban	15-39	2,972	0.5%	(<0.05%)	(<0.05%)	(<0.05%)
Sandwijk, Westerterp & Musterd (1988)	1987	Household	Amsterdam	12+	4,360	—	—	0.3%	0.2%
Sandwijk, Cohen & Musterd (1991)	1989/90	Household	Amsterdam	12+	4,225	1.1%	0.1%	—	(<0.05%)
Kuipers, Mensink & De Zwart (1993)	1992	School	National	12-20	7,216	0.7%	—	—	0.2%
Korf & Van der Steenhoven (1994)	1993	School	Amsterdam	14-22	679	(0)	(0)	(0)	(0)
Korf, Nabben & Schreuders (1995)	1994	School	Amsterdam	14-24	1,761	(0)	(0)	(0)	(0)
Sandwijk et al (1995)	1994	Household	Amsterdam	12+	4,364	1.3%	0.3%	0.3%	0.1%

Table 2: Self-reported "hard" drug use among "high-risk" populations in four field studies in Amsterdam

Sample	Year	N.	Age	Heroin		Cocaine		Amphetamines		Ecstasy	
				Sometime	Current	Sometime	Current	Sometime	Current	Sometime	Current
1 Homeless Youth	1988	137	13-23	39%*	28%*	50%	30%	35%	6%	—	—
2 Coffee shops	1990	332	14-48	18%	1%	48%	15%	34%	7%	38%	9%
3 Non-residential clients	1993	105	13-25	8%	2%	20%	9%	16%	7%	23%	11%
4 Coffee shops	1994	142	15-25	3%	<1%	45%	21%	18%	4%	56%	30%

* Opiates, including heroin. Sources: 1) Korf & Hoogenhout 1990; 2) Korf, Blanken & Nabben 1991; 3) Korf & Van der Steenhoven 1994; 4) Korf, Nabben & Schreuders 1995.

times higher than in the city as a whole (Clayton and Voss, 1991). Results of four field studies that we have conducted in Amsterdam since 1988 also indicate that site surveys among 'high-risk' populations may yield higher prevalence rates (Table 2).

Extrapolations from drug seizures

In the case of licit drugs, extrapolations can be made from direct parameters, such as production figures or tax data. Average consumption – e.g. litres of pure alcohol per capita per annum – can be computed, and the number of frequent or problem users can be estimated by means of mathematical formulae. These kinds of macro-data are not available for illicit drugs.

As an alternative, quantities of confiscated drugs or other criminal justice data on drug offences could be used as indirect parameters. Since data on amounts of illicit drugs seized by customs and police are available in many countries, they seem to be the most appropriate source for cross-national comparisons.

If we know what percentage of an illicit drug destined for consumption is being confiscated, we can extrapolate the total consumption within a certain geographic area, for example a country (for formulae, see Korf, 1995). Assuming we also know the average consumption per user in the same area, we can calculate the total number of users there by dividing the total consumption by the average consumption per user. Where the average consumption is unknown, but may be assumed to be stable, we can still extrapolate trends in the size of the drug-using population: an increase or decrease would then correlate linearly with the extrapolated total consumption. Furthermore, if the proportion being impounded also remains unknown, but may nevertheless be presumed stable, fluctuations in drug seizures will correlate linearly with the number of users.

Heroin seizures

Assuming now that both the average consumption and the percentage confiscated are indeed stable, what can we then conclude from heroin seizures as predictors of trends in the size of heroin-using populations? Figure 1 shows annual heroin seizures from 1981 until 1990 in five EC countries (the United Kingdom, West Germany, Denmark, Belgium and the Netherlands). In these countries, the amount of confiscated heroin soared from around 400 kg in 1981 to some 2,300 kg in 1990. Thus, if seizures are indeed valid indicators for trends in heroin taking, the number of users in 1990 would have been nearly five times higher than in 1981.

A closer look at the heroin seizures reveals marked differences between countries. During the period in question, the amount of heroin confiscated in the Netherlands was substantially higher than that in other 'small' countries such as Denmark and Belgium. One possibility is simply that more heroin was being transported to the Netherlands than to these countries.

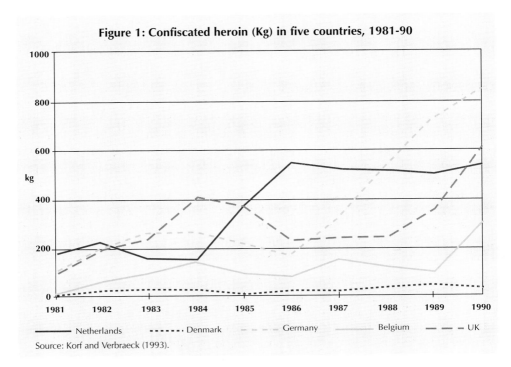

Figure 1: Confiscated heroin (Kg) in five countries, 1981-90

Source: Korf and Verbraeck (1993).

With reference to the assumptions formulated above, the difference could also be explained by three other factors or a combination thereof:

- in the Netherlands a larger share of the total amount of heroin brought into the country was seized;
- the number of heroin users there is much higher;
- the average consumption per user there is much higher.

Between 1981 and 1985, Dutch heroin seizures fluctuated considerably, but from 1986 to 1990 the annual amount confiscated was rather stable (around 500 kg). In Germany, by contrast, it increased sharply during the latter period. Assuming that in Germany average consumption and proportion of the total amount of heroin being confiscated has likewise been stable over the years, this would point to a rising number of heroin users in Germany alongside a stable number in the Netherlands.

Comparison of heroin and cocaine seizures

Another way of verifying the validity of extrapolations based on the amount of confiscated heroin is to look at trends in seizures of other drugs, both cross-nationally and longitudinally. If we posit a linear relationship between seizures and consumption, the seizures would indicate a sharp increase in cocaine use (Figure 2). One could conclude that cocaine use in the five countries more than doubled in just one year, between 1989 and 1990. An overall rising trend is evident for the three illicit drugs illustrated. This is not, however, the case for all drugs, as we showed for amphetamines in another publication (Korf and Verbraeck, 1993). For this drug, fluctuations appeared within such a narrow time window that a constant linear correlation between national seizures and national consumption would be highly dubious.

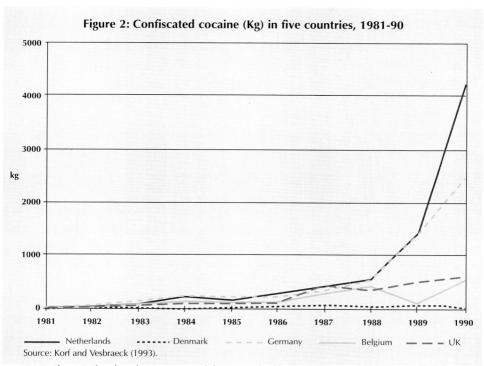

Figure 2: Confiscated cocaine (Kg) in five countries, 1981-90

Source: Korf and Vesbraeck (1993).

In 1990, the Netherlands accounted for over half of all the cocaine seized in the five countries being considered. However, longitudinal trends in cocaine use in the Netherlands show, at least for Amsterdam, a rather stable pattern since the late 1980s (Sandwijk, Westerterp and Musterd, 1988; Sandwijk, Cohen and Musterd, 1991; Sandwijk et al, 1995). The vast differences in the scale of drug seizures between the Netherlands and surrounding countries may also reflect the function of the former as a port of transit for the European drugs market (Korf and Verbraeck, 1993). Moreover, the amount of drugs seized can depend on differences in drug control strategies.

We may conclude that while trends in drug seizures may sometimes parallel trends in other criminal justice indicators, this by no means guarantees the validity of drug seizures as indicators of drug consumption. The correlation could be spurious, the co-variation being caused by a third variable. Trends in both drug seizures and drug use could even be causally related to criminal justice interventions. This leads us to the conclusion that fluctuations in drug hauls correlate linearly with neither drug consumption nor the number of users, all other factors being equal. Drug seizures would therefore not appear to be a valid indicator of trends in drug use.

Extrapolations from drug deaths

Other indirect parameters also suggest a growing number of heroin users in Germany during the late 1980s and early 1990s. One of these parameters is the number of registered drug fatalities. Extrapolation from overdose death statistics is a well-known and, perhaps the most widely applied, procedure to estimate the number of heroin users. In the international literature, mortality rates amongst heroin addicts are normally estimated at one to two per cent per year (Brinkman, 1985). A constant, linear relationship has often been posited between registered deaths and total number of users (Brinkman, 1985). Given this assumption, extrapolation makes it possible not only to estimate the size of local, regional or national populations, but also to make cross-national comparisons.

During the first half of the 1980s the number of registered drug deaths in Germany was roughly 400 per year, but it has risen sharply since then to over 2,000 per year in the early 1990s. As noted above, the amount of heroin confiscated annually in Germany has also increased. Heroin seizures show a significant positive correlation with the annual number of registered drug deaths in Germany (r =.985; p<.05) (Figure 3). It would thus appear at first glance that heroin seizures do linearly reflect trends in numbers of heroin users. This seems to be supported further by the fact that the number of cases noticed and registered by German police as heroin users for the first time climbed from around 2,000 per year in the early 1980s to some 8,000 at the start of the 1990s (Bundeskriminalamt, 1993), which also correlates with drug mortality (r =.937; p<.05). German statistics indeed seem to support the hypothesis 'the more drug deaths, the more drug users'.

There are some considerable complications, however. First, in the Netherlands in the same period, there was a negative, though not significant, relationship between heroin seizures and resident drug fatalities (r = -.481) (Figure 4). Second, there is no direct correlation between incidence of heroin use in Germany and the annual number of new registered cases. Registration is a very complicated and time-dependent process which is influenced by the annual incidence rate of heroin users, mortality, the termination rate of drug users and police activity. Also, there are a number of major potential flaws in the assumption of a constant linear relationship between the number of drug deaths and the number of heroin users. Mortality ratios may vary (i) within a population (ii) over time and (iii) between geographical areas.

- mortality rates mainly involve intravenous users, as death rates are much lower for smokers or sniffers (Brinkman, 1985; Hartnoll *et al*, 1985); numbers of drug deaths can also be affected by changes in heroin purity (Ruttenber and Luke, 1984), or by the number of new users in a given period, as they are thought to run a greater risk of lethal overdosing (Reuband, 1988);

- variations in definition and in the reliability of registration of drug deaths can cause additional complications; for example, towards the end of the 1970s the number of registered drug deaths in Germany increased following a change in the official definition (Püschel *et al*, 1984; Heckman *et al*, 1992).

Figure 3: Confiscated heroin and drug deaths in Germany, 1980-92

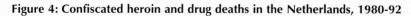

Figure 4: Confiscated heroin and drug deaths in the Netherlands, 1980-92

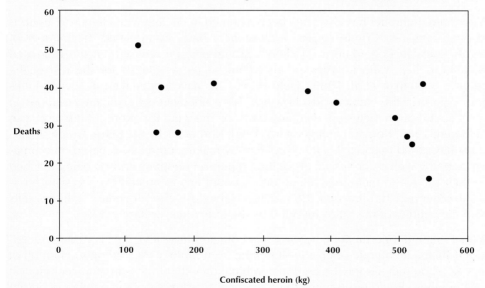

Source: de Zwart and Mensinck (1993).

- an epidemiological study in Amsterdam has shown that clients of methadone services have a far lower mortality rate than non-clients (Cobelans, Scharder and Sluijs, 1990).

Each of these points could explain the difference between the Netherlands and Germany. In the Netherlands, heroin is not usually taken intravenously, in Germany it is. The Netherlands has relatively few new users; and furthermore, it applies a different definition of drug deaths and a different registration method than Germany. Finally, methadone is dispensed to drug users on a far greater scale than in Germany.

Extrapolations from other indirect parameters

Other types of administrative data have been taken to correlate with the number of users. In San Francisco, for example, researchers extrapolated the number of heroin users from registered local crime on the assumption that a certain percentage of users support their habit by burglary (Newmeyer and Johnson, 1976). Burglary rates are thus seen as reflecting the prevalence of heroin use.

Besides crime statistics, general health statistics other than the aforementioned death rates, such as viral hepatitis or HIV for drug users and cirrhosis of the liver for alcohol users, can be employed as indirect parameters. One problem with health parameters, such as viral hepatitis and HIV, is that again they are linked predominantly or exclusively to injecting drug use, leaving out other ways of taking heroin like 'chasing the dragon' (chinezen). The validity of extrapolation is strongly enhanced if the indirect parameter adopted is one which appertains to drug users in a specific population of interest.

A constant multiplier has also often been assumed in dealing with client registrations at drug agencies. Criminologists, for instance, have extrapolated the number of heroin users in Rotterdam from client registrations, presuming that the estimated client/non-client ratio for Amsterdam would be representative for the rest of the country (Bieleman *et al*, 1989). Field studies we have undertaken in several cities and regions in the Netherlands, however, have uncovered significant variations in service utilisation between different parts of the country (Korf, Mann and van Aalderen, 1989; Korf and Hoogenhout, 1990; Korf *et al*, 1990). Other Dutch researchers have tried to solve this ratio problem by making corrections based on estimates made by welfare professionals of the proportion of opiate addicts being reached by their service in their area, taking into account any estimated overlap with services in other regions (Driessen, 1990, 1992). Obviously this procedure stands or falls with the validity of the ratios reported by the individual welfare workers.

A final method for estimating heroin users from administrative data is capture/recapture (CRC), a technique originally stemming from biology. According to Hartnoll *et al*, CRC should preferably be used in combination with other estimating techniques; together they should result in the 'best appropriate estimate' of the number of heroin users in a given area (Hartnoll *et al*, 1985).

Ethnographic mapping, case counting and nomination

The simplest method computationally of estimating the number of heroin users in a community is to count them all. Ethnographic field studies in towns and rural areas in the Netherlands have been shown to achieve a rather complete mapping of users' networks and to yield reliable prevalence data (Korf, Mann and van Aalderen, 1989; Korf, Hes and van Aalderen, 1992).

Such a method is not applicable in the case of big cities, however, where the absolute number of heroin users is many times that of less urbanised areas, and where the social structure of the population is far more complex.

Intermediate conclusions

From this review we can conclude that while survey data may reflect trends in heroin use prevalence, they do not normally permit accurate estimates of the number of current users. Ethnographic mapping of heroin users is an alternative in small communities, but it is not a reliable method for large cities. Extrapolation methods seem most appropriate there. A general problem in extrapolation from one parameter is that the ratio of registered to non-registered cases often has not been empirically verified, and/or cannot be assumed *a priori* to be constant. Alternatively, a ratio can be generated from 'nomination' of institutional contacts by users interviewed in field studies (see below).

When two or more client registrations of users are available, the size of a heroin-using population can be estimated with the CRC technique, which does not rely on data from field samples. Should several field samples from the same population be available, the CRC technique could be applied to them as well. But field studies among heroin users (and other hidden populations) are time consuming and hence costly, especially if data must be collected more than once.

A key advantage of CRC is that it does not depend on an assumption of constant linearity. The extrapolation factor is calculated from the population under study and not from other sources. CRC thus promises more validity than extrapolations from any single parameter. Therefore, I shall now explore this method in more detail. Given that CRC requires more than one official registration, I consider the nomination technique to be a good alternative. I shall focus on this later in the chapter.

Capture-recapture: three criteria for application

Application of the CRC method ideally assumes a closed population during the time frame studied. That is, no new subjects should enter the population within the period under analysis (no new incidence) and also no subject should die, stop taking opiates or otherwise cease to be part of the population.

Samples chosen for application of CRC must satisfy three criteria:

- subjects should be uniquely marked;
- the samples must be drawn randomly and be mutually independent i.e. inclusion in a first sample should not affect inclusion in the second;
- time frame and target population should be defined consistently across samples.

Regarding the independence of samples, it should be noted that registrations of heroin users are seldom perfectly independent in practice. To some extent, the subjects found in one registration will, by definition, be excluded from the second. Such negative dependence reduces natural overlap between registrations and causes overestimation. In the most extreme case, all subjects in one registration would belong to one population and all persons in the second would be from a separate population. Then mutual exclusion is complete, overlap is nil and CRC will yield an infinite population. Examples of such a situation are services for female prostitutes on one side and male prison inmates on the other; or inpatient drug-free treatment and outpatient after care. Conversely, presence in one registration can also increase the chance of being included in a second, for instance, due to referral by professionals. Such positive dependence will enlarge overlap between registrations and cause underestimation. The effects of dependence between registrations are summarised in Table 3.

Table 3: Effects of dependence between registrations in CRC estimates

	Sampling bias	Overlap (denominator)	Effect on estimate of population size
Positive dependence	Mutual inclusion	Enlarged	Under-estimation
Negative dependence	Mutual exclusion	Reduced or zero	Over-estimation
Independence	None	Unbiased	Unbiased

With regard to the third criterion for application of CRC – consistency in time frame and target population – it is implausible that registered methadone clients or arrestees who receive methadone in police stations would represent a random sample from the total population of heroin users. Frequent users will be over-represented, as methadone is dispensed only to daily opiate users ('heroin addicts') who suffer considerable withdrawal symptoms after several hours of abstinence. In most countries, lower-rate users like 'chippers' (Zinberg, 1984) will fall outside methadone programmes.

Application of CRC will be invalid if samples are heterogeneous with regard to traits which affect chances of both capture and recapture. Full homogeneity of populations is usually not a viable assumption. If the chance of being recaptured differs for sub-

populations, this heterogeneity can be corrected by sample stratification. Epidemiological field studies in the Netherlands have shown that heroin-using populations are
socially structured by various characteristics, such as injecting versus non-injecting
drug use and differences in economic behaviour (Grapendaal, Leuw and Nelen,
1991; Grund, Adriaans and Kaplan, 1991; Korf, Hes and van Aalderen, 1992).
Ethnicity and nationality appear to be the most important structuring traits for heroin-
using sub-populations in Amsterdam. The three major sub-populations are: ethnic
Dutch and ethnic minorities (the resident sub-populations) and foreigners (officially
non-resident and mostly European). Figure 5 shows the effect of accounting for this
stratification in applying CRC. Discrepancies between stratified and unstratified total
estimates turn out to be relatively small, but the stratified estimates do reveal that the
overall fluctuations are due primarily to the foreign sub-population.

Figure 5: CRC estimates of opiate addicts in Amsterdam (1984-93), stratified for ethnicity

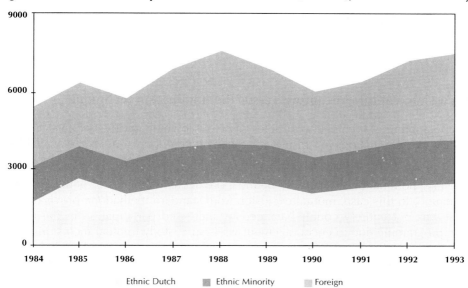

Application of CRC also presumes that the population to be estimated is closed during
the time frame in question. This, of course, is rarely the case. Since year estimates
include anyone coming and going during an entire year-long period, they are necessarily larger than estimates per quarter. An obvious example of subjects who do not
belong to the heroin-using population for extended periods are 'heroin tourists'.
Annual estimates put persons born outside the Netherlands and not belonging to resident ethnic minorities at nearly half the total population of heroin users in Amsterdam;
from 1989 to 1992 the figure was 44 per cent (van Brussel *et al*, 1994). Such a high
percentage is, however, quite inconsistent with systematic field observations and also
with institutional data (Korf and Biemond, 1992).

It may thus be concluded that CRC year figures overestimate the number of users on an average day, because the population is not entirely closed. For the more fluid foreign sub-population the overestimation will be greater than for resident users.

Nomination technique

Sampling bias must also be reckoned with in applying the nomination technique. Table 4 summarises schematically what effects sampling bias can have on estimations derived using the nomination technique.

Table 4: Effects of sampling bias in nomination estimates

	Sampling bias	Denominator	Effect on estimate of population size
Over-representation	Over-inclusion	Enlarged	Under-estimation
Under-representation	Over-exclusion	Reduced	Over-estimation

Discussion: capture/recapture versus the nomination technique

Extrapolation from nomination samples came out lower than CRC estimates for both resident sub-populations in Amsterdam. Since no criterion variables are available, it cannot be established beyond doubt which method yields the most valid estimate.

If we take nomination estimates to be the more accurate, then CRC generated over-estimation. In this case, mutual exclusion from standard methadone provision after arrest was not entirely counterbalanced by increased participation in the methadone programme due to encouragement while in custody (mutual inclusion). If, on the other hand, we take CRC estimates as being more accurate, nomination has produced under-estimation. In that case, registered users would be over-represented in the field sample (over-inclusion). Another possible explanation is that respondents over-reported their institutional contacts, for instance due to telescoping. In the foreign sub-population, comparative analysis of CRC and nomination estimates generated contradictory findings. In one year, extrapolations from self-reported methadone treatment (nomination) were lower than CRC estimates, but a year later they were higher (Korf, 1987). This could be due to the fact that a larger share of the 1986 respondents had been in Amsterdam for a short time, implying a smaller number than had previously participated in a programme. The findings for foreign heroin users underscore once again the specific problems of estimating the size of highly floating populations.

From the preceding overview of methods, we may conclude that extrapolation with CRC from subject registrations is the most feasible method for estimating the size of heroin-using populations in large cities. The reliability of CRC strongly depends on accuracy of registration. Since inaccuracy usually arises from incorrect registration of the same subject under different names, the method will generally yield estimates which are too high. Such errors can be substantially reduced by improving registrations (as was shown for Amsterdam) but full elimination of bias is too much to hope for. The possibility of the same person giving aliases at low threshold programmes, or even at police stations, cannot be fully ruled out. In short, there will always be some underestimation. In the strictest sense, CRC can be applied only to data from independent sources. In the drugs field, full independence of samples (registrations) is not a realistic prospect. Some degree of dependence is unavoidable. Depending on which direction it takes, it will produce overestimation due to mutual exclusion from registrations or underestimation due to mutual inclusion. Certain combinations of registrations are, by definition, unsuitable for CRC.

As has been shown, heroin-using populations are not homogeneous, and overlap between registered samples may be of a different nature for different sub-groups within a local population. Stratification can be helpful in identifying and explaining such variations. From various sets of data, it has been concluded that ethnicity correlates with rates of capture and recapture in Amsterdam. Ethnicity will most probably figure heavily in the use of this method in other cities in Europe. However, in other European cities, populations may be more ethnically homogeneous and/or they may include far fewer 'heroin tourists' than in Amsterdam. Therefore, stratification of CRC estimates by ethnicity may not always be necessary. Gender or age could be more relevant in other cities or countries, but other variables should be explored too in order to find the 'best fit' stratifications.

Application of CRC also assumes a closed population. This condition will generally be violated to some degree due to mobility within the population. If registrations are independent, CRC will then produce overestimation. In Amsterdam, the biggest problems created by this third criterion for CRC were within the sub-population of foreign users, a group of a highly floating nature. Structural fluctuations within a resident population due to voluntary or compulsory drug-free periods should be taken into account as well. Even when CRC findings are not biased by dependence of samples and/or marking irregularities, the number of current heroin users will commonly be lower than year estimates imply.

Comparison of CRC estimates with those calculated from nomination data from our field study suggest that CRC estimates are generally too high. Though rigorous attention was paid to statistical representativeness in the field sample, the possibility that methadone clients were nonetheless over-represented cannot be ruled out. If that was the case, underestimation will have occurred. The reasons for this are: an excess of less sociable users at the zero stage of the snowball chains and bias in chain referrals – clients may have more mutual contacts than non-clients. Another potential source of underestimation under the nomination technique is that respondents may recall certain treatments or arrests as being more recent than they really were (telescoping).

But even if nomination estimates are judged to reflect better the true number of cases, the stability in year estimates produced by CRC (methadone/arrest) for the resident sub-populations of heroin users in Amsterdam (approximately 4,000) is striking. Stronger fluctuations would imply less validity, unless other sources likewise suggested major changes. A clear disadvantage of CRC (and nomination) is that they can be applied only when subject registrations are available. When they are not, estimation will be problematic, if not impossible. Since most registrations in Europe are still confined to, or dominated by, opiate users, application of CRC in other drug-using populations – e.g. cocaine, MDMA – will not normally be feasible. As regards heroin, recreational and infrequent users are generally under-represented in, or even excluded from, registrations. As a consequence, the CRC method will continue to be applied predominantly to estimate numbers of problem heroin users in urban settings.

Although I have referred to nomination as an alternative method, it should be applied in at least some cases as a complement to CRC. Nomination may, at an early stage, reveal biases in CRC estimates. Later, it may help to explain inconsistencies that arise in such approximations.

Conclusions

In this paper I have described various methods which can be used to estimate numbers of problem heroin users. School and household surveys show that no more than a tiny segment of the population has ever used heroin. Such surveys cannot be used to make estimates sufficiently accurate to map trends in the scale of heroin consumption.

Therefore, I proceeded to review indirect parameters such as drug seizures and drug mortality rates. Both in the Netherlands and in Germany, an ever-growing amount of heroin has been confiscated since the early 1970s. In Germany, a sharp rise in heroin deaths was recorded particularly in the late 1980s and early 1990s. The positive correlation between the larger heroin hauls and the greater number of fatalities implies a growing number of heroin-dependent people in Germany. Such a correlation was entirely absent in the Netherlands, however. Statistics on heroin deaths and heroin seizures therefore cannot serve as unequivocal universal indicators of the size of heroin users' populations. One complicating factor is the degree to which heroin is being used intravenously. That is much more often the case in Germany than it is in the Netherlands.

I have devoted a good deal of attention here to CRC. Applying it to the heroin population is a tricky business, given that counting heroin users is not immediately comparable to counting fish in a lake on the basis of several catches. I have made clear that certain circumstances among heroin users foster over- or under-estimation. The direction in which such conditions bias the estimates is known, but determining the exact degree of bias remains a problem. For estimating the scale of populations of a highly 'floating' nature, such as 'heroin tourists', the reliability of capture/recapture was shown to be too low. For resident populations I have compared capture/recapture estimates to those derived from nomination. Population size was estimated on the basis of registration figures from methadone provision and from arrests, processing them with self-reports of provision or arrest. For the nomination technique, too, conditions came to light that can cause over- or under-estimation.

Although no exact estimate of the size of the heroin-using population can be reached, I have argued that CRC furnishes a reasonably trustworthy picture of the evolution in the numbers of resident heroin users.

References

Bieleman. B., Bruggink, G. and Swierstra, K. (1989) *Harddrugs en criminaliteit in Rotterdam.* Groningen: Intraval.

Brinkman, N. (1985) *Over dood en dosis. Een literatuuronderzoek naar sterfte onder heroïnegebruikers.* Utrecht: NcGv.

van Brussel, G.H.A., van der Woude, D.H. and van Lieshout, S.J.M. (1994) *Werkt het Amsterdamse sociaal- medische drugshulpbeleid? Jaarbericht van de drugsafdeling GG&GD waarin opgenomen de jaarcijfers '93.* Amsterdam: Municipal Health Service (GG&GD).

Bundeskriminalamt Wiesbaden (1993) 'Rauschgiftjahresbericht 1992.' In: Hüllinghorst, R., Neß, B. and Wünschmann B. (eds) *Jahrbuch Sucht 1994.* Geesthacht, Neuland: 105-126.

Clayton, R.R. and Voss, H.L. (1981) *Young men and drugs in Manhattan.* A causal analysis. Rockville, Maryland: NIDA Research Monograph 39.

Cobelens, F.G.J., Schrader, P.C. and Sluijs, T.A. (1990) *Acute dood na druggebruik in Amsterdam.* Amsterdam: Municipal Health Service (GG&GD).

Driessen, F.M.H.M. (1990) *Methadonverstrekking in Nederland. Verslag van een inventarisatie onder alle methadon-verstrekkende instellingen in Nederland.* Utrecht: Bureau Driessen.

Driessen, F.M.H.M. (1992) *Methadonverstrekking in Nederland. Verslag van een onderzoek onder methadoncliënten in Nederland, uitgezonderd de vier grote steden.* Utrecht: Bureau Driessen.

Grapendaal, M., Leuw, E. and Nelen, J.M. (1991) *De economie van het drugsbestaan.* Arnhem: Gouda Quint.

Grund, J.P.C., Adriaans, N.F.P. and Kaplan, C.D. (1991) 'Changing cocaine smoking rituals in the Dutch heroin addict population', *British Journal of Addiction,* 86: 439-448.

Hartnoll, R. *et al* (1985) 'Estimating the prevalence of opioid dependence', *The Lancet,* January 26: 203-204.

Hartnoll, R. (1992) Overview of existing research methods. In: Garretsen, H.F.L *et al* (eds) *Proceedings of the invited expert meeting illegal drug use: Research methods for hidden populations.* Rotterdam, 29-30 October, IVO/NIAD: 10-21.

Heckmann, W. *et al* (1992) *Der Drogentod. Eine differentielle Untersuchung zu Prävalenz und Ätiologie von Drogennot- und -todesfällen.* Berlin: Sozial Pädagogisches Institut.

Korf, D.J. (1995) *Dutch Treat. Formal control and illicit drug use in the Netherlands.* Amsterdam: Thesis Publishers.

Korf, D.J., Hes, J. and van Aalderen, H. (1992) *Waar je mee omgaat. Aids-risico's in Alkmaarse drugsecenes.* Alkmaar, Brijder Stichtuing.

Korf, D.J., Mann, R. and van Aalderen, H. (1989) *Drugs op het platteland.* Assen: van Gorcum.

Korf, D.J. *et al* (1990) *Gooise geneugten.* Amsterdam: SPCP.

Korf, D.J. and Biemond, R. (1992) *Effectiviteit van het ontmoedigingsbeleid.* Amsterdam: University of Amsterdam, Faculty of Pedagogigal and Educational Sciences.

Korf, D.J., Blanken, P. and Nabben, T. (1991) *Een nieuwe wonderpil? Verspreiding, effecten en risico's van ecstasygebruik in Amsterdam.* Amsterdam: Jellinek Reeks # 3.

Korf, D.J. and Hoogenhout, H.P.H. (1990) *Zodden aan de Dijk.* Amsterdam: University of Amsterdam, Institute of Social Geography.

Korf, D.J., Nabben, T. and Schreuders, M. (1995) Antenne 1994. *Trends in alcohol, tabak, drugs en gokken bij jonge Amsterdammers.* Amsterdam: Jellinek Reeks # 3.

Korf, D.J., Reijneveld, S.A. and Toet, J. (1994) 'Estimating the number of heroin users: A review of methods and empirical findings from the Netherlands', *International Journal of Addiction,* 29 (11): 1393-1417.

Korf, D.J. and van der Steenhoven, P. (1994) *Antenne 1993. Trends in alcohol, tabak, drugs en gokken bij jonge Amsterdammers.* Amsterdam: Jellinek Reeks # 2.

Korf, D.J. and Verbraeck, H.T. (1993) *Dealers en dienders.* Amsterdam: Bonger Institute of Criminology.

Kuipers, S.B.M., Mensink, C. and de Zwart, W.M. (1993) *Jeugd en riskant gedrag; Roken, drinken, druggebruik en gokken onder scholieren vanaf tien jaar.* Utrecht: NIAD.

Newmeyer, J.A. and Johnson, G.R. (1976) 'The heroin epidemic in San Francisco: Estimates of incidence and prevalence', *International Journal of Addiction,* 11: 417-438.

Plomp, H.N., Kuipers, H. and van Oers, M.L. (1990) *Roken, alcohol- en drugsgebruik onder scholieren vanaf 10 jaar.* Amsterdam: VU-University Press.

Püschel, K. *et al* (1984) 'Forensisch-medizinische und kriminologische Aspekte der Hamburger Rauschgifttodesfälle bis Ende 1982', *Suchtgefahren,* 30: 205-211.

Reuband, K.-H. (1988) Drogenstatistik 1987. In: Neß, B. and Ziegler, H. (eds) *Jahrbuch zur Frage der Suchtgefahren 1987.* Hamburg: Neuland: 41-103.

Ruttenber, A.J. and Luke, J.L. (1984) 'Heroin-related deaths: new epidemiological insights', Science, 226: 14-20.

Sandwijk, J.P., Cohen, P.D.A. and Musterd, S. (1991) *Licit and illicit drug use in Amsterdam.* Amsterdam: University of Amsterdam, Institute of Social Geography.

Sandwijk, J.P., Westerterp, I. and Musterd, S. (1988) *Het gebruik van legale en illegale drugs in Amsterdam.* Amsterdam: University of Amsterdam, Institute of Social Geography.

Sandwijk, J.P. *et al* (1995) *Licit and illicit drug use in Amsterdam II.* Amsterdam: University of Amsterdam, Institute of Social Geography.

Sijlbing, G. (1984) *Het gebruik van drugs, alcohol en tabak. Resultaten van een onderzoek onder Nederlandse jongeren van 15-24 jaar.* Amsterdam: SWOAD.

Zinberg, N.E. (1984) *Drug, set and setting. The basis for controlled intoxicant use.* New Haven: Yale University Press.

de Zwart, W.M. and Mensink, C. (1993) *Alcohol, tabak, drugs en gokken in cijfers.* Utrecht: NIAD.

CHAPTER 20

CASE-FINDING, CAPTURE-RECAPTURE AND DOUBLE COUNTING: A BERLIN CASE STUDY

by Wolf Kirschner

In the Federal Republic of Germany, reliable data on the prevalence of illicit drug use are scarce. To date, estimates of the number of 'hard' drug users have been derived mainly from indirect parameters such as drug-related deaths and drug users first registered by the police. These methods estimated the number of hard drug users in Germany in 1992 to range between 90,000 and 150,000 (IFT, 1994). From these figures, we also have regional estimates. In Berlin (West), for example, the estimated number of injecting drug users in 1992 was between 10,000 and 12,000. Such data serve as the basis for allocating financial or personnel resources in drug prevention and drug treatment.

In 1992, the department for drug control in the Berlin Senate was interested in obtaining more accurate data on the city's injecting drug user population. The research commissioned (Kirschner *et al*, 1994; Grünbeck *et al*, 1993) had two goals:

- to estimate the total number of injecting drug users (IDUs) in Berlin (West) by combining two estimation approaches;
- to describe the population according to socio-demographic and epidemiological parameters.

In this chapter, I will describe the study and some of the methodological problems encountered. In particular, I will discuss problems of double-counting.

Methods and assumptions

In epidemiological field research there are several approaches for reaching target populations. These include population-based approaches, such as representative surveys and snowball samples of hidden populations, where data are gathered on the target population itself; institution-based approaches, where information is gathered from institutions with which the target population has contact (e.g. health care and criminal justice agencies); or a combination of these two methods, for example the nomination technique. This technique is used to estimate prevalence rates of events in small and hidden populations. For example, the number of drug users may be estimated by multiplying the number of drug users in treatment (known from institutional statistics) by the proportion of users in treatment at a given time (known from snowball surveys). It is in this way that the nomination technique combines institution- and population-based methods (Kirschner, 1993).

In this study, comparison is made between capture-recapture and estimations from treated populations adjusted for non-attendance and double-counting.

Capture-recapture

The first 'arm' of the study used a capture/recapture (CRC) approach for estimating the number of injecting drug users in Berlin. This replicated the method used in a Berlin study in 1981 (Scarabis and Patzak, 1981).

From August to December 1992, 41 institutions were enrolled in the study. These included hospitals, welfare institutions, drug treatment centres, prisons and AIDS and drug-counselling services. The participating institutions (n = 22) were asked to complete a short document for each client known to use 'hard' drugs. The documents carried the following information:

- personal identifier;
- date of first contact with the institution;
- date of last contact with the institution;
- date of onset of hard drug use;
- date of onset of injecting drug use;
- type of drugs used.

A total of 6,742 documents were produced for the study. Of these, 1,361 (20 per cent) were identified as having been double-counted within single institutions. This left 5,281 documents for use in the CRC estimations. The estimations were undertaken by a collaborating institute, Intersofia Berlin.

The basic requirements of CRC are that:

- each injecting drug user will be known to at least one of the institutions during his or her drug-using career;
- the institutions have a comparable probability of being contacted by the drug consumer;
- the size of the population is stable.

Anonymous Monitoring (ANOMO)

The second arm of the study utilised the ANOMO approach. The aim here was to elicit reliable information on the socio-demographic and epidemiological parameters of the population, as well as estimating of the number of injecting drug users.

ANOMO is a sentinel-surveillance system based on a representative sample of physicians in 'free' practices. In the German health system, medical services – besides those in the hospital sector – are offered by general practitioners and other specialists who run them in private ('free') practices. The method was first developed in our institute for monitoring the spread of (diagnosed) HIV infections in Germany, as a complement to the administrative reporting systems (AIDS Case Registry, Lab Reporting System). The acronym ANOMO is derived from the practice of 'Anonymous Monitoring' of the target population by physicians (Kirschner and Schwartländer, 1996).

At the end of 1991, there were 1,450 physicians in free practices in Berlin (West), working as general practitioners or internists. From these, a sample of n = 550 (34 per cent) was chosen at random. The physicians were contacted in the last quarter of 1992 and asked to participate in the study. They were required to complete a practice questionnaire – which gathered data on practice size, number of patients and risk groups – and to document each patient whom they knew to be in the target population (i.e. injecting drug users).

Data from these sources would thus allow the target population to be screened and provide information on each patient (e.g. age, sex, HIV status). All data relate to the year 1992.

By the end of the fieldwork in March 1993, 402 physicians (79 per cent) had taken part in the study. Physicians who did not take part were checked to see if they belonged to practices which saw a high number of injecting drug users, but this was not the case.

The number of patients seen by participating physicians serve as the basis for ANOMO estimates. These need to be adjusted due to a proportion of the population not attending the practices and to possible double-counting.

Reasons for selecting physicians for ANOMO monitoring

Given the range of institutions which have contact with injecting drug users, why did we choose physicians in free practices to monitor this population? The two major problems of employing institution-based methods of estimation relate to attendance and selection bias. An institution had to be chosen which is 'visited' by a high proportion of the target population in a given time period and which is subject to minimal selection by different types of users.

For the purposes of this study, the institution also needed to be able to provide reliable epidemiological and medical information.

Compared to institutions such as hospitals, self-help groups, drug treatment centres, criminal justice and social service agencies, we rated physicians in free practices as the most appropriate institution to be involved in the study. The decision to choose these as the monitoring institution was also made in the light of findings from previous studies which show high annual attendance rates by current or former injecting drug users and people with experience of illicit drug use. The attendance rate in these groups of approximately 90 per cent (EFB, 1989; IFT/Infratest, 1990) is significantly higher than in the Berlin general population of a comparable age structure (74 per cent of 18 to 39-year-olds) (EFB, 1993). These high attendance rates have also been found in other countries, such as the Netherlands (Korf, 1995).

While high attendance rates will lower the chance of selection bias, some bias may remain. For example, people with a long drug-using career may be more likely than recent initiates to have a poor health status and, consequently, may visit their doctor more frequently. However, the qualitative interviews we conducted with physicians suggested that this hypothesis was implausible.

Identifier coding systems

The alphanumeric coding system used to identify cases in ANOMO was the same as that used for the AIDS Case Registry. Each identifying code is derived from the case's surname, first name, age and sex.

A different coding system was used in the CRC study. Here, only the case's surname was incorporated into the code, along with the age and sex. Less sophisticated codes were used because of the higher data protection conditions applying in some of the CRC institutions. Also, we assumed that subjects' first names might be documented incorrectly or incompletely in certain settings.

Statistical requirements and assumptions of CRC and ANOMO

Table 1 summarises the main statistical requirements of CRC, and the possible problems and consequences for estimates derived via this method.

Table 1: Statistical requirements and assumptions of CRC, possible problems in the study and consequences for estimation

Assumption/ requirements	Possible problems	Possible consequences for estimation
Each IDU has a probability > 0 to attend one of the institutions at least once	A small proportion will not attend	Under-estimation
IDUs have to be marked completely and identically	Missing data	Over-estimation
Independent random sampling	Overlap of populations	Over-estimation or under-estimation
Stable population	Unlikely with an annual reporting frame	Over-estimation or under-estimation
Target population must be identified completely	Missing data	Over-estimation or under-estimation

The reasons for possible biases in ANOMO estimations are shown in Table 2. To summarise, there will be overestimation (i) if the annual rate of non-attendance of physicians by injecting drug users, derived from previous surveys, is much higher than the assumed 10-20 per cent, and (ii) if double-counting control methods are ineffective.

Taking all these factors into consideration, we assumed that CRC estimations would be higher than the ANOMO estimation.

Table 2: Statistical requirements and assumptions of ANOMO, possible problems in the study and consequences for estimation

Assumption/ requirements	Possible problems	Possible consequences for estimation
Each IDU has a probability > 0 to attend the physicians at least once a year	Not given e.g. for people in prisons ≥ 1 year Not given for the population not attending (10%-20%)	Under-estimation (correctable)
Random sampling of physicians	Clustering of typical IDU groups in single practices may affect the description of population but not the estimation	None
Patients can easily be identified as IDU by the physicians	Few problems with respect to IDU	Under-estimation
Information gathered on the population must be reliable and complete	No problems with respect to estimations Problems with respect to description as not all physicians are documenting all patients completely	None
Double counting must be excluded or reduced	Methods to control double counting may be insufficient	Over-estimation

Results

CRC estimates

Twenty-two data samples (n = 5,381 documents) were used as the basis for CRC calculations. Estimations were made for different populations: users of 'hard' drugs and the sub-population of injecting drug users. This was because data on mode of drug administration were missing on some of the documents used in CRC.

The CRC estimation of Berlin hard drug users in 1992 was 8,923. Of these, 6,335 (71 per cent) were injecting drug users. A further CRC estimation was made which excluded people in continuous detoxification treatment. This resulted in a 'worst case' estimate of 7,123 and a 'best case' estimate of 5,780. The former estimate was based on analysis of 16 of the 41 institutions (90 per cent of documents) while the latter estimate incorporated documents from all participating institutions.

ANOMO estimates

Approximately one third of the free practices taking part in the ANOMO study (128/402; 32 per cent) saw at least one injecting drug user in 1992. The average number of injecting patients seen in these practices was 7.9 although this varied considerably. For example, 21 per cent of the practices had ten or more injecting patients, with an average of 26.5.

The total number of injecting drug users in the ANOMO practice questionnaire sample was 1,013. Of these, 475 (47 per cent) were documented individually.

The projection of cases is based on the total number of drug users identified by the practice questionnaire. The average number of injecting drug users for each practice in Berlin (West) is 2.88. Multiplied by the total number of physicians in the city (n = 1,450) this results in an estimate of approximately 4,200 injectors, with a wide confidence interval between 2,600 and 5,800. The large confidence interval is determined by high standard deviation, based on 21 per cent of practices having 10 or more patients (mean = 26.5). A double counting rate of 10 per cent (discussed below) produces a revised estimate of 3,795 patient contacts (min. = 2,351, max. = 5,238).

To estimate the total population of injecting drug users in Berlin, we must also consider those injectors who do not attend a physician over the course of a year. The assumed non-attendance rate in this population of 20 per cent produces an estimate of 4,744 injectors in total (min. = 2,939, max. = 6,548, 95 per cent confidence interval).

Table 3 summarises the estimates derived via CRC and ANOMO. We can see that the CRC 'best case' estimate (5,780) lies within the confidence-interval of the ANOMO estimate. The maximum ANOMO estimate (6,548) and the CRC estimates lie closely together.

Table 3: ANOMO and CRC estimates of IDU in Berlin, 1992

	Estimate	Range
CRC	6,335	5,780-7,123
ANOMO	4,744	2,939-6,548

Given that the ANOMO estimates exclude drug injectors serving long-term prison sentences, they will be lower than those derived through CRC which included this sub-population. On a fixed day in the study period (30 October 1992), there were approximately 700 injecting drug users in prison in Berlin.

From these analyses, we estimate the total number of injecting drug users in Berlin in 1992 to have been between 5,000 and 7,000. This is approximately half the number estimated by other methods.

Methodological problems

Before describing our procedure for analysing double-reporting in the ANOMO study, we must first consider the possibility of documentation bias.

Documentation bias

Studies using the ANOMO approach must consider the possibility of documentation bias. The approach requires participating physicians to complete a practice questionnaire and a separate document sheet for each patient who is known to inject drugs. In this study, document sheets were completed for only 47 per cent of the cases identified by questionnaire (475/1,013). The question, then, is whether the documented cases are a representative sub-sample of the total recorded patient population.

Our analyses showed a comparatively high documentation rate in practices which had contact with a small recorded number of injectors. For example, 68.2 per cent of cases were documented in practices with one or two injecting patients, compared with 39.6 per cent of cases in practices with ten or more injecting patients. This means that injecting drug users from 'small' practices are over-represented in our sample of documented cases (n = 475).

Documentation bias will only occur if the structure of the injecting population varies according the 'size' of the practice. This was not the case in this study. There were no significant differences between attenders of 'small' practices (one or two patients who inject) and 'large' practices (ten or more patients who inject) with regard to: mean age; percentage <29 years; percentage male; current injecting status; and percentage HIV positive. The only significant difference was that, at small practices, injectors tended to have been in contact with the practice for a longer period of time. Of patients at practices with one or two recorded injectors, 41.1 per cent had attended since 1989 or before. This compares with 13.3 per cent of patients in practices seeing ten or more injectors.

These analyses lead us to conclude that the variable documentation rates in the ANOMO study do not imply documentation bias and that the population documented was indeed a representative sub-sample of the total population.

Identifying double- or multiple-reported cases in ANOMO

Cross-referral between practices. To help us identify double- or multiple-reported cases in the ANOMO study, participating physicians were asked to record referrals of injecting patients to other physicians. In 33 per cent of cases (n = 475) this was unknown. Not surprisingly, doctors' knowledge of their patients' use of other practices was correlated with their overall knowledge of the patient.

The proportion of patients with known referrals who visited more than one practice in 1992 was 20 per cent. Assuming that this group does not differ from patients with unknown referrals, the 20 per cent cross-referral rate pertains to the total ANOMO sample.

Double-counting of the same person. Turning to personal identifiers to calculate double-reporting, we are first confronted by the problem of non-response. Of the 475 documentations in the ANOMO study, 430 (91 per cent) had a complete code.

Calculating the probability of two injecting patients having an identical code as 1:6,536, and taking into account that 430*429/2 = 92,235 pair comparisons will be carried out, the expected number of pairs would be n = 14 (probability 95 per cent). This assumes a Poisson distribution with 92,235/6,536 = 14 (confidence interval: 7-22).

Analysis of codes for identical pairs and triplets produced nine pairs and three triplets (2.8 per cent). This is in the expected range. Checking additionally for sex and age (tolerable range +/- 2 years) left five pairs remaining (1.2 per cent) which are probably identical.

Applied to the estimate of approximately 4,000 patients in contact with free practices, it can be expected that 500 pairs are probably identical persons. This means that 12.5 per cent of contacts are due to double-reporting.

Identical codes for different persons. A sometimes neglected fact is that different persons in ANOMO may be allocated an identical code. Double-counting estimates must therefore be corrected for this. This is important because even a small number of wrongly detected double reports will affect estimations dramatically.

The question of how many identical identifiers may be expected for different persons was addressed in a study for the Robert Koch Institute. Cases from three independent, representative population samples were coded and analysed. In each of the three samples (each containing approximately 5,000 cases), the proportions of identical codes for different persons was about 0.9 per cent. While this proportion is low, the analysis showed the number of identical codes to rise quadratically with rising sample size.

To illustrate how such identical codes may affect estimations, we can analyse a sample of n = 450 in which n = 15 have an identical code. Uncorrected for identical codes for different persons, the estimate would be 13,500 (n = 450* 450/15 = 13,500). The corrected estimate, assuming a rate of 1 per cent, would be 18,409 (n = 450* 450/11 = 18,409).

The difference between the estimates will be smaller if the capture rate is higher. Nevertheless, this problem should be considered carefully in any study design and analysis of data.

Conclusions

This study shows how combined methods of prevalence estimations can improve our understanding of local populations of injecting drug users. Every method has specific limitations and assumptions. Given that some of these assumptions are difficult to test empirically and that study designs may be affected by hard-to-detect selections and biases, congruent estimations may be more reliable.

Nevertheless, it is necessary to have more precise data to test the assumptions. In ANOMO, for example, accurate data on the proportions of injecting drug users not attending practices are required. For CRC, the assumption that each institution has a comparable probability of being seen by clients needs to be investigated more thoroughly.

Besides improving the scope and quality of data available, regional prevalence estimations may also be improved by incorporating indirect parameters, such as drug-related deaths and drug notifications, into the combined approach.

References

E.F.B. (1989) *Sozialhilfestudie.* Berlin.

E.F.B. (1993) *Gesundheits - und Sozialsurvey,* 1991/91.

Grünbeck, P., Markert, S.T. and Tiemann, F. (1993) *Prävalenz des Konsums harter Drogen.* Eine Schätzung zum Umfang der Berliner Opiatszene, AZ-Hefte 21/1994. Berlin.

Institut für Therapieforschung (1994) *Report on methods of estimating the extent of the drug problems in Germany.* Munich: IFT.

Institut für Therapiefirschung/Infratest (1990) *Jugendlichenstudie.* Munich: IFT.

Kirschner, W. (1993) *HIV-Surveillance: Inhaltliche und methodische Probleme bei der Bestimmung der Ausbreitung von HIV-Infektionen.* Ergebnisse sozialwissenschaftlicher AIDS-Forschung Bd, 9. Berlin.

Kirschner, W. and Schwärtlander, B. (1996) *Sentinel-Surveillance von HIV und anderen sexuell übertragbaren krankheiten.* Baden-Baden.

Kirschner, W., Kunert, M., Grünbeck, P., Markert, S.T. and Tiemann, F. (1994) *Umfang und Struktur der Population i.v. Drogenabhangiger in Berlin.* Zusammenfassung der Ergebnisse alternativer epidemiologischer Untersuchungsansätze, AZ-Hefte 22. Berlin.

Korf, D.J. (1995) *Dutch Treat.* Amsterdam.

Scarabis, H. and Patzak, M. (1981) *Die Berliner Heroinszene.* Artbeitsergebnisse aus der Suchtforschung, Band 1. Basel.

CHAPTER 21

DIFFICULTIES IN ESTIMATING
PREVALENCE IN BUDAPEST

by Zsuzsanna Elekes

In Hungary, illicit drug use is a comparatively recent phenomenon, and it has only been over the last decade that attempts have been made to map the extent of the problem. However, the small amount of data available has been questioned as to its reliability. During the 1990s, general population surveys have asked respondents if they have ever taken drugs, but have not provided information on regular drug users. Very few attempts at estimating the total number drug users have been made.

This paper presents two studies conducted by the Epidemiology Research Group of the Sociology and Social Policy Department at the Budapest University of Economics. Both attempt to throw light on the situation regarding illicit drug use in Budapest. The first study uses institutional records to ascertain the number of registered drug users. The second uses snowball methodology to locate opiate users who are not registered in institutional records.

Case-finding: enumerating drug users in contact with institutions

The first study, conducted in 1991, attempted to estimate the spread of drug consumption in Budapest and the number of drug users in contact with institutions, using records from different drug treatment institutions (Elekes and Paksi, 1993). It also aimed to assess the content, reliability and validity of institutional records on drug users which are available.

Data collection methods

On the basis of our previous research, institutions having contact with drug users were classified into three types: the police, health institutions and foster homes. Offices of these institutions were contacted to determine those which had come into contact with drug users in the preceding year. Data sheets were then completed for each person recorded as being a drug user. The sheets recorded socio-demographic information (e.g. place of birth, address, educational qualifications, occupation and marital status) and data relating to the subject's drug use (e.g. current use, reason for contacting the institution, and the date and duration of the contact). Individuals were assigned an identifier derived from their initials, date of birth and sex. To establish the authenticity of the data, interviews were conducted with directors of the participating institutions.

Difficulties of data collection

Difficulties in collecting data were encountered in each of the three types of institution.

Police data: the main difficulty noted was that only the primary offence is recorded in police records. This means that the number of offenders arrested for drug-related crime will be underestimated. For example, if someone was arrested breaking into a pharmacy, the crime would be recorded as 'burglary' or 'breaking and entering', without any indication of whether the crime was drug-related.

Health records: at the time of the research, there were four types of health institution which treated drug users in Hungary – drug treatment centres, alcohol treatment centres or departments, psychiatric departments and crisis intervention or emergency departments. The records from non-specialist agencies were particularly poor, as doctors' initial diagnoses were often inaccurate. For example, patients were frequently recorded as being psychotic, alcoholic or suicidal rather than as having a problem with drug misuse. If a patient was subsequently diagnosed as a drug misuser, this information was seldom recorded. Our research suggested that this was because staff were trying to protect patients from stigmatisation within the institutions.

In institutions where prejudice towards drug users was minimal, or where confidentiality was respected, a patient's drug use was sometimes recorded. However, there was still reason to doubt the reliability of diagnoses as staff were insufficiently trained to recognise drug users. This was particularly the case in crisis intervention and emergency departments and alcohol treatment centres. For example, one doctor commented, 'One of my patients stated that he was a drug abuser and handed over something and said it was marijuana. But I didn't know what it was.'

Difficulties with specialist drug treatment agencies lay in staff suspicion about the research or their general antipathy towards 'statistics'. As a result of these difficulties, only small amounts of data were available from public health institutions.

Records in foster homes: the records kept in foster homes were incomplete. Again, staff rarely recorded clients' drug use in order to protect children from stigmatisation. This could happen when personal files were seen by other institutions. Similarly, school registration records did not hold information about pupils' drug use because other pupils could have access to them. Often drug use went unrecorded because there was no appropriate document to record the information. It became apparent that often drug use was only recorded when it occurred concurrently with other deviant behaviour, such as criminal activity or a suicide attempt.

Findings

Data were collected on 290 drug users: 233 were recorded from health institutions, 30 from the police and 27 from foster homes. Data on types of drugs used were not recorded in emergency departments and outpatient drug treatment centres. However, from health records, it was found that solvents were the only substances used by individuals in foster homes. For illicit drug users identified through police records, opium or cannabis tended to be the most commonly used substances. Data on drug users from health institutions showed the most commonly used drugs to be tranquillisers (24 per cent), opium derivatives (23 per cent) and solvents (17 per cent). The use of cannabis and hallucinogens was found in only a small number of cases.

Concluding comment

The records were found to be unreliable, thereby casting doubt on the validity of the findings. They were incomplete for numerous reasons, but in most cases it was due to institutional staff seeking to protect patients or clients from the stigmatising and legal implications of disclosing their illicit drug use. There also seemed to be considerable mistrust among health personnel towards epidemiological research.

Attempt to estimate the prevalence of opiate use by snowball methods

The second project, undertaken in 1995, was an attempt to locate opiate users who were not registered in any institutions (Elekes and Paksi, 1996). Its aims were:

- to collect data on frequent opiate users;
- to improve the validity of data collected from police and medical records;
- to assess the usefulness of the snowball methodology which had yet to be used in Hungary.

The study focused on the use of all opiates rather than just heroin. This was because previous research indicated the use of other opiates to be more characteristic of drug consumption in Hungary. In 1992, it was found that 3.1 per cent of schoolchildren had taken opiates at least once. A 1990 study showed an equivalent figure of 2.2 per cent for the adult population. Data gathered from police and medical records also indicated that opiate derivatives (along with cannabis) were the most commonly used drugs (Elekes, 1993).

The first stage of the research involved dividing the city into appropriate geographical districts. There was no information to guide this task, other than data from the 1993-4 Budapest School Survey (Elekes and Paksi, 1994). These included demographic variables such as educational qualifications and parental occupation, neither of which were correlated with patterns of drug use. There were relationships between drug use and other variables, such as the way respondents spent their leisure time, and their smoking and drinking habits. However, a general lack of geographical information meant that the data could not be used as a basis for demarcating districts in the capital.

To overcome these difficulties, we used data on registered drug users. First, we categorised users according to the institution where their drug use was recorded. Criminal records were of little use since, as noted above, only the primary cause of arrest was recorded by the police, so medical records were our source of information. Medical institutions are not required to report information about drug users, so we had to check through the case files in every institution to identify those in contact with opiate users.

Five institutions were identified as treating drug users. For reasons of confidentiality, one of these would not release any information to the study. In the remaining four, our objective was to collect data on all opiate users registered during 1994, including their address, profession and level of education, although the last two items were often missing.

Data were collected on 240 cases, and there was great variation in the numbers registered at different institutions (two of the institutions accounted for 95 per cent of cases). Thirty-three per cent of cases were identified as having been double-counted, leaving 161 cases for the analysis.

The amount of information recorded was limited and varied between institutions. This made it impossible to obtain correlations between demographics and opiate use. The selection of districts was therefore based on data detailing the subject's district of residence.

Our analyses showed the rate of opiate use per thousand inhabitants in Budapest to be 0.08 (range = 0.01-0.23). On the basis of these data, districts were assigned to one of three groups: 'below average' districts (rate of known opiate users = <0.06/thousand); 'average' districts (rate = 0.06-0.1/thousand); and 'above average' districts (rate = >0.1/thousand).

Using information on the population density and the profile of inhabitants, a district was then chosen from each group and a key informant was selected for each of the chosen districts. The criteria for the selection of informants required them to:

- be in contact with registering institutions;
- be representative of the average drug user in terms of age and reflect the predominant gender (data from health institutions indicated users were predominantly male, and had a mean age of 27 years);
- have used opiates in the year prior to the research;
- agree to be interviewed;
- have connections with other regular opiate users in their respective districts;
- agree to name their contacts.

Difficulties with data collection

We experienced numerous difficulties in using the snowballing method. First, general mistrust of the research made it difficult to recruit people. Individuals were reluctant to offer information about their contacts as they knew that they would be afraid of such information being released or would suspect the key informant of being connected with the police. This problem was difficult to overcome as we were unable to reassure the informant's contacts directly. Informants also feared they would become ostracised by fellow users. These problems were not alleviated by using ex-drug users and social students in the research.

Informants often failed to maintain contact with us. This meant we had to work with several contacts before the snowball sample could start 'rolling'. The chains of contacts tended to break down easily, normally after the second or third connection. The main reason for this was that individuals declined to be interviewed or wanted to remain anonymous. These difficulties meant that informants often led us only to registered users rather than to those not in contact with institutions.

It proved difficult for contacts to name people from their own districts. To overcome this, we increased the number of districts to include all areas within the three original groupings rather than simply concentrating on one area. This did not make the procedure any easier.

Other obstacles included: difficulties in obtaining users' initials as many were known only by their nicknames; the fact that people often moved away from the city or were imprisoned; or informants sometimes not knowing whether their contacts were registered users. This last factor obviously hindered attempts to estimate the prevalence of opiate use.

These difficulties led us to conclude that snowball methodology was an ineffective way of mapping non-registered opiate users in Budapest and we were unable to use it to produce a prevalence estimate. The overriding obstacle, encountered in every district and with each interviewer, was drug users' mistrust and fear of becoming involved in the study. We would argue that this problem is not peculiar to this project, but stems from the general stigmatisation of drug users by the rest of society.

Conclusions

This paper has outlined two methods for estimating the number of drug users in Budapest. Despite differences in approach, and a three-year gap between the projects, similar problems were encountered.

First, the reliability of institutional records on drug users was poor. This can be solved by improving the way records are compiled and by increasing the knowledge of staff working in these institutions. Second, we were confronted by a general suspicion of epidemiological research. It is possible that, if this type of research is undertaken more frequently and is seen to be useful, the suspicion may subside to some degree.

Finally, we would argue that the greatest problem facing epidemiological research is the widespread negative attitude towards illicit drug users in Hungary. A survey of secondary school students, conducted in 1995, shows this attitude to be on the increase compared with earlier studies (Elekes and Paksi, 1996). This was also found in a survey conducted with an adult sample. Respondents indicated that the idea of having a drug user as a neighbour was more disturbing to them than living next door to people with AIDS, homosexuals, convicted criminals or gypsies. Another survey indicated that the population was less tolerant towards drug users than it was towards people who had committed suicide or who were alcoholics.

Under these circumstances, it is perhaps not surprising that illicit drug users do not trust treatment institutions and that the institutions, in turn, do not register patients as drug users, for fear of stigmatising them. The implication of these attitudes for our research was that drug users would not talk to interviewers or name their contacts. All these factors combined to make it particularly difficult to undertake epidemiological drug research in Hungary.

References

Elekes, Zs. (1993) *A magyarországi droghelyzet a kutatások tükrében.* Országos Alkohológiai Intézet, Budapest.

Elekes, Zs. and Paksi, B. (1994) *Adalékok a magyarországi drogfogyasztás alakulásához* in Devianciák Magyarországon. Közélet Kiadó, Budapest.

Elekes, Zs. and Paksi, B. (1996) Magyarországi középiskolások alkohol és drogfogyasztása. Népjóléti Minisztérium.

Elekes, Zs. and Paksi, B. (1993) *Adalékok a hazai drogprobléma jellegének elemzéséhez.* Esély, 6.

CHAPTER 22

COMPARISON OF DIFFERENT
ESTIMATION METHODS IN POLAND

by Janusz Sierosławski and Antoni Zieliński

Prior to the beginning of the 1980s, drug use was not a publicly acknowledged problem in Poland. Although statistics throughout the 1970s indicated an increased consumption of the home-produced opiate 'Kompot' (a heroin derivative prepared
locally from poppy straw), painkilling drugs and tranquillisers, this went almost
unnoticed by the media. Those articles which did address the issue emphasised the
'capitalist' origin of the phenomenon and did not consider drug dependence to be
the problem of a then socialist Polish society.

With the first legal *Solidarity* period of rule in 1980, all former restrictions on public
discussion were lifted. This prompted a series of alarmist media articles on adoles-
cent 'Polish heroin' use and wild estimations of the number of drug users in Poland
became rife. Initially, this mood was also mirrored in epidemiological estimations
and, at one point, it was suggested that there were 460,000 drug experimenters and
35,000 regular consumers living in Poland (Bielewicz, 1984). As with earlier estimation efforts undertaken in the late 1970s, these assessments were methodologi-
cally limited in their appreciation of national data and often combined them with
multipliers taken from Western studies (Godwod-Sikorska, 1988).

This chapter describes an attempt to use a number of estimation methods not only
to assess the size of the opiate-injecting population in Poland, but also to negate the
influence of mass media and advocacy estimations on national drug policy. The
resulting assessments were based on statistics from drug treatment clinics and police operational data from the wrocławskie and kieleckie regions, and from national
data on drug-related deaths.

Data sources for estimation methods

Four data sources were utilised for the study: results from a snowball study, drug
treatment data, police operational data and statistics on drug-related deaths.

Snowball study data

In 1993, a snowball study of drug users was carried out in two regions of Poland:
wrocławskie and kieleckie. The areas were deliberately chosen as they represented

the two extremes of Polish drug use. In wrocławskie, drug consumption had been reported as high, whilst in kieleckie there was a relatively low reported rate of use.

Although the aim of the study was to estimate the number of opiate injectors in both regions, the logic of the snowball method dictated that both opiate users and individuals who used any drug on a regular basis should be contacted. The rationale behind this was that non-opiate users could have introduced researchers to opiate users.

Contacted individuals were interviewed about their pattern of drug use in the 30 days prior to the interview, the age at which they first started using drugs, their present health status and any previous treatment they had received. Socio-demographic data were also collected.

In wrocławskie, the study was implemented by staff in a drug dependency counselling centre which also undertook outreach work. Here, selected individuals treated in the centre or contacted during outreach were asked to introduce staff to other drug users they knew. In kieleckie, the study was carried out by students and individuals attached to a prevention centre operating within the educational system. Here, individuals familiar with other drug users introduced these to staff.

The study lasted six months. During this time 169 drug users in the wrocławskie region and 48 in the kieleckie region were interviewed. From this number, 107 individuals (63 per cent) in the wrocławskie region and 27 individuals (54 per cent) in the region of kieleckie were found to be opiate users, the majority of which, in both regions, used opiates every day (70-80 per cent).

Drug treatment data

In Poland, the drug dependency treatment system was set up in the late 1970s and is part of the psychiatric care system. There are two separate clinical systems: inpatient and outpatient.

Inpatient services are found in psychiatric hospitals, detoxification units and rehabilitation centres. These also include services run by non-governmental organisations (NGOs) which have a medical centre status.

The Institute of Psychiatry and Neurology collates all records relating to inpatient services. These are collected individually (the record being sent when a patient is discharged from treatment) and, at the beginning of each year, all clinics send information on patients in treatment on 31 December of the previous year. All records are marked with the initials and birth date of the patient. On the basis of these records, we were able to construct three indicators relating to the total number of patients: the numbers admitted, discharged and treated in a given year.

Inpatient records also provided a drug use profile for each patient. This is contained in the primary and secondary diagnoses. In accordance with the ICD (9) classification system, the first diagnosis is coded with four digits whilst the secondary diagnosis only receives three digits. The first three digits of either diagnosis denote whether the patient is drug dependent (code 304) or non-drug dependent (code 305). The fourth digit of the primary diagnosis denotes the main type of drug consumed.

Consequently, no information was available within the secondary diagnosis concerning the patient's drug of choice and this had to be excluded from the analysis regarding the type of dependency. The above limitations result in minor errors, which do not exceed 2-3 per cent with regard to the first group and 10 per cent with regard to the latter.

Outpatient services are found in drug treatment, mental health and alcohol treatment centres. NGOs are not included. Aggregate reports are kept on patients' sex, age and primary diagnosis according to ICD (9).

Police data on drug users

In Poland, the personal use or possession of drugs is not a criminal offence. However, the cultivation or production of a drug, including its import, export and supply to other individuals, is punishable by imprisonment. This is laid out in the Prevention of Drug Abuse Law passed in 1985.

There are no official statistics on police arrest rates. However, socio-demographic data are recorded on drug users who may become involved, or are already suspected of being involved, in crime. These are collected through local police operations penetrating drug environments which are then reported to regional headquarters. These data do not include any information on the type of drug used.

There are two main problems with such data:

- as there are no official procedures on how to collate the data, we cannot assume that every local police operation utilises the same definition of what a drug dependent individual is;
- as drug users are geographically mobile, they may be included in the register more than once.

Despite these difficulties, the long-term trends indicated by law enforcement and drug treatment data were remarkably similar; this may support the value of such an indicator.

Data on drug-related deaths

The basic source of information concerning deaths in Poland is the electronic database and archive at the Central Statistical Office (GUS) where every death is recorded. The database records the date and location of death, the socio-demographic details of the deceased and three contributing causes of death (one primary and two secondary).

The GUS database and archive were not, however, used for this study for three reasons:

- death from intoxication with opiates rarely appears in the GUS data, mainly due to the death classification system which does not allow for such a precise distinction;
- studies have suggested that a significant proportion of deaths regarding drug dependents are often classified as being of an undefined cause (Moskalewicz and Sierosławski, 1992; 1996)
- no names or initials are recorded in the electronic database. Only the date of birth and sex of the deceased can be used as identifiers. This would compound the problem of double counting when attempting to compare a number of different data sources. Although the archive death records contain given names and surnames, obtaining this information is difficult due to confidentiality regulations.

The main source of information on deaths of drug dependents used for the study were police records on drug overdoses. Again, these were based on non-standardised reports from local police stations to regional headquarters. They contained no information on the type of drug implicated nor any socio-demographic data. The completeness of such collected data also remains unclear. For instance, deaths involving volatile substances may be neglected by some police stations if the local police does not include glue sniffing into the concept and definition of drug dependence.

Assessment of validity and reliability of data sources

The reporting systems detailed above should be evaluated in terms of the quality of the data they produce. This, and other salient indicators of quality, are outlined in Table 1.

Table 1: Quality of data sources in Poland

	Validity	Reliability	Early warning	Analytical capability	Confidentiality
In-patient clinics	good	good	poor	satisfactory	good
Out-patient clinics	satisfactory	good	poor	poor	good
Police (drug users)	poor	unknown	good	poor	good
Police (deaths)	poor	unknown	good	poor	good
HIV register	good	good	poor	satisfactory	good

Primarily, this assessment is undertaken in terms of its validity and reliability. By validity, we refer to the degree of confidence one can have in the data produced as being reflective of what it proposes to measure. Reliability refers to the data being collected according to a standardised procedure or definition, for example 'drug dependency'.

'Early warning' ability refers to the regularity by which data become available, and the month of the year when data become available. It is assumed that the earlier the data are available the easier it is to target policy interventions effectively.

'Analytical capability' is coterminous with the type of data available. Therefore, those systems which collect data on an individual's socio-demographic background and their drug use profile are deemed as more desirable.

Estimations

Three different types of estimation were undertaken: (a) estimations based upon the snowball study, using treatment experience as a multiplier and applying this to city and national treatment statistics; (b) drug-related deaths statistics, using mortality rate multipliers; (c) capture-recapture approach, using data from the snowball study and drug treatment and police data.

Snowball study estimates

Data collected in the wrocławskie and kieleckie regions through the snowball procedure were used to estimate the number of opiate users in Poland. This estimation was based on the number of opiate users who had undergone inpatient treatment in the previous year (1993).

It was found that in the region of wrocławskie, 49 per cent of all opiate users interviewed were treated as inpatients, whilst this was the case for only 19 per cent of opiate users in the kieleckie region. Of course, this may have been due to the lesser availability of treatment in kieleckie and it could also have been influenced by the different starting points of the snowball in each region. However, if generally representative, then the total population of opiate dependent individuals in wrocławskie is approximately twice as big as the number of individuals who had received inpatient treatment. The total number of opiate users in kieleckie would be five times higher than the number of treated individuals.

In 1993, 250 residents of the wrocławskie region and 60 residents of the kieleckie region were treated as inpatients because of opiate dependency. Therefore, the total number of opiate users would amount to approximately 500 in the wrocławskie region and to 300 in the kieleckie region.

If we apply these two multipliers for estimation using national inpatient statistics, the following results are obtained: on the basis of the wrocławskie findings the number of opiate users in Poland may be estimated as being around 8,300 and on the basis of the kieleckie findings around 20,000.

Estimates derived from drug-related death statistics

Estimations were also made on the basis of police statistics on the number of drug overdoses in Poland in 1995. This employed a multiplier constructed from three previous studies.

The first two studies examined the mortality rates of drug dependent individuals in inpatient clinics over a four-year period beginning in 1974 and 1984 respectively (Moskalewicz and Sierosławski 1984; 1992). These yielded mortality rates of 1.6 and 1.7.

The third study assessed the mortality rate of injecting drug users from a detoxification unit in Warsaw between 1983 and 1992. The study was a part of an international project initiated by the World Health Organisation and revealed a mortality rate of 2.6 for men and 1.4 for women (Moskalewicz and Sierosławski, 1996).

From these findings, it was possible to estimate the mortality rate to be approximately 1-2 per cent. A more sophisticated measure was not available for two reasons. First, the mortality rate has significantly increased in the last couple of years. Consequently, those studies addressing an earlier period are perhaps out of date. Second, the study conducted in Warsaw is limited to only one centre and in the last period of this study (1991-1992) only 34 deaths were notified. This is too small a number to use as a base for a multiplier. However, if 1-2 per cent is adopted as the mortality rate, the 177 cases of deaths reported by the police in 1995 produce an estimate of 9,000-18,000 opiate users nationwide.

Capture-recapture estimate

The capture-recapture (CRC) method entailed the use of various data sources to produce an estimate. This was the first time that drug treatment and operational police data had been combined to produce a national estimate (Moskalewicz and Sierosławski, 1995). Furthermore, unlike in previous studies, the presence of identifiers in the original snowball study, drug treatment and operational police data meant it was possible to avoid including an individual more than once.

The estimation was broken down into five steps. First, a single health register comprising the total population of patients undergoing treatment for drug use was created. To avoid the problem of double-counting, all records collected from in- and out-patient clinics were compared. It was found that 40 per cent of the number of individuals treated in out-patient clinics had been treated in in-patient clinics in the same year. From this, the total number of individuals treated in a single year was estimated by adding 60 per cent to the number of patients treated solely in outpatient clinics.

Second, all opiate users were selected from this single health register and also from the snowball sample. Although the operational police data did not contain information which allowed this, it was assumed for the purposes of the study that opiate users constituted the majority of individuals registered by the police. This could result in an overestimation of the number of opiate users.

Third, the opiate users from the single health register, the snowball study and operational police data were compared. Adjustments were made to these figures if any opiate user appeared in more than one data source. These comparisons are shown in Table 2.

Table 2: Capture-recapture estimates of the number of opiate addicts in the population

	wrocławskie	kieleckie
Snowball-police	1,200	401
Snowball-Treatment	907	140
Police-treatment	1,435	258

Source: Moskalewicz and Sierosławski (1995).

The number of opiate users in wrocławskie was estimated to range between 900 and 1,400 individuals. The estimate for kieleckie was approximately 140-400. The median of these assessments, i.e. 1,200 individuals in wrocławskie and 258 individuals in kieleckie, were then used as the figure for those regions.

Fourth, a multiplier was created. The estimated number of opiate users in wrocławskie and kieleckie was compared with individual datasets from inpatient treatment clinics and police operational data.

From this, it was found that the median assessment of the number of opiate users in both regions was, on average, 2.4 times higher than the number of drug users registered by the police. This figure rose to 4.6 times higher when compared with the number of drug dependent patients at inpatient treatment clinics.

Finally, this multiplier was applied to national statistics from inpatient clinics and police operational data. The results are shown in Table 3.

Table 3: Estimated number of opiate addicts based on police and treatment statistics in Poland

	Treatment	Police
Statistics	4,232	16,598
Multipliers	4,6	2,4
Final estimate result	19,467	39,835

Source: Moskalewicz and Sierosławski (1995).

It was estimated that the total number of opiate users in Poland can be located within the range of 20,000-40,000. The lower figure was calculated on the basis of inpatient treatment data and the higher number was based on operational police data.

Assessment of estimation methods

Although the estimation methods described in this section are reflective of an increasing sophistication in Polish epidemiology, they must be considered as only the beginning of an attempt to construct a set of valid estimators. It is possible to identify three main areas where improvements could be made.

First, in conducting the snowball study, the zero-stage point was not randomly selected: this could influence the final results. In the region of wrocławskie, for example, the zero-stage point consisted of patients in a dependency treatment clinic. This could explain the high proportion of treated individuals in the snowball sample. Equally, the smaller number of treated individuals in the kieleckie sample could be explained by the zero-stage point being established among individuals without experience of drug treatment.

Second, the comparison of the treatment register, the police operational data and the snowball study resulted in three different estimations. On the basis of common sense this resulted in a median figure for each region. A model for all three sets should be developed instead.

Third, the multipliers used in the CRC studies were derived from only two regions. However, regional variations of drug use in Poland are high, as indicated by the regional rates of hospitalisation for drug addiction (Figure 1). This ranges from 42.0 per 100,000 of the population in Jelenia Góra region to 0.97 in Nowy Sącz region. Rates for wrocławskie region and kieleckie region are 23.5 and 7.1 respectively (Sierosławski 1995). To improve the validity of the findings and the multiplier on a nationwide basis, it is desirable to undertake further CRC studies in other regions of Poland.

Summary of estimation methods

The attempts to estimate the number of opiate users in Poland have produced a number of assessments: 8,300-20,000 individuals when using the snowball method; 9,000-18,000 users when using police overdose data; and 20,000-40,000 persons with the CRC approach. The best estimate is approximately 20,000 individuals.

Conclusions: relevance of estimation to drug policy

Large numbers will always appeal to the imagination and it would be unrealistic to expect media estimations to have changed much from the early days of *Solidarity*. Indeed, according to *Wprost Weekly*, for example, not only are there now 300,000 addicts in Poland but the number will rise to 3,000,000 in a few years (Szumińska,

Figure 1: Rate of hospitalisation due to drug dependence per 100,000 inhabitants by region, 1994

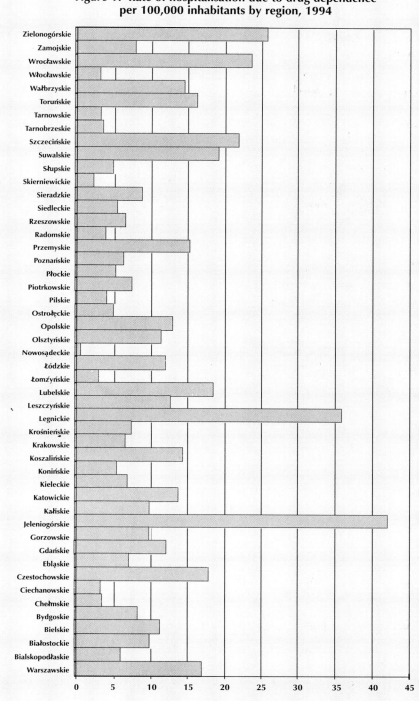

1994; Mazur, 1994). In the past, the role of epidemiologists has been encroached upon by activists and advocates. Unlike those derived from the media, epidemiological estimates do not evoke immediate interest and often refer to situations over the past couple of years. Consequently, politicians have often preferred to listen to the 'estimates' presented by activists and journalists.

However, due to their increasing methodological sophistication, presentations of epidemiological estimates are becoming increasingly difficult to ignore. At the 1996 meeting of the Inter-Ministerial Commission of Co-ordination of Drug Control, the latest epidemiological data regarding the situation in the country in 1994 were presented. Although neither the exposition of the systematical methodology nor the accurately presented figures provoked any significant discussion, it did, for the first time, discourage activists from presenting their own opposing assessments based predominantly on intuition and selective interest. This growing reputation has also been partly recognised by the inclusion of a government representative and several epidemiologists in the Pompidou Group.

Poland is currently engaged in a public debate over the proposed content of a new law addressing the status of personal drug possession. Although the mass media will always be prone to publishing inaccurate estimates and advocacy groups will continue to lobby the government, it is likely that, more than ever, attention will be paid to epidemiological estimates of the number of Polish drug users.

References

Bielewicz A. (1984) 'Rozpowszechnienie zjawiska nadużywania leków w Polsce', in: A. Śliwowski, W. Górecki (ed.) *Medycyna Środowiskowa, część IV, Problemy Diagostyki i Terapii*, Warszawa, Centrum Medycznego Kształcenia Podyplomowego.

Godwod-Sikorska C. (1988) 'Uzależnienia lekowe w Polsce', *Terapia i Leki*, Nr 4-5.

Godwod-Sikorska C. (1993) 'Rozpowszechnienie uzależnień lekowych w Polsce w latach 1989-1991', *Alkoholizm i Narkomania*, Wydanie Specjalne: Zagrożenia AIDS.

Mazur M. (1994) Złota żyła, *Wprost*, 21 August, 1994.

Moskalewicz J. and Sierosławski J. (1984) 'Umieralność wśród uzależnionych od leków', in: A. Śliwowski and W. Górecki (eds) *Medycyna Środowiskowa, część IV, Problemy Diagostyki i Terapii*, Warszawa, Centrum Medycznego Kształcenia Podyplomowego.

Moskalewicz J. and Sierosławski J. (1992) 'Umieralność wśród osób uzależnionych od substancji psychoaktywnych, *Alkoholizm i Narkomania*, 9.

Moskalewicz J. and Sierosławski J. (1995) 'Zastosowanie nowych metod szacowania rozpowszechnienia narkomanii', *Alkoholizm i Narkomania*, 4 (21).

Moskalewicz J. and Sierosławski J. (1996) 'Umieralność osób uzależnionych od narkotyków przyjmowanych w iniekcjach', *Przegląd Epidemiologiczny*, 50-3.

Sierosławski J. (1995) 'Rozpowszechnienie uzależnień lekowych w 1993 r.', *Alkoholizm i Narkomania* 1, 18.

Szuminska H. (1994) Szkoła uzależnienia, *Wprost*, 06 March, 1994.

COMPARISON OF KEY INFORMANT
AND MULTIPLIER ESTIMATES IN SLOVENIA

by Dušan Nolimal

It is only comparatively recently that illicit drug use in Slovenia has been perceived as a problem. In the last five years, media attention to this issue has rapidly grown and there has been mounting public concern. This has been accompanied by a considerable growth in the number of governmental and non-governmental bodies set up to deal with illicit drug use. Heroin injecting, in particular, has become an important political issue, not least because of its association with HIV transmission. This concern culminated in 1991 with the opening of the first specialist treatment services for heroin users.

The planning of these services was made in the absence of reliable epidemiological information. The data which were available indicated the number of problematic heroin users in Slovenia to be between 2,000 and 10,000 (Nolimal and Premik, 1992; Flaker *et al*, 1992; Nolimal *et al*, 1993; Nolimal and Onusic, 1993). While the figures indicate fewer heroin users than may be found in Western European countries, they were still deemed significant, given the comparatively small size of the country and its population.

The paucity of epidemiological data led the National Institute of Public Health to ask some basic questions such as: What data are available for estimating the number of heroin users? How reliable are these data? Are the numbers of users likely to change? How many users will continue to use drugs over time? What proportion of users have suffered social or health consequences of drug-taking? What proportion of the drug-using population are seeking treatment?

To answer these questions satisfactorily, a number of practical, methodological and conceptual problems needed to be addressed. This paper reviews these issues and presents three methods we used to estimate the prevalence of heroin use:

- secondary data analysis;
- key informant estimation;
- snowballing.

It should be emphasised that the primary goal of all three studies was to identify high risk groups in order to help target interventions for problem drug users, rather than to estimate prevalence.

Secondary data analysis

The first systematic attempt to collect data on illicit drug use was undertaken in 1989 by the National Institute of Public Health. Some useful data were available from health and social services, pharmacies, law enforcement agencies, schools and prisons. These allowed us to provide an approximate estimate of the size of the problem. Statistics on the prescribing of methadone and other psychoactive substances provided an indicator of the extent of heroin use. The increasing number of methadone prescriptions was one of the first warning signals that heroin use was on the increase. The number of prescriptions for methadone rose from 2,943 in 1989 to 7,656 in 1991.

The police held information on people arrested for drug-related offences. Available from the Ministry of Interior Affairs were data on the number of people arrested for drugs possession and on the quantity of drugs seized. Between 1989 and 1996 the number of heroin seizures increased significantly, indicating a rise in the quantity of heroin entering the country. The quantity of heroin seized in Slovenia rose from 494g in 1989 to 8,723g in 1991. Other sources of data included the courts, which held records on people charged with drug-related offences, and schools, which recorded data on drug use among pupils. Finally, there were the epidemiological data on AIDS and HIV infection, collected by the National Institute of Public Health. These showed a comparatively low number of drug injecting-related HIV cases through the 1990s.

Comments

Access to the secondary data was dependent upon the co-operation of agency representatives. This made it important to explain the study to them and to earn their trust. The quality of available information was found to be lacking in most instances, thereby undermining the validity of prevalence estimates derived by this method. Nonetheless, analysis of secondary data pointed to a rapid increase in the extent of heroin use since 1989-90.

Key informant estimation

Having identified the available secondary data, we interviewed a range of professionals who had contact with drug users. These included doctors, pharmacists, social workers, teachers, community workers and police officers. The aim of the interviews was to obtain impressions of the nature of drug-related problems in Slovenia. The qualitative data were used to inform the design of a standardised questionnaire on drug use, which was distributed to key informants in the nine Public Health Institutes and eleven regional Criminal Investigation Bureaux. Those involved drew on data from their own networks of key informants. Participants were asked to consult their records and use these to estimate the number of registered heroin users in their respective areas and to make informed 'guesstimates' as to the numbers at regional or local levels. The issues addressed via the questionnaire included: the extent of illicit drug use; community perceptions of drug use; the number of heroin users; the proportion of these who are known to the police; the number who had received treatment; the number of current and former heroin users; and the prevalence of HIV infection. Estimates from police personnel generated an aggregated estimate of 1,026-1,226 heroin users. The aggregated estimate from public health informants was 743-1,045.

The study produced other information which was useful for the planning of interventions. For example, two of the country's largest cities – Ljubljana and Koper – were identified as holding a high proportion of the country's heroin users; heroin was highlighted as the drug associated with the most acute health and social problems; a general awareness of the link between injecting drug use and HIV was indicated; and a large number of problem drug users were found to have only sought treatment once the country's first methadone programme had opened.

Comments

Key informant estimation has an obvious weakness, namely that it relies entirely on 'guesstimates' of local experts whose reports may be distorted by incomplete knowledge or personal bias. However, it can provide useful data on 'visible' heroin users for minimal cost.

Snowballing and multiplier estimation

The third study was conducted in 1993 by the Institute of Public Health in Koper and the National Institute of Public Health (Krek *et al*, 1995). Its aim was to identify high risk groups and to examine drug users' risk behaviour. The data were used to generate a retrospective prevalence estimate of heroin addiction.

Method

The first part of the study was designed to estimate the proportion of heroin users who had been treated. The existence of the methadone maintenance programme in Koper, which treated 263 heroin users between 1991 and 1993, helped us gain access to illicit drug users. Twenty-six of its patients were selected as 'indigenous fieldworkers' for the study. The main selection criterion was area of residency as we wanted to ensure that fieldworkers would recruit nominees from throughout the country. The task was made easier because, at the time of the research, there was only one other methadone treatment centre, so the Koper centre clientele was drawn from across Slovenia.

Those selected were knowledgeable about, and respected by, heroin users. This enabled them to gain access to other heroin users relatively quickly and smoothly, collect first-hand information on local drug scenes and recruit 'hidden' heroin users. Their role was to nominate individuals whom they knew used heroin regularly. A questionnaire, exploring risk behaviour and previous treatment experiences, was then administered by the fieldworker. To minimise double-counting, participants were assigned a unique identifying code. This part of the study produced estimates of the proportion who had received treatment at some time. In the second part of the study, existing documents relating to drug treatment were also reviewed. Most of these were available at the two methadone maintenance treatment centres. The National Institute of Public Health kept documentation on patients who had been hospitalised through their heroin use (e.g. cases of overdose) rather than on those in treatment for their addiction. These documents provided benchmark information on the number of treated heroin users and were used for the prevalence estimation.

Results

A total of 890 heroin users completed the questionnaire. The study consisted of at least 21 sub-samples. One fieldworker recruited 139 nominees (19 per cent), although most recruited approximately 15 to 20. Of the total sample, 616 (72 per cent) were male and 241 (28 per cent) were female. Respondents were recruited from different areas of the country, but most lived in Koper (24 per cent). Forty per cent of the sample (362) had received treatment at least once in their lifetime. This percentage was used as the multiplier for the prevalence estimations. In addition to those who had ever received treatment, 160 were reported in the same period to have been hospitalised as a consequence of their heroin use. These figures were used as the benchmark for the calculation. It was assumed that most of those who had received treatment in the past would have done so after the first treatment centres were opened in 1991. The following approximate estimate was produced applying the benchmark-multiplier calculation to the figures:

$$E = (n1 + n2) \times \frac{100}{m}$$

E = prevalence estimation for the period 1991-1993
n1 = total number of the treated methadone patients (approximately 360)
n2 = total number of heroin users hospitalised (160)
m = multiplier (% of heroin users who were in treatment – 362/890 = 0.40)

$$E = 520 \times 100 = \frac{1300}{40}$$

In this way, the population of heroin users in Slovenia between 1991 and 1993 was estimated to be 1,300. However, the confidence limits within which this estimate lies are extremely wide.

Comments

There is insufficient information to assess the quality of the data, for example with regard to the consistency of fieldworkers' approaches to recruitment and the reliability of self-reported data. We had to review the fieldwork process retrospectively, relying on anecdotal information and using the indicator of missing data. Given the data at our disposal, simplifying assumptions also had to be adopted for the prevalence estimation. But, despite the methodological limitations, the analysis offers a reasonable first answer regarding the size of the heroin-using population in Slovenia.

The recruitment of drug users as the indigenous fieldworkers was critical to the success of the study. It enabled us to gain access to hidden heroin users and to map areas where heroin use is most prevalent. The fieldworkers made this possible through having credibility with other drug users and their ability to establish trusting relationships with them. Drug users in the treatment programme also offered the study a wealth of information and ideas. We would recommend, therefore, that future studies of this type should actively seek the help and support provided by indigenous drug users.

The snowball sampling method is not without its problems, however. We have been unable to ascertain how many successive stages of snowballing were produced by different fieldworkers or to assess, retrospectively, double-counting in the nominee sample. There was also a lack of information on nominee refusal rates, as well as errors in the reporting of nominees' treatment status. The medical records reviewed for the study were incomplete and double entries of patients were not excluded. There were also considerable variations in the way treatment centres recorded information. For example, some records did not distinguish between different types of addictive drugs nor did they differentiate between patients who had ever used a drug and those who were current problem users.

Conclusions

Two recent reports estimate that there are between 2,000 and 4,000 heroin users nationwide (Nolimal 1996; Kastelic and Kostnapfel, 1996). The snowball and multiplier approach, presented above, generated a lower figure of 1,300 for the period 1991–93, although, as stated, the confidence limits are extremely wide. Using the systematic key person approach, the maximum number of heroin users in 1992 was estimated to be between 1,045 and 1,226. These two methods, therefore, produced similar estimates. Both procedures used treatment population as the source group, so it is likely that the treatment population is over-represented in our samples. From these studies, comparatively little is known about users who have never had contact with statutory institutions.

The Pompidou Group assistance programmes in 1993-96 were the first to introduce basic concepts in drug use estimation (Council of Europe, 1994). The introduction of standardised methods and indicators has heightened awareness about drug issues in public health and emphasised the importance of collecting drug-related information, including information on addiction prevalence (Hartnoll, 1995). One of the results of this programme is the research described in this paper which presents the first attempt to use scientific approaches to estimate the extent of illicit drug use in Slovenia.

In the light of growing public concern about illicit drug use and competition for public funds, we should be sceptical of prevalence estimates based on anecdotal evidence. It is important to increase the number of epidemiologists and, we argue, there is a fundamental need to establish a national unit which would be responsible for collecting, processing and analysing information on the use of drugs. The unit could monitor trends over time and take responsibility for improving the quality and relevance of information used to inform drug policy.

The economic and political climate in Slovenia is conducive to further rises in the prevalence of drug use. The increasing availability of heroin, limited economic prospects and the loss of traditional values have encouraged heroin use among the population. The development of policies and services concerning drug misuse has been handicapped by the lack of reliable epidemiological information. If knowledge about methodological and conceptual issues is limited, and if the resources are scant, the response to drug problems will be based on inadequate knowledge. Given the preliminary nature of the research presented in this chapter, it is hazardous to speculate about the true extent of heroin use in Slovenia and on the adequacy of existing services. If drug policy and treatment services are to be well informed, and not merely the product of wishful thinking, it is vital that the quality of the epidemiological research is improved so that we can collect reliable information on visible and hidden drug-using populations.

Acknowledgements

The preparation of this report was facilitated by many individuals and agencies. Special thanks go to the key persons from the Ministry of the Interior and the Regional Institutes of Public Health, in particular to Dr. Milan Krek (Regional Institute of Public Health of Koper), Nino Rode (School for Social Work), Vladimira Rejc and Viktor Nolimal for their assistance.

References

Council of Europe (1994) *Report Information Systems and Applied Epidemiology of Drug Misuse Follow-up Seminar*, Strasbourg.

Flaker, V. *et al* (1992) *Project "Stigma": The interim report to WHO.*

Hartnoll, R. (1995) *Recent trends in drug consumption, policy and research 1994: synthesis of national reports*, Strasbourg: Council of Europe.

Kastelic, A. and Kostnapfel, RT. (1996) 'Treatment of addicts of prohibited drugs in Slovenia', *Euro-Methwork Newsletter*, 8, 11-14.

Krek, M., Krek-Misigoj, J. and Nolimal, D.(1995) 'Difficulties with field research of the illicit drug use', in Nolimal, D. and Belec M. (eds) *Anthology of the papers presented at the Information Systems and Applied Epidemiology of Drug Misuse Follow-up Seminar.* Ljubljana-Piran: Institute of Public Health.

Nolimal, D. (1996) 'Self-help and methadone in Slovenia', *Euro-Methwork Newsletter*, 7,15.

Nolimal, D., Globonik, M., Rebec, A., Krek, M. and Flaker, V. (1993) 'Descriptive epidemiology of the group of street injecting drug users in the regions of Koper and Ljubljana in the year 1991', *Zdrav Var 32*, 161-4.

Nolimal, D. and Onusic, S. (1993) *Overview of drug misuse in Slovenia: epidemiology and research*, Ljubljana: Institute of Public Health of Slovenia.

Nolimal, D. and Premik, M.(1992) 'Some social-medical aspects of drug abuse', *Zdrav Vestn*, 61, 133-6.

CHAPTER 24

CROSS-VALIDATING AT LOCAL LEVEL

by Richard Hartnoll

This final chapter concentrates on how to assess the validity of prevalence estimates, especially when prevalence and drug use patterns are changing, and on how to interpret the prevalence rates that are obtained in terms of what they mean within the context to which they refer.

All methods for estimating prevalence are based on assumptions and have important limitations and sources of error. The problem is that there is no method that gives a 'gold standard' against which to validate any particular estimate. An alternative approach is to compare estimates based on different methods that make different assumptions. If it is possible to assess the likely direction of error of each estimate (i.e. whether it is likely to be too high or too low, or whether certain sub-groups of users are excluded) then it may be possible to define a range within which the 'best estimate' is likely to lie. During periods when the prevalence is changing, it is necessary to obtain separate estimates for successive years, rather than combine data from a period of several years. This is the subject of the first section of this chapter.

Even a series of 'best estimates' obtained from several different estimates over successive years remains a rather abstract figure (or range) based on assumptions and inferences that may or may not be valid. Such estimates should not be accepted in isolation from other information on the situation to which they refer. Otherwise there would be no way of knowing whether they are indeed reasonable estimates that make sense, nor any means of understanding how to interpret and use them within the wider, dynamic picture of problematic drug use and responses to it. A complementary approach is thus to examine the relationship between prevalence estimates and other indicators and sources of information on the drug situation, including indirect indicators of drug trends and consequences, and more descriptive information on drug use patterns and on the activities and responses of agencies that are the basis for those indicators. Although this, in itself, may not improve the validity of any estimate in terms of giving a more precise figure, it does set estimates within a more meaningful context so that they can be useful. This is addressed in the second section below.

The examples that are used to illustrate these points are drawn from a broader series of detailed studies of drug use and drug indicators carried out by the author and his colleagues in London in the 1980s. These included: studies of the utility of data on drug problems available from different agencies and other sources of information as possible indicators of drug trends; pilot studies to estimate the prevalence of problematic drug use (with an emphasis on regular opiate use); and fieldwork studies of drug users both in and out of treatment (Hartnoll *et al* 1985a, 1985b).

The purpose of this chapter is not to discuss the data themselves, but rather to draw out some of the lessons that can be learned about assessing the drug situation from an epidemiological point of view. It must be noted that this is facilitated by the benefit of hindsight. It should also be noted that the original studies were of an exploratory nature and aimed at identifying feasible methodologies that could be applied at local level. Estimation techniques have become increasingly sophisticated since then, and other researchers, including many of the contributors to this monograph, have played an important role in this. However, the main theme of this chapter is not to add to the discussion of specific methods but rather to emphasise that no level of technical development is adequate unless it is accompanied by critical reflection on the relationship between the data and the phenomenon they are assumed to reflect, and by adoption of a holistic approach in which the consistency between different methods and the coherence of the different parts in terms of the whole are carefully analysed.

Although these principles are as relevant at national level as at local level, it is often more feasible to apply them locally, where context and relevant circumstances can be taken into account. The researchers involved in the examples given below had been working in London with a range of services and drug users since the early 1970s, especially in the area selected for intensive epidemiological investigation in the 1980s. This local knowledge undoubtedly made it easier to assess the results of each method or indicator within the overall local setting.

Cross-validation of different prevalence estimation methods

This section describes how a series of 'best estimates' for the prevalence of regular opiate use in inner north London was derived for successive years based on estimates obtained from four different methods: capture-recapture, addict-death multiplier, nomination, and extrapolation from a survey of GPs (Hartnoll *et al*, 1985a). Where it was possible to apply different methods to the same year, then the different methods indicated relatively similar prevalence levels, though differences also emerged that need to be discussed more closely, especially regarding the death multiplier.

As far as we are aware, apart from a case-finding and capture-recapture study in Sweden (Socialdepartementet, 1980) and apart from several case-finding studies in the United Kingdom (Arroyave *et al*, 1972; Bishop *et al*, 1976; de Alarcon and Rathod, 1968) and an application of nomination methods (Blumberg and Dronfield, 1976), this was the first systematic attempt to apply simultaneously different prevalence estimation methods in Europe, although various methods had been used in the United States (DuPont and Piemme, 1973; Greene, 1974; Greenwood, 1971; Hughes, 1977; Hunt and Chambers, 1976; Newmayer, 1976; Person *et al*, 1977).

Since these estimates were feasibility sub-studies rather than major research investigations of prevalence, the detailed data are not reproduced here. As with all initial efforts, more can be learnt from mistakes and careful reflection on the nature and direction of the likely errors in the estimates rather than from the results themselves.

For the purpose of these estimates, the operational definition of a case was a person aged 16 to 44 years who had used an opiate on a daily or almost daily basis (6 days per week) for at least a month during the course of the calendar year and who was living in the Inner London boroughs of Camden and Islington (population around 300,000). It was not always easy to apply these definitions precisely and some of the problems are described below.

Capture-recapture

For the capture-recapture estimates, four different samples of opiate users were obtained from sources covering the defined population. The sources were: a specialised outpatient drug treatment centre, a hospital for infectious diseases, the death records at a Coroner's Court, and court cases identified through local newspaper reports.

There were few problems in applying the case definition at the outpatient treatment centre. This was due to the fact that treatment was aimed primarily at opiate dependents, that all those attending had been carefully assessed, and that clinical records were systematic and of high quality. The situation was similar at the hospital for infectious diseases (cases were opiate injectors with acute hepatitis). At the Coroner's Court, it was necessary to review in depth the records of all unnatural deaths between the ages of 16 and 44 where there was a possibility of drug involvement, since death certificates or Coroners' verdicts were not usually adequate for deciding if the criteria for a case had been met. Relatively extensive information was often available from these records on dependent or regular opiate users who died through a variety of causes although, if there were any arising from road traffic accidents, then these would have been missed.

In order to include a sample drawn from law enforcement sources, it might have been preferable to use records based on arrests of opiate users by the police. However, it was not possible to obtain data that identified individuals. In any case, it is unlikely that police data would have provided information on most of the opiate users they arrested, since usually the alleged offence involved theft rather than a drug offence such as possession of opiates. Similar limitations applied to court statistics.

As an experimental alternative, we used reports from the local newspapers, which routinely covered the local courts and which, every week, would contain pages of cases including names, age, street or district of residence, offence and, when applicable, whether the accused was described as an addict. The (coincidental) fact that the fieldwork office was based above one of the two local newspapers was useful in verifying the unorthodox sampling procedure! Even if coverage of court cases was not comprehensive, we could find no indications of systematic bias in the resulting sample, though it was clearly an assumption that this was a representative sample of opiate users passing through the local courts. Cases were included only where there was information to justify a reasonable assumption that they met the study criteria, although it is quite possible that some did not. In these respects, however, the sample was probably no worse than any other drawn from law enforcement sources.

For all four samples, full names, as well as other information, could be obtained for research purposes, thus making the task of identifying overlaps between samples relatively easy. Since this was an exploratory study of the capture-recapture method in a fairly restricted area, the samples were relatively small and the overlaps between pairs of samples in single figures. It was thus only possible to apply the two-sample model, albeit for different combinations of sources taken two at a time. The confidence intervals (estimated subsequently by Colin Taylor) were also too large to allow reliable comparison between the estimates produced by different pairs of samples.

However, one can use this experience as a basis for discussing how one might try to understand whether combinations of given pairs of sources might lead to a higher or lower estimate. Even when samples are large enough to apply three or more sample models and allow for positive or negative dependency between pairs of samples, it is also valuable to reflect, in non-statistical terms, on how case definitions, as actually applied in the different samples, as well as the possible dependencies between samples, might affect the estimate. At the same time, the reader should be warned that this can lead to serious headaches!

Thus, during the period of this study, it was observed in a separate sub-study of opiate users not in treatment that sniffing or smoking heroin was becoming more common. At first, with some exceptions, this was not reflected in the treatment sample, though subsequently the proportion of non-injectors in treatment increased.

Throughout the study, the sample from the Coroner's Court consisted largely of injectors, again with a few exceptions, and the sample from the hospital for infectious diseases contained only injectors. Thus, if injecting users were more likely to go for treatment and also more likely to die and/or to be admitted to hospital for drug-related diseases such as acute hepatitis, then capture-recapture estimates based on overlaps between treatment and deaths or drug-related infectious diseases would underestimate the extent of opiate use by other routes. An under-estimate would also have arisen if cases were referred from the hospital for infectious diseases to the treatment centre. However, when the number of non-injectors in treatment subsequently increased, then the estimates also increased, since non-injectors had a lower probability of dying or contracting drug-related infectious diseases and the overlap was therefore lower.

Conversely, estimates based on the overlap of treatment and court samples might be expected to give lower overlaps, and thus higher estimates, if the case definition in the court sample was broader and included cases of individuals who were not so heavily dependent and thus less likely to go for treatment, or if a significant proportion were sent to prison and thus unable to go for treatment.

It is not always possible to describe the effect on the estimate of differences in the application of the case definition in practice, nor is it easy to assess the likely direction of error resulting from dependence between samples in the simple two-sample model. Attempting to do this does, however, force the researcher to think hard about how the case definition is applied in practice and about whether inclusion in one sample means that cases are more or less likely to be included in the second. Many of these effects are likely to be rather specific to local circumstances. Such reflections thus push one towards trying to understand the relationship between different sources of information and the conditions under which drug users are more or less likely to be identified by those different sources.

Addict death multiplier

The second estimation method applied was based on a projection from the number of regular opiate users who died each year - the addict death multiplier described by Martin Frischer and Henrik Sælan in Chapters 12 and 15 of this monograph. Several studies in the United Kingdom had suggested that the mortality rate from all causes for opiate-injecting addicts was between one and two per cent per year. The mid-point of this range was taken as the basis for the multiplier that was then applied to the annual number of regular or dependent opiate users who had been living in the area when they died and who were identified through the comprehensive review of Coroner's Court records described above.

Two possible sources of error in these estimates were the assumption that all relevant cases were identified in the review of the Coroner's records, and that the mortality rate was correct and constant. As noted earlier, if there were any deaths of regular opiate users due to road accidents, then these may have been missed. In such a case, the estimates would have been too low. Furthermore, the rise in the use of heroin by sniffing, and especially by smoking, over the time period concerned meant that the annual mortality rate based on injecting drug users became progressively too high as non-injecting modes of use increased, leading to a growing degree of underestimation. It is thus likely that estimates derived from the death multiplier tended to be too low and by an increasing margin in the years following 1980. A further factor, described below in the second part of this chapter, also reinforces this interpretation.

Extrapolation from a survey of general practitioners

The third estimation method used was an indirect form of capture-recapture. Rather than identify the overlap between two sources (agencies) by counting individuals, we attempted to estimate the overlap, in this case between general practitioners and the drug treatment centre. Surveys of general practitioners gave estimates of the number of cases whom they saw for whatever reason and of the proportion who had been in treatment at the treatment centre during the previous year. Since the numbers treated at the centre each year were known, the same two-sample capture-recapture formula was applied to give an estimate of total prevalence.

One should be especially cautious about estimates derived in this indirect manner. In this particular example, there was also good reason to assume that there was a positive dependency between the two sources, since some addicts had been referred to the treatment centre by the GP and others became known as addicts to their GP as a result of going to the treatment centre. It is quite likely that this led to an under-estimate.

Nomination technique

The fourth and final estimation method was based on nomination techniques. Over 100 opiate users interviewed in an ongoing community-based fieldwork study in the area served by the treatment centre were asked to nominate friends who were also regular opiate users and to indicate whether those friends had been in treatment at the centre during the previous year. The ratio of 'attended treatment centre' to 'not attended' was averaged across all respondents and the ratio was used as a multiplier to extrapolate the estimated prevalence from the known figures for the number attending the treatment centre.

As with all other methods, there are biases. If interviewees were unaware that some of their friends had been to the treatment centre, then the multiplier would have been too large and the estimate too high. Conversely, if respondents included as 'attending' the friends who had only been referred to the treatment centre but who had not actually attended, or who had attended but only in the past, prior to the specified time period, then the multiplier would have been too small and the estimate too low. It was not possible to assess which direction of error was more likely. At the time, the services offered by the treatment centre often included methadone. It was apparent from the interviews and observations made during the fieldwork study that regular opiate users were very aware of the drug use patterns of their friends. Also, one of the salient topics for conversation amongst them was whether or not these friends were receiving a 'script' (prescription for methadone) and from whom.

Even if the nomination information used to obtain the multiplier was reasonably reliable, there remained problems of sampling, discussed in Chapter 16 of this monograph by Colin Taylor, and also of case definition as it was understood by the interviewees. In particular, among the interviewed sample, the proportion of injectors was lower than at the treatment centre and, furthermore, many respondents knew larger numbers of intermittent or occasional users (who did not inject).

Whilst the interviewers stressed that they were interested only in nominations of friends who were regular, probably dependent opiate users, and excluded occasional users, it was not easy to be certain how strictly the case definition was applied in practice. It was nonetheless interesting, and reassuring, that the estimates given by a multiplier obtained from opiate users were rather similar to those achieved through capture-recapture. Beyond this, the sub-study was valuable for indicating that estimates based on samples biased towards injecting users would understate the population of regular opiate users who were not injecting.

The 'best estimate'

Figure 1 shows the results of the prevalence estimates for the age range 16 to 44 years derived from the different methods from 1980 to 1982. For 1980, five estimates were obtained, and four for each of the remaining two years. As would be expected, there was a range of estimates for each year, but the 'best estimate', which was taken as a simple average of all the estimates for that year, showed a near doubling in prevalence between 1980 and 1982. In retrospect, as described below, it is clear that the period from the late 1970s through to the mid 1980s did indeed witness a major rise in the prevalence of opiate use and dependence in London (and in other parts of the country). The trend in Figure 1 can thus be considered to be validated to a degree that is acceptable for the practical business of policy making and planning, even though considerable uncertainty surrounds each individual estimate.

Several provisional comments can be made on the value of the different methods. It can be noted that the death multiplier did appear to underestimate prevalence as non-injecting modes of administration of heroin developed, emphasising the message that the mortality rate on which the method depends must not be assumed to be constant over time or between places. Extrapolations from the estimated overlap between general practitioners and the treatment centre also gave lower estimates, adding to the discussion of statistical interdependence between samples and the value of looking in non-statistical terms at the relationship between the clientele of different agencies. The overlap between treatment and reported court cases gave a higher estimate, suggesting, although not conclusively, that covering both health and law enforcement sources, as suggested by Antònia Domingo-Salvany in Chapter 8, is preferable in that it gives an estimate of a population that is broader than that which may utilise health services. Finally, we would agree with the conclusion of Dirk Korf in Chapter 19 that nomination methods offer an acceptable alternative to capture-recapture, with the proviso that it is always preferable to apply at least two different methods rather than rely on one.

It might have been interesting to have had the possibility of comparing the estimates obtained through the indirect methods described above and elsewhere in this monograph with the results of surveys based on random population sampling. This was not possible, since no such surveys were conducted over that period which would have allowed comparisons to be made. In any case, it is unlikely that the results would have added much information, since traditional population surveys are not usually sensitive to rare, socially marginalised groups.

A final comment in this section is that, in a period when incidence is rising and prevalence is changing fairly rapidly, it is necessary to derive estimates based on relatively short successive time periods. If this is not done, then the assumption of a closed population is seriously compromised. In this example, it would not have been appropriate to combine data from several years in order to increase sample sizes and statistical power. An alternative strategy, especially when sample sizes in local studies may be relatively small, is to set the estimates in a wider context that includes other trend indicators, a longer time perspective, and the findings, both qualitative and quantitative, of research studies on drug use patterns and drug using groups. This is the topic of the second section of this chapter.

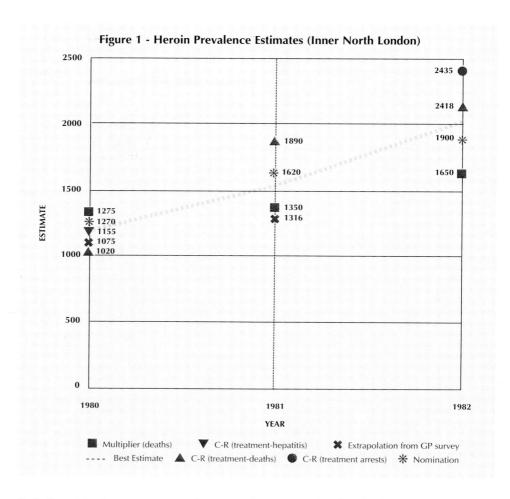

Figure 1 - Heroin Prevalence Estimates (Inner North London)

Relationship between prevalence estimates and other indicators

A variety of different agencies and institutions generate information that can be used as indirect indicators of trends in drug use, or at least of certain aspects, consequences or correlates of drug use. These indicators include the demand for treatment for drug dependence or other problems, drug-related emergencies treated in hospital emergency rooms, drug-related infectious diseases notified by public health services, drug-related deaths, police arrests of drug users or arrests for offences against the drug laws, seizures of illicit drugs made by the police and so on. The same problem arises for individual trend indicators as for single prevalence estimates - there is no 'gold standard' against which to validate the trends observed in any given indicator. Thus, a strategy is required to analyse the different indicators as a package and to cross-refer between them rather than treat them individually in isolation. Even if the validity of a particular indicator is doubtful, greater confidence can be placed if several relatively independent indicators all point in the same direction.

Multiple indicator analysis of trends in regular opiate use in London

Figure 2 shows a selection of different indicators of trends in opiates (or in some cases only heroin) in London from 1977 to 1985. The data were collected as part of the same series of exploratory epidemiological studies of methods, including prevalence estimation, that could be used to assess local patterns of drug use and drug-related problems (for full data, see also Hartnoll and Grey, 1987; and Hartnoll, Perera and Gorman, 1992). The indicators refer to London as a whole (apart from drug-related deaths) and not just to the population of the area to which the prevalence estimates described above refer. This is because it was not possible to disaggregate the data for all indicators for inner north London alone. This should not affect the broad thrust of the analysis developed in the rest of this section, since the analysis focuses on relative trends rather than on absolute prevalence and because it is clear (again with the benefit of hindsight) that the increase in heroin availability, use and dependence was not limited to one area of London alone, but was a more widespread phenomenon occurring across London and in other parts of the country as well.

In Figure 2, 1979 is taken as the reference or index year with a value of 100 for all indicators. The figure thus shows the relative changes in each indicator over time compared to other indicators. Where relevant, the indicators, like the prevalence estimates, are based on data for the 16 to 44 year age range. The indicators presented in Figure 2 are: first notifications of new heroin addicts requesting treatment; drug-related deaths of opiate users or involving opiates identified from reviews of the records of the three Coroners' Courts covering inner London (acknowledgements to Mr. John Harvey for his data); the number of seizures of heroin made by the Metropolitan Police; and the retail ('street') price of heroin per gramme based on fieldwork studies (Lewis and Hartnoll, 1985) and other sources. The thick line refers to the estimates of total prevalence of regular opiate use described in the first section, with additional estimates for the years before and after the 1980-1982 period included.

We also collected data for other indicators, including in-patient hospital admissions with a primary or secondary diagnosis of drug dependence (morphine type), drug injection-related cases of hepatitis B, arrests by the police for possession of heroin, the total quantity of heroin seized each year, and, for some years, the purity of heroin at user level. For the sake of visual clarity, these are not included in the figure, but are commented on in the text below.

It can be seen that the number of new addict notifications from treatment centres and doctors (treated incidence) showed very modest changes from 1977 to 1980, but then increased rapidly from 1981 to 1985. Hospital admissions (not shown) of patients with a diagnosis of opiate dependence also increased from 1981 but at a much slower rate. Drug-related cases of hepatitis increased from 1983, though again the increase was not dramatic. Concerning law enforcement indicators, the number of seizures of heroin made by the police increased at the same rate as first treatment notifications, especially from 1981, though unlike treatment notifications, they had also shown an increase from 1977. The number of people arrested for possession of

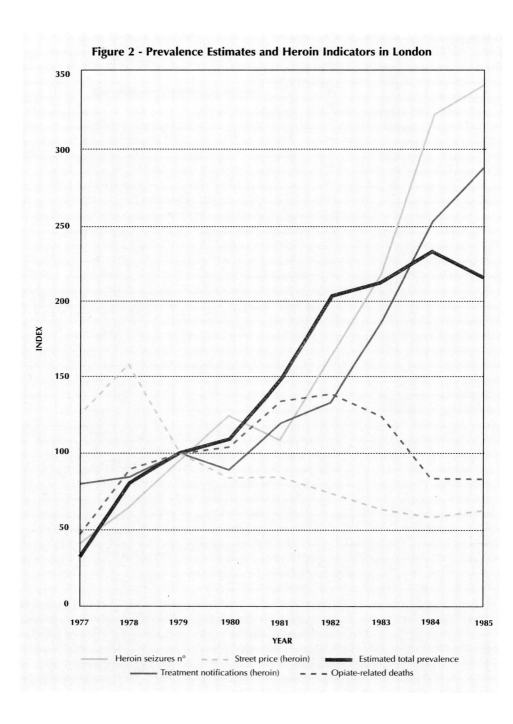

Figure 2 - Prevalence Estimates and Heroin Indicators in London

heroin (not shown) followed an almost identical curve to that for the number of seizures. The quantities of heroin (not shown) also increased over this period whilst the street price of heroin fell sharply in 1979 and continued to fall until 1984.

The indicator of opiate-related deaths generally paralleled the increases observed in the number of seizures and new treatment notifications until 1981-1982, but then decreased whilst seizures and treatment indicators were rising rapidly. Closer examination of death data showed that deaths involving heroin continued to increase after 1992, and that the fall was due to a large drop in deaths involving a synthetic opiate (dipipanone) which caused particularly dangerous complications when injected and which was involved in as many deaths as heroin in 1982. Stronger restrictions were placed on the prescribing of dipipanone and deaths related to the use of this drug dropped sharply, producing a fall in the overall number of deaths. This indicator subsequently stabilised from 1984.

Interpretation of the relationship between indicator trends and prevalence

How is one to interpret the changes in the different indicators described above? In what way do they reflect changes in incidence and prevalence? Considering the first question, it is possible that changes in an indicator such as treatment notifications reflects the availability, type, attractiveness or capacity of treatment centres, or that police arrests and seizures reflect the priorities of the police and the resources they devote to drug enforcement.

There was little change in the overall level of provision of drug treatment in London from the second half of the 1970s to 1983. One change that was taking place, however, was a shift in treatment policy towards substitute prescribing - away from maintenance (usually on methadone) and from the prescribing of injectable drugs (also usually methadone, sometimes heroin) towards a more confrontational, abstinence-oriented approach in which prescribing was often limited to oral drugs only for a period of, for example, six months during which the dose was steadily reduced.

It is very unlikely that this change increased the proportion of heroin addicts going for treatment, and possibly the reverse. The most likely explanation for the increase in treatment notifications was an increase in prevalence. Subsequently, in 1983, additional resources became available to expand treatment services, but this could not have had a major impact on treatment demand until 1984.

Similarly, there were no major changes in police priorities and resources regarding drugs in London until around 1983. Furthermore, the increase in the number of seizures was not observed for other illegal drugs, but only for heroin. This suggests that there was no general increase in police drug enforcement. Taken together with the absence of a significant switch of priorities to target heroin users by the Metropolitan Police across London, it also suggests that the best interpretation of the rising number of seizures, at least in the latter 1970s and beginning of the 1980s, reflected a rise in the availability of heroin amongst drug-using groups encountered by the police (it should be added that the large majority of seizures involved small quantities found in the possession of individual consumers, rather than large quantities seized from dealers).

The increasing number of seizures, and the rising quantities that were being seized by customs officials over the same period, could have reflected an increased success rate by law enforcement authorities. Set against this, however, was a sharp fall in the street prices of heroin from 1979 onwards, suggesting rather that increasing figures for seizures reflected greater availability of heroin. The reasons for this have been described elsewhere (Hartnoll 1987) but included political developments in heroin producing countries of South West Asia and conditions within Britain, and especially London, that facilitated the expansion of heroin use and especially heroin smoking.

Thus, taken as a 'package', these indicators were strongly suggestive of a large rise in heroin use and addiction from the latter 1970s through to the mid 1980s, a conclusion confirmed by subsequent experience.

The second question concerns the relationship between these indicators and changes in 'real' prevalence. The estimates of the prevalence of regular opiate use in London suggested that heroin use had started to increase from 1977, a couple of years before the trend became apparent in the indicators. The first indicators to show a change were drug-related deaths (though the absolute numbers were quite low) and indicators of the illicit heroin market, rising numbers of seizures and a fall in price. Hepatitis B data were not available before 1979, so these could not be used as an indicator of incidence, though they did not appear to be the most useful of the indicators examined. However, in a similar situation in Dublin, this was the first indicator to show a change (O'Hare, 1992). Hospital admission data were not a useful early indicator.

New treatment notifications showed a longer delay before the trend became clear. This was consistent with research data from treatment centres suggesting a typical time lag of three or four years between first heroin use and first treatment demand. The slower rise in deaths linked to heroin was consistent with research evidence from treatment centres, and especially from ethnographic research amongst untreated heroin users, indicating that a significant part of the increase in heroin use was associated with sniffing or smoking heroin, rather than injection. Otherwise deaths involving heroin would almost certainly have increased more rapidly. As noted above, the rise and fall of the total number of opiate-related deaths were affected by the increased use and subsequent restriction of dipipanone.

Although not an indicator in the statistical sense, the other information source that picked up the evolving trend, was the community-based fieldwork being carried out amongst drug users, and especially heroin users. The emergence of heroin sniffing and subsequently heroin smoking, the adoption of this practice amongst groups that had not traditionally been involved in heroin use, the fall in price and the shift in patterns of availability were all observed in the course of these studies.

Subsequent evidence (Hartnoll, Perera and Gorman, 1992) suggested that incidence of heroin use started to level off around 1983 or 1984 though treatment and enforcement indicators continued to rise for another year or two, the former because of the time lag between initiation and treatment, the latter because of increased police attention on heroin. The number of seizures stabilised in 1985 and the price in 1984. Subsequently the seizures fell and prices drifted upwards.

The above, simplified example is given to emphasise the importance of using indicators in combination with prevalence estimates and other available sources of information. Fitting information together in this fashion is rather like doing a large and complicated jigsaw puzzle - the result is a picture that makes sense, the individual pieces make very little sense at all. Another example of a multiple indicator approach is the work of the expert epidemiology group of the Pompidou Group in the Council of Europe (Hartnoll *et al*, 1989; Hartnoll *et al*, 1994).

Conclusions

This chapter has emphasised a point raised throughout this monograph, that the mechanical application of statistical techniques is insufficient for achieving meaningful and valid prevalence estimates. It has further stressed that it is vital to examine prevalence estimates, not only in terms of the methodological requirements of each method, but to understand where the data come from and what they signify, and to cross-check any interpretation of those data against information from other sources and methods.

The final point relates to the usefulness of a prevalence estimate within a policy context, an important issue that is covered in the first section of this monograph. In the description of the research on prevalence and indicators described here, it was noted that treatment and law enforcement policies and resources did not change significantly until much of the increase in heroin use and dependence had already occurred. This information was used to assist in the interpretation of the indicators based on those sources. However the same information can also be used to comment on the responsiveness of services and policies to changing patterns of drug use. Viewed from this perspective, it becomes apparent that changes in treatment and law enforcement responses occurred too late to have any impact on the development of the 'epidemic', although they did develop in time to deal with the aftermath.

When the research described in this chapter began in 1980, the general perception amongst the different agencies that we contacted was that the big changes in 'drugs' had occurred in the late 1960s and early 1970s, and that since then the situation had stabilised. A similar view could be observed in much of the media and in the (lack of) political interest. There was some awareness of changing patterns of drug use by more perceptive individual observers within the health and social care sector and among specialised police drug squads, but this did not translate into action.

Subsequently, it was widely accepted that there had been a substantial increase in heroin use and dependence over that period, and media and political interest escalated in the mid 1980s, but at first the reaction to the estimates and analysis of trends was that they must be too high.

Since the research had been concerned with feasibility and pilot studies at a local level, it was not possible to make strong generalisations to the national level, even though we were confident of the conclusions for Inner London based on the cumulative evidence from different sources and methods. However, once political interest did 'take off' (stimulated, it must be added, not by research but by sensational and almost certainly baseless stories about, for example, drug dealers adding heroin to the milk provided for primary school children) these same estimates were quoted in justification for increased funding, and criticised in other quarters for being too low.

Many of the difficulties in the relationship between research and policy have been covered in the first part of this monograph and so only one aspect is raised here. The sort of situation described in the preceding paragraphs generates a dilemma for both researchers and policy makers.

Policy makers say they need information for policy making and planning but the reactive nature of much policy making on social problems, combined with the time lag between changes on the ground and the reflection of those changes in the indicators, often means that research findings arrive even later. It thus becomes necessary to think of the future of prevalence estimation not simply in terms of improving the quality of individual cross-sectional estimates of prevalence in a given year, but in terms of developing them in the context of dynamic modelling techniques that take account of different indicators and that offer the possibility, despite the limitations of such models, of projecting trends on a more scientific basis.

To do this requires not only an extension in scientific methodology, but also a willingness to adopt a broad and holistic approach to integrating a diversity of sources, methods and sorts of information into future work on prevalence estimation.

References

Arroyave F., Little D. and Letemendia F. (1972) 'Misuse of heroin and methadone in the city of Oxford', *British Journal of Psychiatry*, 120, 505-506.

Bishop B.P., Cave G.H., Gay M. *et al* (1976) 'A city looks at its problem of drug abuse by injection', *British Journal of Psychiatry*, 129, 465-471.

Blumberg H. and Dronfield E. (1976) 'Nomination techniques in the study of largely invisible groups: opiate users not at drug dependence clinics', *Social Science and Medicine*, 10, 415-422.

de Alarcon R. and Rathod N.H. (1968) 'Prevalence and early detection of heroin abuse', *British Journal of Addiction*, 69, 225-229.

Dupont R.L. and Piemme T.E. (1973) 'Estimation of the number of heroin addicts in an urban area', *Medical Annals of the District of Columbia*, 42(7), 323-326.

Greene M.H. (1974) *Estimating the Prevalence of Heroin Use in a Community*, Special Action Monograph series A, no. 4, Special Action Office for Drug Abuse Prevention, Executive Office of the President, Washington, DC.

Greenwood J.A. (1971) *Estimating Number of Narcotic Addicts*, Drug Control Division, US Bureau of Narcotics and Dangerous Drugs, Washington, DC, U.S. Government Printing Office.

Hartnoll R.L., Lewis R.J., Mitcheson M.C. and Bryer S. (1985a) 'Estimating the prevalence of opioid dependence', *The Lancet*, i, 203-205.

Hartnoll R.L., Lewis E., Daviaud E. and Mitcheson M.C. (1985b) *Drug Problems: Assessing Local Needs. A Practical Manual for Assessing the Nature and Extent of Drug Misuse in a Community*, London, Birkbeck College: Drug Indicators Project.

Hartnoll R.L. and Grey D. (1987) 'The drug situation in Greater London', in Pompidou Group, *Multi-City Study of Drug Misuse*, Final Report, Section I, 135-188, Strasbourg, Council of Europe: Pompidou Group.

Hartnoll R.L., Perera, J. and Gorman, A. (1992) 'London report', in Pompidou Group, *Multi-city Study of Drug Misuse, 1991 update of data*, Strasbourg, Council of Europe: Pompidou Group.

Hartnoll R.L. (1987) 'Patterns of drug taking in Britain', in Heller, T., Gott, M. and Jeffery, C. (eds.) *Drug Misuse: A Reader*, 74-79, London, John Wiley in association with the Open University.

Hartnoll R.L., Avico, U., Ingold, F.R., Lange, K., Lenke, L., O'hare, A., and De Roij-Motshagen, A. (1989) 'A multi-city study of drug misuse in Europe', *United Nations Bulletin on Narcotics*, 41(1&2), 3-27.

Hartnoll R.L. (1994) *Multi-city Study: Drug misuse trends in thirteen European cities*, Strasbourg, Pompidou Group, Council of Europe Press

Hughes P.H. (1977) *Behind the Wall of Respect*, Chicago, University of Chicago Press.

Hunt L.G. and Chambers C.D. (1976) *The Heroin Epidemics: A Study of Heroin Use in the United States, 1965-75*, New York, Spectrum.

Lewis R.J., Hartnoll R.L., Bryer S., Daviaud E. and Mitcheson M.C. (1985) 'Scoring smack: the illicit heroin market in London', 1980-83, *British Journal of Addiction*, 80, pp. 281-290.

Newmayer J.A. and Johnson G.R. (1976) 'The heroin epidemic in San Francisco: estimates of incidence and prevalence', *International Journal of the Addictions*, 11(3) pp. 417-438.

O'Hare A. (1992) 'Dublin city report', in Pompidou Group (ed.) *Multi-city Study of Drug Misuse, 1991 update of data*, Strasbourg, Council of Europe: Pompidou Group.

Person P.H., Retka R.L. and Woodward A.W. (1977) A method for estimating heroin use prevalence, National Institute on Drug Abuse Technical Paper, DHEW Publication No. (ADM) 77439, Washington, DC, U.S. Government Printing Office.

Socialdepartementet (1980) *Tungt narkotikamissbruk - en totalunders-kning 1979*, Rapport från utredningen om narkotikamissbrukets omfattning (UNO), Stockholm, Ds S 1980:5.

GENERAL CONCLUSIONS

GENERAL CONCLUSIONS

by Richard Hartnoll

One of the main conclusions of the Scientific Seminar on *'Addiction Prevalence Estimation: Methods and Research Strategies'* was that the question 'How many addicts are there?' has neither a simple solution nor a single answer. The variety of approaches described in this monograph reflects the scientific struggle to quantify the complexity of the phenomena that lie behind this apparently simple question. However, despite the difficulties of defining what it is that we wish to measure, and the problems of finding ways to do so, the quality of the contributions contained in this volume also suggest that the art of scientific prevalence estimation in Europe has a healthy future.

I suggested in my introduction that neither the Seminar nor this monograph represent a final state of knowledge but rather a starting point for the future. In this spirit, the research agenda for this future can be summarised as follows.

One of the first priorities is to clarify case definitions. The word 'addiction', that was used as a short hand term in the Scientific Seminar, has been changed in this monograph to 'problem drug use'. This is no accident, but this broader concept raises its own difficulties. It becomes even more necessary to operationalise and specify, as far as the sources on which the various estimates are based allow, who is counted and to what the final estimates refer. In many situations it may not be possible to specify this precisely in advance, since researchers often have limited control over the type of data that has been recorded in the registers or other sources on which they rely. However, it is essential to try to assess and, if possible, stratify what it is that the estimates they produce can reasonably be assumed to represent, for example in terms of the main drugs involved, the frequency of use, the routes of administration, whether or not people in treatment are included, and so on.

It is equally important to clarify the measures that are used. These include: the time frame of the study; whether estimates refer to point or period prevalence; how well the area of study is defined; what the reference population is and how issues concerning non-residents are dealt with; whether the population is assumed to be open or closed; whether longer time periods are studied; how incidence and cessation of drug use or other movements in and out of the population are handled; whether rates are reported rather than numbers and, finally, whether they are broken down by age, gender and other relevant demographic variables (e.g. urban/rural).

Data analysis, and especially analysis of sources of error, needs to be improved. This can only be achieved through improved methodological rigour, from relatively basic issues - such as presenting estimates in terms of confidence intervals rather than a number or, if this is not possible, in terms of likely ranges - to more sophisticated analyses of possible biases in the estimates. Furthermore, this is not just a statistical issue. Measurement errors may be very important.

There is no point in developing more sophisticated analysis methods if the data on which they depend is unreliable or of unknown quality. Thus, it is essential to improve the quality of basic data collection procedures and of the databases on which all estimates rely.

It is apparent that there is a particular need to improve national estimates, not only because of the political demand for such estimates, but also because many of the methods used are more easily applied at local level. However, since it is known that prevalence is not evenly distributed across a country, it is also important to aim for regional and socio-demographic breakdown.

A vital need is to move beyond estimates based on a single method and to develop strategies to integrate different methods into the estimation process. Different estimates can then be compared and cross-validated. It is also important to include approaches that go beyond static estimates and analyse trends over time and the relationship of prevalence to other indicators. These should not only deal with trends in the overall prevalence but should also aim to differentiate patterns in different areas or different groups within the population.

Alongside improvement in the methodological quality, greater attention needs to be given to the interpretation of the estimates: how they should be viewed in the wider context of society and of the nature and extent of drug taking; what they mean in terms of problems and needs; what the implications might be for services. To answer these questions, it is necessary to move beyond prevalence and complement the estimates with information on other aspects of the situation, not only statistical studies, but also qualitative studies. This brings us back to one of the key purposes for trying to answer the question of 'How many addicts?' in the first place. It is a major challenge for researchers to aim to analyse the relationship and relevance of prevalence estimates to policy.

CONTRIBUTORS

Dr. Pierre-Yves Bello
Observatoire Régional de la Santé en Midi-Pyrénées, Toulouse, France.

Dr. Geneviève Chêne
INSERM U 330, Université Victor Segalen, Bordeaux 2, Bordeaux, France.

Dr. Peter D. A. Cohen
Centrum voor Drugsonderzoek (CEDRO), Universiteit van Amsterdam, Amsterdam, The Netherlands.

Dr. Marina Davoli
Department of Epidemiology, Lazio Region Health Authority, Rome, Italy.

Dr. Antònia Domingo-Salvany
Institut Municipal d'Investigació Mèdica, Barcelona, Spain.

Dr. Zsuzsanna Elekes
Department of Sociology and Social Policy, Budapest University of Economics, Budapest, Hungary.

Dr. Michael Farrell
National Addiction Centre, Institute of Psychiatry, London, England.

Dr. Martin Frischer
Department of Medicines Management, Keele University, Staffordshire, England.

Paul Griffiths
National Addiction Centre, Institute of Psychiatry, London, England.

Richard Hartnoll
European Monitoring Centre for Drugs and Drug Addiction, Lisbon, Portugal.

Matthew Hickman
The Centre for Research on Drugs and Health Behaviour, Imperial College School of Medicine, London, England.

Samantha Howes
National Addiction Centre, Institute of Psychiatry, London, England.

Ali Judd
The Centre for Research on Drugs and Health Behaviour, Imperial College School of Medicine, London, England.

Dr. Wolf Kirschner
Forschung, Beratung + Evaluation GmbH. Berlin.

Dr. Dirk J. Korf
Amsterdam Bureau of Social Research and Statistics, Amsterdam, The Netherlands.

Dr. Ludwig Kraus
Institut für Therapieforschung, Munich, Germany.

Prof. Dr. Philip Lazarov
National Centre for Addictions, Sofia, Bulgaria.

Conchi Moreno Iribas
Instituto de Salud Pública, Navarra, Spain.

Dr. Dušan Nolimal
Institute of Public Health of Slovenia, Ljubljana, Slovenia.

Dr. Börje Olsson
Department of Criminology, University of Stockholm, Stockholm, Sweden.

Prof. Dr. med. Klaus Püschel
Institute for Forensic Medicine, University of Hamburg, Hamburg, Germany.

Alan Quirk
The Centre for Research on Drugs and Health Behaviour, Imperial College School of Medicine, London, England.

Assoc. Prof. Clive Richardson
Consultant, Greek REITOX Focal Point, University Mental Health Research Institute, Athens, Greece.

Dr. Henrik Sælan
Stadslægen, Copenhagen, Denmark.

Janusz Sierosławski
Department of Studies on Alcoholism and Drug Dependence, Institute of Psychiatry and Neurology, Warsaw, Poland.

Roland Simon, Dipl. Psych.
Unit of Clinical Epidemiology, Institut für Therapieforschung , Munich, Germany.

Prof. Gerry Stimson
The Centre for Research on Drugs and Health Behaviour, Imperial College School of Medicine, London, England.

Colin Taylor
National Addiction Centre, Institute of Psychiatry, London, England.

Mikel Urtiaga Dominguez
Instituto de Salud Pública, Navarra, Spain.

Dr. Antoni Zieliński
Department of Studies on Alcoholism and Drug Dependence, Institute of Psychiatry and Neurology, Warsaw, Poland.

PRACTICAL INFORMATION

Address:
The European Monitoring Centre for Drugs and Drug Addiction
Rua da Cruz de Santa Apolónia 23-25
P-1100 Lisbon, Portugal.

Telephone numbers:
351 1 - 811 30 00 / 813 13 18

Fax:
351 1 - 813 17 11

E-mail:
General: info@emcdda.org or emcdda@reitox.net
Private: firstname.surname@emcdda.org or firstname.surname@reitox.net

Printed in Italy

EMCDDA, November 1997

European Monitoring Centre for Drugs and Drug Addiction

Luxembourg: Office for Official Publications of the European Communities

1997 - pp. 272 - 16 x 24 cm

ISBN 92-9168-006-0

Price (excluding VAT) in Luxembourg: ECU 28